# Parting

# Parting
## The Aftermath of Separation and Divorce

**UPDATED EDITION**

# Graham B. Spanier
# Linda Thompson

 **SAGE** PUBLICATIONS  Newbury Park Beverly Hills London New Delhi

Copyright © 1987 by Sage Publications, Inc.

All rights reserved. No part of this book may be reproduced or utilized in any form or by any means, electronic or mechanical, including photocopying, recording, or by any information storage and retrieval system, without permission in writing from the publisher.

*For information address:*

SAGE Publications, Inc.
2111 West Hillcrest Drive
Newbury Park, California 91320

SAGE Publications Inc.
275 South Beverly Drive
Beverly Hills
California 90212

SAGE Publications Ltd.
28 Banner Street
London EC1Y 8QE
England

SAGE PUBLICATIONS India Pvt. Ltd.
M-32 Market
Greater Kailash I
New Delhi 110 048 India

Printed in the United States of America

Library of Congress Cataloging-in-Publication Data

Spanier, Graham B.
 Parting : the aftermath of separation and divorce.

 Includes index.
 1. Divorce--Pennsylvania--Centre County--Longitudinal studies. 2. Divorced people--Pennsylvania--Centre County--Attitudes I. Thompson, Linda. II. Title.
HQ835.P4S6   1987       306.8'9'0974853         87-9796
ISBN 0-8039-3109-3 (pbk.)

**SECOND PRINTING, 1987**

# Contents

| | | |
|---|---|---|
| *Preface* | | 7 |
| 1. | Parting: Introduction | 9 |
| 2. | Moving Toward Separation | 27 |
| 3. | Outsiders | 59 |
| 4. | Relief and Distress | 103 |
| 5. | The Partners After Marriage | 131 |
| 6. | Friends and Relatives | 163 |
| 7. | Dating and Sex | 187 |
| 8. | Well-Being | 209 |
| | *References* | 235 |
| | *Index* | 243 |
| | *About the Authors* | 249 |

# Preface

The transition from marriage to divorce is an immensely complex event in the lives of those who experience it. The complexity of this experience makes research on the topic challenging yet rewarding. We were not fully aware of this challenge when the project that led to this book began nearly a decade ago. Since that time we have learned much about marital separation and its aftermath; this book, then, summarizes what we have discovered about separation, divorce, and the adjustments that follow.

Our project began in 1974, the first year that more marriages in the United States were dissolved by divorce than by the death of a spouse. A proposal was submitted to the National Institute of Mental Health and funded in 1976. This provided a modest sum of money to conduct the first phase of the research, 50 open-ended unstructured case-study interviews done in the fall of 1976. A small additional grant from the American Council on Life Insurance provided the opportunity to continue the study. The objective was to develop a survey instrument that could tap most of the salient dimensions of separation and divorce experience. The survey was conducted in 1977. Because there was very little known about divorce and its aftermath by the early 1970s, we decided to let the qualitative case-study interviews inform the development of the structured interviews. Later, a follow-up study was conducted, allowing us to turn a cross-sectional study into a longitudinal one. The longitudinal data and specifically the transition from divorce to remarriage are featured in a companion volume, *Recycling the Family*, written by Frank F. Furstenberg, Jr., and Graham B. Spanier.

A project of this scope requires the cooperation and efforts of many individuals, particularly as the funding for the research presented in this book only covered a small fraction of the overall effort. We are grateful to our many dedicated and generous colleagues and students at The Pennsylvania State University and at our current universities who participated so enthusiastically in the project. We would specifically like to mention Elaine Anderson, Robert Casto, Rodney Cate, Margie

Lachman, Mary Hart, Randie Margolis, Anthony Mixon, Carol Pfeiffenberger, Judy Shea, Catherine Surra, Sandra Hanson, James Shockey, Patricia Dalto, Rebecca Hicks, and Marilyn Cavell, who worked with us as interviewers, research assistants, or as coauthors on articles based on these data which have appeared in journals. Although most of the material found in the pages that follow was written especially for this volume, we occasionally draw on work done earlier in collaboration with our colleagues. Without the cooperation and the dedication that they all brought to the project, this book might not have been possible.

This book was first published in 1984. The current edition updates demographic data on American marriages and families presented in Chapter 1. Material in subsequent chapters remains unchanged.

We think of this book as a product of a long association that began when the first author was on the faculty and the second author was entering graduate school. Ten years later, the association and the effort on this book can only be viewed as a full-fledged collaboration.

—Graham B. Spanier
*State University of New York
at Stony Brook*

—Linda Thompson
*Virginia Polytechnic Institute
and State University*

CHAPTER 1

# Parting
## Introduction

> Do you want me to characterize divorce in one sentence? It's hell, sheer hell.
>
> I'm really excited about what's going on in my life right now and the changes I see in me and everything.

As with most life transitions, marital separation can be liberating, depressing, frustrating, exciting, scary, traumatic, or any combination of these emotions. In the last two decades—when divorce rates soared to a record high—we have all been bombarded with information and opinions about divorce. What we see and read ranges from interesting case studies to speculations about why there is so much divorce, from careful research about who divorces and why to claims that contemporary divorce is ruining the family. In this book, we hope to put some of this in perspective by presenting data from our research on the adjustment to marital separation.

The quotes above illustrate the diversity of experience following the breakup of the marriage, and this theme is highlighted in this book. There is no universal response to the end of a marriage, although there are many common threads found in the experiences of certain individuals. We seek to capture the similarities while not losing sight of the diversity. The study had its beginnings nearly a decade ago, after it was clear that the dramatic increases in divorce rates seen in the 1960s and early 1970s were likely to be with us to stay. It was clear that the community of social scientists had largely ignored divorce as a topic for careful research, with only one comprehensive study (Goode, 1956) attempted in the postwar period.

This book, and books and papers by others which have appeared in recent years, demonstrates a marked increase in the attention of social scientists to divorce. Social scientists have discovered in this effort that divorce is much more complicated than many had thought. Most of us who have conducted research in this area have concluded that the study of broken marriages has been the most challenging work we have attempted in our careers. There is so much to discover, there are many different approaches to making the discovery, and the interpretations of what is discovered are virtually unlimited. Thus, we have made choices about what to study and what not to study. We chose to examine the social, psychological, economic, and legal aspects of marital separation through 50 case-study interviews and, subsequently, face-to-face interviews with more than 200 recently separated men and women. It was beyond our resources and inclination, however, to interview children or other family members as well. Thus, our research focuses on the adults involved in the termination of a marriage, not the children.

This book is about marital separation. Strictly speaking, we studied individuals who *decided* to divorce and consequently separated. As we shall detail later, 76 percent of our sample of 205 men and women had actually divorced by the time of our interviews with them. The other 24 percent eventually divorced, but not until after our initial interviews. The distinction between marital separation and divorce may appear to be trivial, but it is not really; conceptually, the decision to separate and the physical separation that follows is more important socially and psychologically than the legal designation of divorce per se—something we learned in our initial case-study interviews.

Our goal in this book is to describe the aftermath of marriage. Divorce is now an everyday occurrence throughout America, yet we still know very little about what it is, why it happens, and how it affects those involved. The purpose of this book and the research which underlies it is to propose some answers to these questions. Our research can be said to raise as many questions as it answers; but one could argue that this is a mark of good scholarship, not of incomplete scholarship.

The data presented in this book are from the first phase of a longitudinal study of the adjustment to marital separation, divorce, and remarriage. A companion volume, *Recycling the Family*, written by Frank F. Furstenberg, Jr., and Graham B. Spanier, features the transition to remarriage, taking advantage of the data available throughout the entire course of the longitudinal project.

We begin this chapter with a discussion of divorce in relation to the changing family in contemporary America. We then focus more specifically on the background of the study for this book, the procedures for sampling and data collection, and the background of the respondents who participated in our research.

## Divorce and the Changing Family

"The contemporary American family, currently in ill health, is in critical condition and may soon die." We hear this prognosis often. It is an opinion which is argued persuasively by respected scholars, policymakers, and service providers. It is, however, *not* an opinion we share. We intend to challenge the view that the high divorce rate signifies the demise of the American family. We wish to acknowledge the very real problems families and the society they live in face today, but also to put current demographic and social changes into a more appropriate perspective.

Perhaps the most honest view of the social history of the United States is that the family has never been as healthy as our nostalgic reminiscences would have it. Indeed, as contemporary social historians probe into the past and reconstruct accurate American family history, we find that none of our current problems are new; and many of them are less burdensome today than they were a generation or even a century ago. What we find is a strong argument that family life is *changing*, not deteriorating.

Of course, there is ample evidence of the ill health of the family today and much justification for our continued concern. Divorce rates reached a record high during the past decade; more children now live in an arrangement other than the traditional two-parent family household than ever before; and family problems such as child abuse, spouse abuse, institutionalization of the aged, runaway adolescents, lack of suitable day care, unintended or unwanted pregnancies, and unemployment are among a long list of troublesome social problems.

Thus, there are persuasive arguments that suggest (1) that the family system in America has always been plagued by significant problems; (2) that these problems are likely to persist; but (3) that the current state of affairs does *not* suggest the demise of the modern American family. In short, the family is here to stay, problems and all. The picture of family turmoil that is often seen coexists within a frame of widespread individual commitment to family life and considerable stability in the social institution of the family.

Marriage is still the norm in this society and is likely to continue to be. In 1987 we can anticipate that five million persons will marry—a figure which will resemble the number for each of the first six years of this decade. Indeed, the marriage rate climbed during the last half of the 1970s and has remained at a sustained high level in the early 1980s. More than nine in ten Americans eventually marry; and many of those who do not have a particular profile of demographic characteristics which, in effect, restricts their field of eligibles.

Much of the marriage experience today, of course, comes in the form of remarriage. About three-fourths of all divorced persons remarry, nearly half within three years of the final divorce decree. From an adult's perspective, we remarry quickly (although three years can be a very long time to a young child). This propensity to marriage, for both never-married and previously married individuals, suggests to us a very strong continued interest in the family inasmuch as marriage forms the core of most families.

This trend, in conjunction with other well-documented trends, is heartening. For example, there have been improvements in the ability of married couples to plan the number, spacing, and timing of their children, allowing for better coordination of family and work commitments, better use of economic resources, and greater realization of lifestyle preferences.

The endurance of the family seems possible as long as marriage continues to attract so many. Young adults today seem as committed to the possibility of marriage as previous cohorts, but there is one difference. The average age of first marriage has been delayed. Despite impressions in the media to the contrary, the rate of teenage marriage has declined over the past decade. Those who marry in their teens *do* increase their prospect for divorce substantially, but fortunately this particular phenomenon has not contributed disproportionately to the increase in the divorce rate in recent years.

The increase in the marriage rate has thus occurred during a time when American youth are not in as much of a hurry to marry as were the youth of the previous generation. The median age at first marriage is now 25½ for men and 23 for women. This is an increase of nearly three full years since the 1950s. To a small degree the explanation for this trend may lie in the state of the economy in that it may be difficult to be secure enough to launch a marriage. But undoubtedly the most persuasive argument centers around the increased freedoms experienced by young adults today. As a large majority of young men and women are now sexually experienced before the conclusion of adolescence, it is less likely than before that access to a sexual partner will be a reason for marriage. Effective contraception can virtually eliminate the chance of an unwanted pregnancy—a fear that in the past encouraged some early marriages, and a reality that in the past forced some early marriages.

The availability of cohabitation as a life-style also may make marriage seem less critical. The average age at marriage has always been greater for those at higher educational levels, and the population is becoming more highly educated. Thus, some marriages may be postponed because of undergraduate and graduate college work. Finally, the increasing movement of women into professional careers and the concomitant economic independence and mobility may work to delay some marriages.

Of all the trends relating to the family, none has had so profound an impact as has the dramatic upturn in the divorce rate. Figures for 1985 show approximately 1.1 million divorces involving nearly 2.3 million adults and more than one million children. Thus, divorce touches many lives every year. Although the increase in divorce seen during the past two decades—when the rate more than doubled—has finally slowed, there is no evidence to suggest that the divorce rate will do anything other than level off or decline slightly—a trend which it now seems safe to acknowledge with some confidence. The divorce rate is unlikely to turn downward to a significant degree in the next decade.

Divorce does not affect all social groups equally. Divorce rates are higher for blacks than for whites. Generally speaking, the higher the educational level, the lower the divorce rate. One interesting exception is women with graduate degrees; they have a disproportionately high divorce rate, due perhaps to increased economic security and social independence. Although divorce can strike couples of any age and circumstance, those who divorce tend to do so relatively early in their marriages. The peak period for divorce is two to five years after the marriage, a statistic that has not changed much. Given the time required to make the decision to divorce, separate, file, and wait for a final decree, this peak period reflects evidence of serious marital problems very early in the relationship for most couples who eventually divorce.

Projections based on Census Bureau and Vital Statistics Bureau data and assumptions that future divorce experience will remain relatively constant tell us that about one half of all first marriages formed in recent years are likely to end in divorce. Considering separation, divorce, remarriage, and redivorce, it can be projected that a majority of all marriages among young adults today will not remain intact.

Numbers of this magnitude might seem to challenge the notion of family stability mentioned earlier. One wonders how the future of the family can be assured when more than one half of all families are structurally broken by separation or divorce. An optimist would note that approximately one half of those who divorce do so relatively early in their marriage, many before they have children. These divorced individuals may still look forward to a so-called "traditional" family life following remarriage, with little obligation to a spouse from an earlier marriage. Moreover, many divorced persons with children develop acceptable and sometimes innovative ways of coping with their disrupted status, and the concept of the family may still be maintained for them. The pessimist would point to the emotional, financial, and social damage that can be done by divorce, and there can be little argument with such an assessment.

Most important for objectively evaluating the future of the family, however, is a point obvious to some but missing from most discussions about the family: Divorce is a response to an unsuccessful marriage relationship in which the spouses reject each other; *they are usually not rejecting the idea of marriage or the family per se.* Thus, divorce is not so much a statement about the viability of married life or about family stability as it is a realization of poor mate selection, lack of personal commitment, disenchantment with one's partner, or some other personal or social problem surrounding a particular relationship. Persons approaching divorce usually report that they are no longer in love, that they have grown apart, or that they do not get along with each other any more.

The data on remarriage say more to some social scientists than do the data about marriage or divorce. Nearly one-fourth of divorced persons remarry within the first year following the termination of the marriage. Even though many recently divorced persons claim to be "soured" on marriage for a time after their divorce, one-half have changed their minds and married again within three years.

When trying to determine if the increase in divorce means that marriages today are less happy than marriages of earlier generations, it is important to differentiate between a definition of marital stability (whether or not a marriage remains intact) and marital quality (how well an intact marriage is working). Marital stability indicates outcome, whereas marital quality tells something about a couple's happiness in their relationship. This distinction is needed to understand the plausible argument that the quality of marital relationships has not changed much historically; only stability has changed.

In 1950, a special issue of *The Annals of the American Academy of Political and Social Science* titled "Toward Family Stability" was published. In that year, the divorce rate was only a fraction of what it is now; even the dramatic postwar divorce activity increased the rate momentarily to a level that was below the sustained rate of today. The contributors were 25 of the most eminent family scholars of the time. In his 1950 contribution, Ernest Burgess noted that the divorce rate had "excited alarm two generations ago." One may wonder if there was ever or will ever be a time when the divorce rate will be viewed without alarm, and not defined as a threat to the family institution.

We all know the tragedy of marriages that remain intact structurally yet have failed in terms of the quality of the relationships. Americans today are more likely to seek divorce when a marriage is unhappy. This has occurred because much of the social stigma associated with divorce has disappeared (although it has not vanished entirely). There have always been barriers to divorce, thresholds that must be negotiated, but these thresholds have become much less formidable.

For example, religious doctrine has diminished as a barrier to divorce. The importance of maintaining an appearance of marital stability for the corporate or political arena is less important. No-fault divorce laws have made it easier to go through with a divorce if that is considered to be the best solution. There is greater willingness on the part of women in particular to leave a marriage that is intolerable to them because of physical or emotional abuse. This latter threshold has changed in part because of the greater independence that many women experience and the possibility in modern America that women can be economically self-sufficient. These and other thresholds have changed dramatically, and with them so has marital stability. Evidence to demonstrate that marital quality has changed, however, is difficult to find.

Much of society's uneasiness with regard to family instability stems from its concern about children. About two of every five divorcing couples have no children under 18 years of age when they divorce; three in five couples have at least one child. On the average, two children are involved in each divorce in which there are any children under the age of 18 years. The impact of family disruption on children cannot be ignored. Psychologists have summarized the problems children sometimes face following divorce: psychological stress, economic hardship, guilt, and discontinuity in parent-child relations, to name just a few.

On the other hand, family experts say that it is far better for a child to grow up in a loving home with one parent than in a battleground with two parents who live together but are terribly unhappy. Some experts also point out that children are remarkably resilient, often showing an uncanny ability to survive emotionally in some very oppressive family situations. This has been demonstrated many times over by children who grow to be very well adjusted and seemingly unscarred by their family experience. There seems to be some truth in all of these assertions, but the data are not clear enough yet.

The number of family households maintained by a man or woman with no spouse present has increased substantially since 1970. The dramatic increase during the decade in divorce and separation rates as well as in the rate of births out of marriage to females in their teens has resulted in a rapid growth of one-parent households, the overwhelming majority headed by women. Approximately three-fourths of white children and 90 percent of black children born out of wedlock are kept by their mothers. Whereas 85 percent of children under 18 lived with two parents in 1970, only 75% were found in this status in 1984. Married couple households with children under 18 constituted 40 percent of all households in the United States in 1970, but the percentage of such households declined to 29 by 1984.

There is a popular belief, spurred no doubt by movies such as *Kramer vs. Kramer* and affectionately written feature stories in newspapers and magazines, that a greater proportion of children are living with their fathers than ever before. Actually, the proportion of children living only with their father remained small over the last decade. Although the number of children living with only their father increased by about one-third between 1970 and 1984 (from 748,000 to 1,378,000), the proportion of children living only with their father but not their mother still remains about 2 percent. By contrast, 15 percent of white children and 50 percent of black children live with their mother but not their father. Only about one-tenth of the children living with a currently divored parent live with their father; this percentage is about the same as it was in 1960. This is likely to change in the next decade, although slowly and mostly among the middle and upper-middle classes. Although there is some debate about the relative merits for the children of single-parent fatherhood versus single-parent motherhood, researchers have found that there is little continuity between the quality of pre- and postseparation parent-child interaction, particularly for fathers. This finding challenges the historical judicial guidepost known as the "tender years doctrine," a tradition of awarding young children to their mothers.

If the institution of the family is to change into the future, the change is not likely to be seen in its structural arrangements or in its functional tasks. Change is most likely to be found in the dynamics of family interactions. Family relationships will need to change as the times change, and this will require family members to act toward each other differently, to meet each others' needs better than they have in the past, to communicate better about those needs, and to change their habits to perform more adequately the familial function—emotional support— that has become dominant in recent decades. While some of the family's functions (such as religion, education, and economics) are being taken over by other institutions (the church, schools, the political and economic systems), one function has remained for the family to struggle with more than any other—namely, the function of providing emotional support for family members.

Humans have a great need for intimacy. As society becomes more urban, industrial, and mobile, it also becomes more impersonal. In short, a growing need for personalization is found in a society that is becoming more impersonal; and one looks to the family to meet this need. Love is sought from parents, children, and other intimate companions because it is unlikely that this need will be met elsewhere. Perhaps paradoxically, then, the family may become stronger and more valuable as other social institutions such as the church and state erode its traditional responsibilities. Marriages and families are able to meet these needs in ways that alternatives to marriage and family life may not be able to. For a variety of reasons, the family has been the most efficient mechanism for coordinating the complex dynamics of intimacy, reproduction, socialization of the young, and emotional support.

Divorce, then, must really be seen as one symptom of a complex family system found throughout Western societies. Divorce is a response to a failing marriage, not a failing institution. The family system can remain strong even while divorce rates remain high. Although this situation may not be ideal, it would be incorrect to say that it is unworkable. We attempt to approach our research, then, in a rather nonjudgmental way—looking at divorce not so much as a social problem but as a critical, often chaotic, and usually stressful transition in the life course of a substantial number of Americans.

## Overview of the Study

The study on which this book is based had its origins about a decade ago when it became clear that divorce had rapidly become a significant life event for perhaps millions of Americans each year. By 1975, there were more than one million divorces each year, affecting two million adults and more than one million children. Thus, at least three million persons in nuclear families were confronted with divorce each year; and undoubtedly millions of other family members, friends, and coworkers were touched indirectly. Now, of course, the numbers are even higher. Yet by the early 1970s there was still a dearth of literature on the subject.

Given the scarce research on which to base any serious survey study, we determined that it would be most fruitful to do an exploratory, unstructured study in which detailed case-study interviews were conducted before launching into a full-fledged survey. The goal of the initial phase of the research was to learn what the salient issues were for the individuals who were going through a divorce.

Four graduate students in Human Development and Family Studies at Pennsylvania State University were thoroughly trained in participant observation and field interviewing techniques. They observed "practice" interviews conducted by Graham Spanier, who had been trained in this method by Howard Becker at Northwestern University. Following this training, we spent the fall of 1976 conducting lengthy, unstructured interviews with individuals who had filed for divorce within the preceding year. The interviews were guided only to the extent that we tried to get a general idea of the couple's premarital and marital history, a detailed picture of the determinants of the separation, and as much information as possible about its process and problems. We therefore tried to focus on the problems that the respondents felt were of primary importance. This method seemed most appropriate because in the 20 years since Goode's (1956) pioneering study of divorce, virtually nothing new on the subject had been published; thus, it wasn't even clear as to what questions should be asked if a survey were to be conducted.

The interviewers used the technique, characteristic of Becker's method of observational research, of conversing with the respondents, probing, and changing the direction of the conversation often to follow up interesting leads. Notes were not taken at the time of the interview but were transcribed from memory immediately following the interviews. Approximately 1,000 pages of field notes were collected from the 50 interviews.

The data from the case studies were used to develop hypotheses, suggest areas of importance for further research, and generally to serve as a basis for theory building and construction of the fixed-choice interview schedule to be used in the first wave of what would eventually become a longitudinal study. The case study material is used in this book as a source of quotations to feature certain ideas generated by the structured interviews, and to provide more vivid examples than the fixed-choice responses can of the perspectives of men and women who experience the breakup of their marriages.

The case-study interviews often revealed insights into causal relationships that have been the source of speculation among social scientists in the past. For example, we began our research with little understanding of the role that extramarital sexual involvements played in marital disruption. Our qualitative data began to reveal that there were both instances where marital discord seemed to develop or increase following an extramarital relationship—a finding many would expect; we also found cases where extramarital relationships developed following months or years of discord. These findings prompted us to examine the bidirectional influences between marital disruption and extramarital sex, eventually leading to the conclusion (elaborated in Chapter 3) that the presence of extramarital sex has different meanings for different individuals and couples.

The following quotations illustrate the point. In one statement, a man reveals a pattern of frequenting bars, picking up women, and drinking, due to loneliness.

> One night I met this girl at a bar and picked her up for the night. Anyway I told my wife about it right afterwards, and that caused another fight and messed things up again. . . . I met another girl in the same bar and went home with her for the night. Then I told my wife about it right after also. My timing always seems to be really lousy. Also I don't know why I always have to tell her immediately when I did something wrong. Maybe it's my Catholic upbringing. I think I need to be punished or something. They were both so senseless they didn't mean anything. I was just feeling lonely, and both times I was also drunk.

Another man told us of how his marriage began to deteriorate, suggesting that his wife's involvement with a professor signaled the beginning of the end. When asked by the interviewer "When would you say the problems started that led to the divorce?" he replied:

> Probably some time in the late 60s when she had gone back to graduate school. . . . She had an affair with her advisor. That really hurt me bad. She said then that she really didn't want to be married, and that was pretty hard to take at the time. Consequently, shortly after that I got involved with another woman for about a two-year period.

We then turned our attention to developing a survey instrument. Following two frustrating and challenging pretests, 210 individuals in Central Pennsylvania were interviewed in the spring of 1977. These were in-depth, structured, face-to-face interviews focusing on the social, psychological, and economic adjustments of males and females who had experienced a marital separation within approximately two years preceding the interview, whether or not they were divorced.

These individuals were reinterviewed in the summer and fall of 1979, approximately two and one-half years after the initial interview, as part of a follow-up study focusing on remarriage. Of the 210 respondents interviewed in 1977, we were able to obtain complete interviews in 1979 with 181 respondents. In addition, partial interviews were completed with an additional nine respondents. The data collected in the follow-up study (which included interviews with the new married or unmarried partners of the original sample) and in subsequent unstructured tape-recorded interviews with remarried couples are not included in this book but serve as the basis of another volume.

## Sample and Data Collection

Respondents for the initial case studies were recruited through public records available in Centre County, Pennsylvania. Three types of records were used as a basis for sampling: divorce decrees granted, divorce petitions filed, and child and spouse support agreements filed in conjunction with separation. In Pennsylvania, such records reveal all separated and divorced respondents except those who have separated informally but have neither filed for divorce nor requested support.

Potential respondents were individuals who had either filed for divorce or were divorced within the previous two years.

We eventually contacted in person or by phone 37 percent of the persons whose names we had obtained from the county records. The remainder were primarily people who were no longer residents of the county. Of the 37 percent we personally contacted, 61 percent agreed to be interviewed. The other 39 percent refused to participate in the study.

Interviews ranged from one and one-half to three and one-half hours, with a mean length of two and one-half hours. Immediately following each interview, the interviewers prepared field notes, as nearly verbatim as possible. The project director and the interviewers read each others' notes and met weekly to share ideas and to suggest topics or questions to be included in future interviews.

Following two pretests, sampling and data collection began for the in-depth, structured interviews. Nonprobability, purposive-sampling techniques were used. The population from which the sample was drawn consisted of all those separated persons in Centre County, Pennsylvania, whose separation had taken place between January 1975 and the time of the interview, March or April 1977. The selection and location of individuals was accomplished through various methods.

Feature articles describing the project were placed in several local newspapers. The purpose of these articles was to alert the community about the study and to attempt to set a tone for the study that might elicit cooperation and better response rates than is customary for research on this topic. This strategy proved to be a most helpful technique for increasing response rates as most of the respondents had read about the study and "felt it was legitimate" as a result of the newspaper write-up. Letters were sent to all attorneys in the county informing them of the study, and the domestic relations office staff at the county courthouse also was contacted for cooperation. These contacts and calls in response to the article produced a few respondents.

The primary method for obtaining participants involved procuring from public documents in the county courthouse names and addresses of those who had recently separated or divorced. A team from the project abstracted the files of eligible persons. Eligible respondents included persons still living within 50 miles of the county who had either (1) filed for divorce but had not yet received a decree; (2) obtained a divorce decree; or (3) separated and filed (or were filed against) for custody or support. Individuals who were informally separated but had not sought custody or support were obtained by the forms of solicitation mentioned above and, additionally, through snowball sampling techniques.

Letters were then sent to possible participants describing the study and requesting a response. Interviewers attempted to contact by telephone individuals who did not respond so that interview appointments could be arranged. Once persons were contacted and agreed to participate, respondents were given the choice of being interviewed in their homes or in the project offices. Babysitters were offered. Interviews ranged from one and one-half to three hours, with a mean length of two and one-quarter hours. The interview schedule, reproduced in the appendix to the book, contained approximately 550 questions.

Locating and recruiting a sample of separated and divorced individuals is a heroic task because of their reticence and mobility (Dean and Bresnahan, 1969). A total of 918 potential respondents were identified in the county. After three follow-up letters and numerous attempts via telephone to contact persons directly, 344 (37 percent) of the potential respondents were contacted. Of these persons 210 (61 percent) agreed to be interviewed and actually completed the interview. Five interviews were discarded after it was determined that the persons had been separated for longer than 26 months. This left 205 respondents available for analysis in the study.

Our response rates are low by standards typically used to judge the methodology of surveys but consistent with the success rates found in other studies that seek to interview separated or divorced men and women. These, after all, are individuals who tend to be highly mobile following separation, often have unlisted numbers, and sometimes are reluctant to talk to an interviewer because of their current distress. Why, then, do so many individuals agree to participate? We found two prevalent themes of respondent cooperation: wanting to have a sympathetic listener to hear one's story, and wanting to provide information that might ultimately help others. There were also a few individuals who were mostly curious. Said one respondent, "I would like to see the results [of the study] to sort of see how I measure up to other people."

## The Respondents

The respondents in our 50 case-study interviews were 28 females and 22 males, all caucasion. They ranged in age from 21 to 63 years old, with a mean age of 36. The mean length of marriage was 12 years, with a range of 1 to 38 years. Of the respondents, 32 were divorced at the time they were interviewed while the remaining 18 were separated but not yet divorced. The time since the couple last separated ranged from less than 1 month to 12 years, with a mean of 21 months and a median of 12 months. Only six respondents had been separated for more than three years.

Of the respondents, 29 were the plaintiffs in their divorce actions while 21 were the defendants. Sixteen of the respondents were childless, while 34 cases involved a total of 82 children including the adult children of older respondents. The respondents were fairly evenly distributed across the working, middle, and upper-middle classes.

The 205 respondents in our structured interviews consisted of 50 separated persons and 155 divorced persons. About 9 percent (N = 18) of the divorced persons had remarried at the time of the interview. In the sample 44 percent (N = 91) was male and 56 percent was female (N = 114). All respondents were white. The ages of the respondents ranged from 20 to 67 with a mean of 33. For both the respondent and his or her former spouse, the mean level of education was 14 years.

The sample was 12 percent Roman Catholic and 60 percent Protestant. Other religious preferences were stated by 9 percent, and 19 percent were atheist, agnostic, or had no religious preference. The total yearly income was less than $5,000 for 28 percent of the sample. As to yearly income 31 percent of the respondents earned between $5,000 and $9,999 while 23 percent had an income range of $10,000 to $14,999. The remaining 18 percent of the respondents had incomes greater than $15,000.

In 70 percent of the cases in which a divorce had been filed, the plaintiff was the wife. Of the divorces granted, 96 percent had not been contested. It was stated that both the respondent and his or her spouse were responsible for the break-up of their marriage by 47 percent of the respondents; 31 percent stated that their former spouse was responsible for the marriage breaking up. Of the respondents, 7 percent said they were responsible for the marriage breaking up, and an additional 7 percent stated that another person, such as a lover, was responsible for their marriage dissolving. The remaining 9 percent of the respondents felt no one should be blamed for the break-up of the marriage. The men and women in our sample had been separated between 1 and 26 months: 15 percent were separated 6 months or less; 20 percent between 6 months and a year; 25 percent between a year and 18 months; and 40 percent had been separated between 18 and 26 months. The median length of separation was 16 months.

The mean length of marriage was 9 years, with a range of 4 months to 45 years. In this sample, 8 percent had been divorced more than once. There was a total of 279 children in the 128 cases involving children (including the adult children of older respondents), although 38 percent of the respondents were childless. Of the 128 respondents with children, the wife had been awarded custody of the children in 73 percent of the cases. According to respondent reports, custody was decided by mutual agreement between the spouses of 68 percent of the respondents. The court decided the custody arrangements for 22 percent of the respondents, and in 7 percent of the cases the children primarily determined their own custody arrangement. Of the respondents, 74 percent expressed some degree of satisfaction with the custody arrangement. Child support was being received by 27 percent of the respondents while 19 percent were paying child support.

## The Legal Context

At the time of the study, Pennsylvania was one of three states that did not have no-fault divorce procedures. Recently, Pennsylvania has provided an additional option for individuals or couples contemplating a divorce—a provision for a no-fault divorce to be granted following a mandatory period of separation. However, at the time of the study grounds for divorce had to be specified under a traditional adversary system. This fact provided two opportunities: the chance to consider how divorce under an adversary system affected postseparation adjustment, and the ability to compare findings from our study with those of companion studies being conducted in California by Chiriboga and by Weitzman, and in Ohio by Kitson and Sussman. California had a fully operational no-fault system, and Ohio had a system of mixed grounds—that is, the opportunity to seek divorce either through traditional fault grounds or under the more liberal no-fault provisions. We shall say more about the impact of the legal system on the adjustment to marital separation in Chapter 3.

## Overview of the Book

The book features seven broad areas of importance as revealed to us by our respondents. These areas form the outlines of the chapters for the book. The chapters are organized to reflect the process of ending a marriage and moving on with one's life after separation. The organization reflects this chronology.

Chapter 2 addresses the marriage going sour and the couple moving toward separation. Chapter 3 considers the part played in the process of breaking up by people and forces outside the marital pair. The emotional response to breakup is featured in Chapter 4. In the next three chapters we consider continuity and change in various realms of life after separation. Chapter 5 looks at the partners after marriage. Chapter 6 focuses on friends and relatives after separation. Dating and sex are considered in Chapter 7. Finally, Chapter 8 highlights well-being after separation and how circumstances of ending a marriage and putting a new life together influence physical and mental well-being.

We begin with a consideration of the process of moving toward separation, considering the failing marriage in its final months, marital adjustment, sexual activity with the spouse, feelings toward the spouse at the time of separation, steps toward divorce, and issues of blame and reconciliation.

CHAPTER 2

# Moving Toward Separation

In order to understand the aftermath of separation and divorce, it is important to examine the events leading up to the breakup. In this chapter, therefore, we look back at the marriages that were to end eventually and chart their progress toward separation and divorce. The recollections of marriage provide portraits of misalliance between husband and wife and, more importantly, bestow an understanding of what the alliance has bequeathed to its partners.

In the sections that follow, we link the recalled characteristics of marriage to the process of marital breakup. Previous information available about afflicted marriages before dissolution is based on retrospective reports of former spouses (Cuber and Harroff, 1965; Goode, 1956; Kitson and Sussman, 1982; Levinger, 1966; Weiss, 1975). To find out how the divorce was experienced, Goode (1956) simply asked divorced women what they thought was the main cause of their divorce. A content analysis of these complaints revealed several themes. Among the 12 themes were nonsupport, drinking, incongruent values, disagreement about authority, another woman, and neglect of home life. Goode offers two dimensions that underly the themes of complaint: disagreement and involvement in the home. Using a similar method with divorced men and women, Kitson and Sussman (1982) report a historical shift in the content of complaints since Goode's study: Complaints in more recent breakups emphasize the affectional and sexual (rather than instrumental) involvement in marriage, and disagreement over gender roles. Even though the content may differ, the themes of disagreement and involvement persist.

Weiss (1975) presents different styles of bringing about the end of a marriage. Some marriages are relatively satisfying although one partner feels compelled to leave. By unilateral withdrawal or by convincing the mate to agree, separation occurs. Sometimes, in these cases, the end comes suddenly and unexpectedly. A woman contentedly married a little over two years described her husband's leave-taking:

> I didn't realize anything was wrong. To this day I don't know what went wrong. . . . I could tell something was on his mind. He was distant. When we woke up Saturday, he didn't touch me. He came up and hugged me really sadly in the kitchen. I said to him, "What's the matter? Don't you love me anymore?" He couldn't answer. Just cried. I tried to talk to him. He said, yes he loved me, but he didn't know. He had to get away. . . . He packed his suitcases and left. He said he needed to get away. . . . Later, I talked to him once. . . . I said "Please come back and talk." He said, "I can't." I got angry then, and I asked him if he didn't owe me something. He said, "No". That was it . . . I never ever heard from him again.

Most separations come about, however, after the marriage has been going badly for months, perhaps years (Cuber and Harroff, 1965). The final stage of marriage may be quarrelsome—filled with anger and anguish. One man described his 25-year marriage as "one long conflict." "It was never good," he said, "not any time that I can remember." Another man characterized the final months of his 3-year marriage in the following way:

> We argued about everything. . . . She was a lousy housekeeper, and we argued about that; she thought it was as much my responsibility as hers and maybe it was but we argued about it a lot. We argued about the dog. I don't know what else, all sorts of things.

He went on to explain his leaving at the end:

> I don't think there was anything special that caused it. . . . I'd been thinking about it for a while. It really happened sort of gradually. I would come home less and less frequently. I would stay away overnight and then for more and more days at a time, until finally I just moved out altogether.

In some instances, the anguish is worsened by one partner's refusal to talk or argue about the disintegrating marriage. One woman was separated only three weeks when we talked with her; she had filed for divorce. She told us her husband just started staying out late. He told her he has so much on his mind that he just "rides around."

> One week everything's fine, and the next week, everything's a mess. ... That's what makes it hard. It was so sudden. He was never late before; he never stayed away like this. ... He won't talk at all. Whenever I would bring something up, he'd say, "We'll talk later," or "I don't want to argue about it now." ... I don't want a divorce, and my husband says he doesn't either. But I just couldn't go on; I didn't know what to do.

She went on to describe the separation:

> He called last night; that was the first time. I've been a wreck. I cry all day at work. When he called, though, I forced myself to be calm. I didn't ask him anything, about where he's been or anything. He called back four times. I think he expected me to ask. He wants to know where I'm at, what I'm thinking, but he still won't tell me what he's thinking about.

The ambiguity and anguish of such a breakup are grievous.

Other couples have long ago dissipated the anger, and the final months before actual separation are spent with partners leading emotionally and behaviorally separate lives. When we asked a woman married 22 years what events led up to the final separation, she started her chronicle of trouble with, "It was years. We were married young." She ended by saying: "I had to try to build a wall around myself. I'd be in bed and tell myself I had to separate myself. It was a matter of survival." Separated men and women would often use phrases such as "drifted apart" and "gone our own separate ways" to account for their eventual separation. One middle-aged woman put it this way: "There was no warmth and affection anymore for him. It just eroded. Years and years. I didn't casually decide to end my marriage."

Notice the overriding themes of disagreement and involvement—or noninvolvement—in home life in all these characterizations. The disagreement and involvement themes are useful because they can be linked to the aftermath of separation and divorce. The amount of disagreement (incompatability, bickering, dissension, anger) and involvement (emotional and instrumental overlap of partners' lives) determines, in part, how painful it is to break out of a marriage and how painful it is to leave it behind. A person may experience relief rather than distress upon leaving an irritating and frustrating marriage (Kitson and Sussman, 1982). On the other hand, the accrued overlap in partners' lives does not dwindle to nothing as an immediate consequence of separation and divorce, and a high level of involvement during marriage may intensify the distress of a breakup (Chiriboga and Thurnher, 1978; Hetherington et al., 1976; Hunt, 1966). The linkage between conditions of marriage and the sequel of separation and divorce is the focus of later chapters.

The disagreements can be long-standing grievances in marriage or the acute discomforts of a relationship nearing its end. Involvement, as well, can be a stable characteristic of marriage or the approach and disengagement attempts of the final months. Some of our questions to respondents refer to general recollections of marriage while other questions refer to the terminal stage, the final months, of the relationship. Rather than asking the separated individual to generate the "causes" of his or her breakup, our approach was to have the respondent evaluate the marriage along dimensions associated with marital stability. Using the span of marriage as a referent, we asked about the degree of disappointment with the partner's performance across a range of instrumental and expressive domains, task participation at home, financial instability, and marital sex relations. Then we asked about involvement (companionship, affectional compatibility, sexual relations) and disagreement (consensus and marital harmony) in the final months of marriage. We consider general recollections first.

## Recollections of Marriage

We asked respondents to what extent their husband or wife lived up to their expectations in a variety of family and marital roles. Response choices ranged from very much to not at all. Disappointment with role performance differed for husbands and wives; of those who were parents, 40 percent of the women and 20 percent of the men reported that their spouse lived up to their expectations as a parent very little or not at all. As a group, the wives were more disappointed than the husbands in most domains of partner performance: As a helper with household tasks, 56 percent of the wives, as compared to 15 percent of the husbands, reported in the lower two categories of satisfaction. As leisure-time companion, 56 percent of the wives and 35 percent of the husbands expressed very little satisfaction with their partner's performance. As someone with whom to talk things over, 60 percent of the wives and 43 percent of the husbands were disappointed in their partners. Wives were slightly more disappointed than husbands in their spouse's performance as a sexual partner, and husbands were slightly more disappointed than wives in their partner's contribution to family income. The differences between husbands and wives were small in these two role domains, with about 30 percent reporting very little or no satisfaction with their spouse's performance as a provider and sexual partner.

To understand more fully the respondent's disappointment in the partner's role performance, we looked more closely at the housekeeper and provider roles. Table 2.1 shows the connection between division of household tasks and disappointment in the partner as a helper around the house. Task participation ranged from the partner usually doing the job, through sharing the task, to the respondent usually doing the job. Among both men and women, but particularly among women, the more responsibility a person has for doing the traditional female tasks around the house—grocery shopping, cleaning, and doing the dishes—the more disappointed the person was in the partner as a housekeeper. Participation in traditional male household tasks—repairs, servicing the car, keeping track of money and bills—was not as important in evaluating the partner's role performance. It seems that having to do more than one's fair share of traditional "housework" made a husband or wife judge his or her partner harshly when it came to the realm of maintaining the household; the tasks that men have traditionally done were not considered.

It was common during our interviews to hear men and women complain about household tasks and express their dissatisfaction with

TABLE 2.1
Correlations Between Participation in Household Tasks
and Disappointment in Partner as Housekeeper

| Task Participation* | Disappointment in Partner | |
| --- | --- | --- |
|  | Women | Men |
| Repair things around the house | .27** | .13 |
| Service the car | .02 | .09 |
| Keep track of money and bills | .03 | .04 |
| Do the grocery shopping | .30** | .23** |
| Clean the house | .51** | .38** |
| Do the evening dishes | .38** | .24** |

*A high score reflects greater self-participation in household tasks relative to partner's participation.
**$p < .01$

their former marital partner as homemaker. In each case, the overriding issue was conflict over gender role expectations. Marital power and the wife's employment were part of the wrangle, but dishes and dirt would set off the dispute. One man, who described his wife as always "wanting her own way about everything," characterized his marriage in the following way:

> Actually, her running around didn't bother me as much as her not doing any of the housekeeping duties. . . . I would not say anything about the filthy house, and then I would finally do the dishes, the laundry, and pick up the house. That didn't bother me so bad when she was working, but when she wasn't, I figured she would do it. . . . The fight would usually start after I would get home from work and see how sloppy the house was. We usually would argue at first about something else, but it usually ended up with me griping about the house. I couldn't understand why she didn't have the time to keep the house straight. I sometimes cleaned the whole house, and it would only take me about eight hours total. I never could convince her it was easier to do the dishes right after each meal rather than letting them pile up. . . . I should have been the dominant one from the beginning of the marriage. Instead, I just let things get out of hand since it's just not my nature to hassle people.

Another husband, who described his wife as "cold, unaffectionate, independent, assertive, domineering, and short-tempered," told us about the end of his 25-year marriage:

> A sort of resentment just built up over that two year period. I guess I'm pretty chauvinistic. I get tired of there never being meals, the house not being clean, and other things. Her starting to work full-time only made things worse. She thought I should help more than I did, even though I really didn't want to. . . . I had kept all of this to myself pretty much over the years. . . . So, we just gradually drifted apart. I became very unhappy and I'm sure she did too. She just wasn't the sweet, loving housewife I wanted.

We heard complaints from women as well. A young woman who told us her husband resented her return to school put it this way:

> He had an old fashioned idea that I should do all the housework. He had silly ideas from his Mom. I guess he carried it over. Like, he expected me to wash walls twice a year.

Another woman, married almost 15 years, described the frustration of her marriage:

> I cooked and cleaned; he brought home the paycheck. I was home with two small children and no adult to talk to, and he would go out all the time. . . . If we went to a party, he left me with the coats, and I had to find someone to talk to; otherwise, he just picked me up with the coats on his way out. . . . Someone was visiting us once and asked Hal why he dropped his clothes on the floor when he was standing right next to the hamper. And he told them it was easier to train me to pick them up than to do it himself. He'd always been very dominant; I liked him originally because he was so powerful. But he got extremely domineering.

After bemoaning his wife's transgressions as a homemaker, one man said, "I never was one for sitting around talking about trivial things." For many couples, housework is not trivial.

Looking more closely at the provider role, we found vast difference between wives and husbands in the connection of financial stability and the evaluation of the partner's performance. Among wives, financial stability in marriage and satisfaction with the husband's role as a provider were strongly connected ($r = .52$). A woman whose husband was always changing or losing jobs said, "He kept saying he always wanted to provide for me and take care of me, but it probably never would happen. I couldn't wait forever." Among husbands, the association between financial stability in marriage and satisfaction with the wife's performance in the provider role was negligible ($r = .15$). Only about one-fourth of the respondents considered their income before separation to be somewhat or very unstable.

In some marriages, of course, the respondent recalled that the partner had very much lived up to his or her expectations although this satisfaction was most likely to occur when respondents were rating the partner's traditionally gender-assigned role performance. That is, over half of the husbands chose the highest response choice in regard to their wife's performance as a parent and housekeeper, and over half of the wives seemed very content with their husband's performance as provider. In general, then, expectations were met in these marriages in areas of instrumental role performance where expectations are most clearly defined by gender-role norms. In domains where the expectations are expressive and shared (for example, someone to talk things over with) or where the partner is rating the other's performance in an area traditionally assigned to one's own gender (for example, women evaluating their husband's help with household tasks), disappointment is typical. In addition, wives were more disappointed in their husband's role performance than the other way around.

Many men and women were perplexed that they had done responsibly their traditional duties and, still, the marriage had fallen apart. As one woman said,

> For 26 years we had a good marriage. We were financially comfortable and owed no bills. . . . I don't know what else I could have done. I gave him his freedom; he needed it. I was understanding. Took care of him—meals and all.

A man who could have been responding to the woman above said the following:

> One thing about my wife is that she always took care of her duties. I mean that I always had clean, neat clothes and dinner always ready when it was time. But in other ways, she didn't think of me at all. . . . My wife never wanted to do anything with me. We really had no life together.

A young woman described what many of these people may have been searching and settling for in marriage:

> I could never depend on Jim. I couldn't talk to him. I couldn't open up. I wanted to tell him what was deep inside my heart, but I never did. Like I don't want you to do this or that because I feel like you don't care about me. He'd say I was stupid. See, he never showed any emotion except anger. I was his slave. Get me this. Get me that. Take off my boots. He felt that's what a wife is for. He needed love, too, I think, but I couldn't give it. It got to the point where I was so angry inside I hated him.

## Sex and Separation

It is not surprising that sexual relationships, inside and outside of marriage, are important dimensions in the path to divorce and in the adjustment that follows. As critical as sex is in contributing to marital quality, it similarly becomes critical in contributing to or detracting from marital stability. Many social scientists have written about the reciprocal, causal influences between sexual interaction and marital interaction, and we find in our study that this interdependence is important to keep in mind. In other words, the quality of one's sexual relationship influences the quality of the marital relationship; but the reciprocal is also true: the quality of one's marital relationship affects the quality of one's sexual relationship.

This obvious interaction takes on special meaning as separation approaches, when sex can become a very visible arena for demonstrating to one's husband or wife just how bad he or she feels or how intolerable the marriage is becoming. It is, of course, very difficult to show affection for your spouse when you are experiencing the deterioration of your marriage. Even if one wants to attempt to rescue the marriage by expressing a renewed degree of intimacy, such expression is likely to be emotionally difficult, unnatural, and strained. Consequently, as our data will illustrate, sex can become part of a vicious cycle contributing to the deterioration of the marriage in its final months, although for a small minority of the sample, sex and affection appear to be remarkably untouched by the turmoil of a failing marriage—in these cases being overwhelmed by other, more fundamental problems facing the couple. In this section, then, we follow the sexual relations of the couple from before the marriage to the final months before their final separation.

### SEX AND DATING BEFORE MARRIAGE

Our sample is not atypical of what would be found in a cross-section of similarly configured marriage cohorts in contemporary America. One in six respondents did not have sexual intercourse with anyone before marriage. One in four respondents had coitus with only one person, usually the eventual marriage partner. Another third had between two and five partners. And one-fourth of the sample had more than five partners (one respondent claimed to have more then one hundred partners, but we did not insist that he provide the exact number).

About half of the respondents began sexual relations with their future spouse during the six months before the marriage, about three-fourths of the sample within a year. Surprisingly, nearly one in ten respondents had been sexually involved with their future spouse for three years or more before they married. Seven individuals were sexually experienced but avoided coitus with the spouse before marriage. All but 10 percent of the respondents reported that they enjoyed sexual intercourse before marriage a great deal or somewhat; respondents provide quite similar reports of their spouse's degree of satisfaction.

One in five respondents was involved in a pregnancy before marriage, a figure roughly consistent with national norms. In our sample, where 41 respondents had experienced a premarital pregnancy, the most common outcome was a baby born after the wedding (45 percent). In another 23 percent of the cases, the baby was born before the wedding and kept by the mother. Only one respondent gave an illegitimate child up for adoption; three respondents reported miscarriages or stillbirths. It was reported by 23 percent of the respondents that they had terminated the pregnancy by abortion.

It is interesting to note in the qualitative reports several instances where men and women report problems relating to sex and dating before the marriage even began. These often become the themes of more serious problems later. One woman, commenting on her initial attraction to her husband, stated,

> My parents hated him and forbade me to see him. I think that made me like him more. He had money and a car.

A man made the following statement:

> Yes, we had sex before marriage. Our sexual relations really weren't very good, especially after we got married. She didn't enjoy sex very much and when I realized that, then I didn't either. She was inhibited.

Others recalled that things were pretty good before marriage, but turned sour later.

> Yes, we had sex before we were married. I think we had good sexual relations before marriage and especially early in the marriage, but our sexual relations seemed to deteriorate as other areas of the marriage deteriorated.

One respondent, half joking but half serious, noted, "I sometimes think if we could have stayed engaged there would never have been any problems."

Still others avoided sexual intercourse before marriage. In some cases, the avoidance of coitus before marriage was not reported to be tied to later consequences, whereas in other cases it was.

> The major problem after marriage was sexual, but I couldn't tell much about how she would be about that because we never had intercourse before marriage. It just wasn't as prevalent then as now, so I couldn't get an indicator there. We got into heavy petting but that was as far as it ever went. It became quite clear after marriage that there were different intensities of sexual interest.

## SEX AFTER MARRIAGE

Things tend to change after the wedding. Only 36 percent of our respondents report that sex remained about the same after the marriage. Although 34 percent report that sex became more pleasurable, 30 percent report that it became less pleasurable. We have no comparable data from other studies to suggest whether this pattern might be typical of marriages that remain intact; thus, it is difficult to surmise whether the distribution of changes might be at all predictive of subsequent alterations in the quality of marriage.

The conclusion that the quality of the sexual relationship begins to deteriorate for many couples early in the marriage is bolstered by several statements made in the case-study interviews. One man complained that his sexual relationship with his wife began to deteriorate immediately after the marriage:

> I don't think we had sex more than half a dozen times [in a year]. She just couldn't get interested enough and then, when we did it, put [such] pressure on me to make it really good for her that it just wasn't good for either of us. I really felt like I had to succeed every time.

In other instances, sex was fine early in the marriage and began to decline later. This is illustrated by the following exchange between interviewer and respondent:

> I: How was your sexual relationship during marriage?
>
> R: They were fine for awhile but then in the later years they became very difficult and then nonexistent.
>
> I: In what way, difficult?
>
> R: Well, when we weren't communicating and were having troubles it was hard to have good sex.
>
> I: Then would you probably say that the other problems caused the sexual problems and not that the sexual problems were a cause of the other problems?
>
> R: Yes, it was only when the other problems got bad that sex became difficult.

In order to contrast the nature of the sexual relationship early in the marriage with the period closer to the time of separation, we asked our participants for their recollections of the frequency of intercourse, how satisfied they were with the level of frequency, and the degree of satisfaction they experienced. The contrast is striking.

During the beginning of marriage, about half of our respondents report a frequency of intercourse of 15 times a month or more (an average of every other day or more often). Only 10 percent of the sample was having coitus once a week or less frequently. By the time the marriage had significantly deteriorated and separation was within months away, only 7 percent of the respondents were having intercourse 15 times a month or more while nearly three-fourths of the sample were having intercourse once a week or less. Almost a third of the men and women report that they had no sexual involvement with their partner in the final months. The median for frequency of intercourse during this period is two times per month. As one man said, "We didn't have any problems about sex until we had the other problems, and then the problem was mostly not wanting to have sex with someone you are mad at."

More than 70 percent of the respondents reported that they were having sexual intercourse about as often as they liked early in the marriage, but this fell to 39 percent as separation neared, as might be expected. Nearly half of the respondents reported that they were having sexual intercourse less often than they would have liked in the months before separation, a figure which is twice that reported for the beginning of marriage.

Satisfaction with sexual intercourse varied considerably at both times although, as would be expected, satisfaction deteriorates over the course of the marriage. Table 2.2 shows this comparison. Early in the marriage, more than half of the respondents say that they found their sexual relations very satisfactory. A similar proportion in the months before separation report that sexual intercourse was either a little unsatisfactory or very unsatisfactory. There were differences between men and women in satisfaction with the frequency and quality of sex during the final months: 62 percent of the men, compared to 39 percent of the women, would have liked sexual contact more often. Of the women 22 percent felt they already had sexual contact more often than they would like; no men felt this way. The remaining 40 percent of men and women were content with their level of sexual activity in marriage.

While men were more dissatisfied with the frequency of sexual activity than women, women were more dissatisfied with the quality. Half of the women found sexual relations with their husband to be very unsatisfactory in the final months, while only 28 percent of the men found sexual relations so unsatisfactory. Very few (8 percent of women and 16 percent of the men) found the final months of sexual involvement a very satisfying experience. As others record (Goode, 1956; Weiss, 1975), the process of disengagement begins long before the final separation.

A further indication of the deterioration of sex in the marriage is the specific nature of the sleeping arrangements. Perhaps a symbol of one's

**TABLE 2.2**
**Satisfaction with Sexual Relations During the Beginning of Marriage and in the Months Before Final Separation**

|  | Early in Marriage | | Before Separation | |
|---|---|---|---|---|
|  | Number | Percentage | Number | Percentage |
| Very satisfactory | 105 | 51.2 | 18 | 8.8 |
| Somewhat satisfactory | 60 | 29.3 | 37 | 18.0 |
| A little satisfactory | 27 | 13.2 | 39 | 19.0 |
| Very unsatisfactory | 10 | 4.9 | 64 | 31.2 |
| Not having intercourse | 3 | 1.5 | 47 | 22.9 |
| Total | 205 | 100.0 | 205 | 100.0 |

feelings more than anything else, men and women approaching divorce often redefine appropriate sleeping arrangements. Seven of our respondents had taken to sleeping in separate beds in the same room. More striking is that fully 29 percent of the sample had moved to a separate room in the same house.

Although the data in this section adequately reflect the reality that sex becomes a symptom of the deteriorating marriage, it is important to ask whether or not sex itself contributed significantly to the deterioration of marital quality. The data that follow mostly reveal that it did. Of course, we are aware from an earlier study (Spanier, 1976) that there is a tendency to downgrade one's evaluation of all aspects of marriage following divorce or separation—a reverse halo effect—and thus such reports must be evaluated cautiously. Of our respondents, 28 percent reported that sexual relations were a major problem in the marriage; another 27 percent report that it was a minor problem. About one-third of the sample reported that it was neither a problem nor a help to the marriage. Interestingly enough, and certainly illustrative of the diversity of experience, we found that about one in ten respondents reported that sexual relations actually helped hold the marriage together, presumably keeping the relationship going longer than it might have had the sexual bond not been so strong.

The men and women in our sample had much to say about the connection between marital discord and sexual satisfaction. One man commented,

> She could never really enjoy it, and then we fought more, that probably made it harder. Then, of course, when she wasn't interested that destroyed my confidence and made things worse.

A woman who had thought about the connection summarized it this way:

> Well, when we weren't communicating and were having other troubles it was hard to have good sex.

Another women said simply, "I think the sex problem was a reflection of our other problems."

## The Final Months

It is not surprising that most men and women recall the final months of their previous marriages as unhappy. Rating the overall happiness of marriage, a third of the men and almost half of the women recall their marriages as extremely unhappy—the lowest point on our preferred scale. The vast majority of separated and divorced people remember unhappy marriages, with only 8 percent of the men and 4 percent of the women reporting any degree of prevailing happiness. Half of the men and women report that they never or rarely thought that things between them and their spouses were going well. Characterizing the discord, the majority of both men and women did not frequently regret that they married or frequently discuss or consider marital termination. The majority, however, did recall quarreling or getting on each other's nerves at least more often than not. These marriages were apparently endured rather than enjoyed in the final months by most husbands and wives. Not all of the recollections of marriage, however, are so bellicose and grim; a considerable number of men and women recall marriages where calm and detachment reigned.

An account offered earlier in the chapter illustrated that calm and detachment may reign because one or both partners refuse to participate in conflicts of interest. We asked participants how they approached disagreement and conflict in the final months of their waning marriages: 22 percent said they tried to avoid it at all costs, 50 percent said conflicts was something they disliked but lived with, while 28 percent accepted conflict as normal. In the unstructured interviews, many men and women referred to their own or their partner's conflict tactics to explain the end of their marriage. Rands and her colleagues (1981) suggest three styles of conflicts: avoid, attack, and compromise. The separated men and women we spoke with did not talk much about compromise; they talked about avoidance and attack.

A middle-aged man described his manner of avoiding conflict in the following way:

> I never was very good at talking about my feelings and often, in order to avoid conflict, I would suppress the way I was feeling and defer to my wife. I think it bothered her when I was too passive, also when I would suppress or not face openly some issues just to avoid conflict. . . . I think if I would have been able to express

my feelings earlier while things were good that would have helped us to solve our later problems much easier.

Another man pointed to his wife's avoidance of conflict:

She just didn't want to talk about any problems. . . . I mean we always talked to each other but not about problems or how we were feeling. She never could really talk about what was bothering her.

It was clear from several reports such as this one that avoidance of conflict had undermined intimacy in marriage. Frustration and anger are common outcomes. A young woman tersely summarized the conflict process in her marriage: "My husband always ran away. Whenever we'd start to argue, he'd leave. He'd never work anything out, and I'd be left fuming."

Attack tactics in conflict can take many forms. A coercive style may include maligning the partner, threats, flagrant self-interest, demands, shouts, and violence. Attack tactics are cruel and uncompromising. They require that the other partner simply give in. One man characterized his wife and marriage in the following way:

She seemed to be very domineering. I could feel how she needed to be dominant. . . . She would never admit to being wrong about anything. She wanted her way about everything. . . . I just didn't like to get in a hassle, so I would let her have her way a lot of the time.

Another man put it this way:

Mostly she would start screaming at me, and I would just leave the room. I wasn't used to being screamed at as a kid, so I just didn't like it. . . . I would always give in to her. She always had to have her way.

As another man noted, seething or pouting can be an effective strategy:

When we would have a disagreement, she would stay angry for quite awhile, kind of pout and not have anything to say to me. I usually would end up apologizing in the end to get things back to normal. Things never got really loud because I just find that sort of thing very unpleasant.

Coercive conflict tactics can escalate into violence (Straus, 1979). A young woman with an explosive husband recalled the conflict in her marriage:

> Usually it was just hysterical screaming and throwing and smashing things. Then he'd start throwing things at me. It was never anything that showed on me; he always seemed to do things that wouldn't leave marks, like hair pulling and arm twisting. It was like he felt, "you're my wife and I'm the boss," and he had to prove it.

Over and over again, the people who had given in to their partner's demands would say, "I should have put my foot down a long time ago." Some were martyrs; some were submissive. Others avoided conflict at all costs. Putting one's foot down means taking an unwavering stand. Coercive tactics by one partner elicit the same from the other (Gottman, 1979; Raush et al., 1974). Particularly in the final months of marriage, many of the participants found mutual compromise or problem-solving impossible.

The content of disagreement provides an overview of the loci of strain in contentious marriages. Affectional and sexual issues seem to be particularly thorny: Over 70 percent of the men and women recall not showing love as a problem in the final months of marriage, while half report that they frequently to always disagreed about demonstrations of affection and sex relations. Disagreements about philosophy of life, things believed important, and the amount of time spent together are also frequent occurrences, while other issues lag somewhat behind in their persistence.

Disagreement about the amount of time spent together suggests the second major theme of disrupted marriages—involvement. The so-called estranged marriage is often just that: Partners keep their distance from each other and lead emotionally and behaviorally separate lives (Goode, 1956; Weiss, 1975). Although having a stimulating exchange of ideas and working on a project together are rare occurrences in these dissolving marriages, half of the husbands and wives continued to confide in their mates more often than not. About half of the men and women also recall laughing or calmly discussing something with their mates at least once or twice a week in these final months of marriage. For many, then, companionship persists until the end of marriage, although not at the level of more stable relationships. Concerning interests outside of the home, a third of the men and almost two-thirds of the women report sharing none or very few of these activities with their wives and husbands.

The waning attractiveness of marriage is reflected in the diminution of personal commitment to its continuance. One-fourth of the men and women chose the statement representing the lowest level of commitment: "My marriage could have never succeeded, and there was nothing more that I could have done to keep it going." The vast majority recall that by the final months they had already done everything possible to help the marriage succeed with only the desire and hope for success varying among them. Only 12 and 15 percent of the men and women, respectively, desperately wanted their marriages to succeed and would have gone to almost any length to see that it did by the final months. Table 2.3 shows how the respondents felt about their partner by the time of the final separation. Men were more likely than women to still love their partner or to feel numb, while women were more likely to feel ambivalence, mild affection, or even hate.

Marriage is notoriously different for men and women, and the reconstruction of failed marriages in this study is no exception. In rating dimensions of the dissolved marriage, men recall greater consensus, companionship, compatibility in affectional realms, and harmony than women recall; the first three dimensions noted are significantly different for men and women. Researchers must be cautious about interpreting these differences as indicating actual differences in the emotional and behavioral experience of marriage. Nevertheless, a close examination of the distributions reveals that with very few exceptions, women as a group rate every item evaluating their previous marriage more negatively than men. Supposing that the items

TABLE 2.3
Feelings for Partner at the Time
of the Final Separation (in percentages)

|  | Women (%) | Men (%) |
|---|---|---|
| Still loved him/her | 17.7 | 35.2 |
| Still liked, but didn't love him/her | 21.2 | 15.4 |
| Didn't feel much of anything | 17.7 | 27.5 |
| Hated him/her | 18.6 | 4.4 |
| Both loved and hated him/her | 24.8 | 17.6 |
| TOTAL | 100 | 100 |

do not have a drastically different meaning for men and women and that there is no gender-linked propensity to blacken the memory of a bygone marriage, it is safe to conclude that the final months of marriage hold fewer positive attractions and are more costly for women than for men.

Previous research with intact and failed marriages supports this conclusion. In global assessments of marital satisfaction and happiness, women typically report their marriages as less satisfying and happy than men (Campbell et al., 1976; Glenn and Weaver, 1978). Such findings are often taken to mean that marriage is less rewarding and more costly for women than for men (Bernard, 1972). In remembrances of failed marriages, women seem to be more sensitive to the problems that existed. In the case of premarital breakups (Hill et al., 1979) and interviews with divorce applicants (Levinger, 1966), women cited more problems and complaints with the relationship than did men. Finally, women reportedly experience more distress in the predivorce period of marital dissolution than do men (Albrecht, 1980; Nager et al., 1977), while men are more apt to evaluate the predivorce time favorably than are women (Albrecht, 1980). It may well be that the terminal stage of marriage is more unpleasant for women than it is for men.

The portrait of the end of marriage just offered is an aggregated one. It represents the typical experience of separated and divorced men and women rather than the actual experience of any individual. Unfortunately, the richness of exceptional cases is lost. The woman who considered herself contentedly married only to come home one day to a note on the kitchen table from her deserting husband is lost in a sample where the overwhelming majority of couples endured a deteriorating marriage and deliberated about its dissolution for months or even years. There are not enough cases where the marriage was truly a happy one for at least one partner to glean an understanding of this exceptional experience. The reports are also reconstructions of marriage—painfully and deliberately constructed accounts of what went wrong (Weiss, 1975). As such, it is unlikely that the descriptions of marriage are objective or would be similar to reports of dissolving marriages gathered concurrently; but recalled experience has an importance of its own (Goode, 1956).

## Deliberation and Decision

Most separations and divorces are preceded by a period of conflict and deliberation. We asked our respondents about the timing of events in their marital histories that mark phases in the move toward final dissolution. Respondents recalled when they first thought their marriage might end in separation or divorce, first openly discussed divorce with their partner, were first certain that their marriage was going to end, first separated even for a short time, finally separated, and filed for divorce. Similar to Goode (1956), we wanted to look at the timing and sequence of these markers.

Three events of divorce deliberation vary in timing but not in sequence: (1) foreboding of possible breakup; (2) certainty about the end of marriage; and (3) filing for divorce. On the other hand, both discussion about divorce and actual separation can occur anywhere in the sequence. The order of the events and the swiftness of deliberation tell us a lot about the circumstances and anticipation of the end of marriage. Diversity in the spacing of the three deliberation events is presented in Table 2.4.

As we might expect, the period between thinking separation or divorce might occur and certainty about the event is longer than the period from certainty to filing. In general, the decision period from certainty to filing took about 3 to 4 months in our sample, and the

**TABLE 2.4**
**Time Between Events of Deliberation and Decision (in percentages)**

| | Phases | | | |
| | Foreboding to Certainty | | Certainty to Filing | |
| Time in Months | Women | Men | Women | Men |
|---|---|---|---|---|
| less than 1 | 11.7 | 21.2 | 32.7 | 22.7 |
| 1–6 | 17.1 | 17.6 | 25.7 | 42.6 |
| 7–12 | 9.9 | 10.6 | 20.8 | 12.0 |
| 13–24 | 18.1 | 16.5 | 10.9 | 6.7 |
| more than 24 | 43.2 | 34.1 | 11.9 | 16.0 |
| Total | 100 | 100 | 100 | 100 |
| median | 22 mo. | 12 mo. | 4 mo. | 3 mo. |

timing is similar for men and women. Length of deliberation between foreboding and certainty, however, differs for men and women. The duration for men is about a year (median = 12 months), while women were aware of the possibility of separation and divorce for almost two years (median = 22 months) before certainty settled in or struck. Women considered the possibility of breakup earlier in their marriages than men; for example, 16 percent of the women as compared to 8 percent of the men recall experiencing foreboding in the first month of marriage. One woman said, "I knew in the back of my mind from the beginning it would never work." A young woman married three years described her foreboding in this way: "The first year, I kept thinking, 'Oh, it's the first year, it'll get better.' Then it didn't during the second year, and soon I knew that was it." A man married almost 20 years recalled doubts he had had early in the marriage: "I think we both knew as early as the first two years that we had made a mistake. We knew it was not working but we just sort of muddled through." Both foreboding and certainty are subjective markers and may be very different for the two partners involved. The timing of events that apply to both partners—discussion of separation and divorce, actual separation, and filing—have very similar distributions for men and women.

Length of marriage is, of course, associated with the duration of deliberation about separation and divorce. The longer the marriage endured, the more time was spent anticipating and moving toward the end of marriage. Time spent in one phase of deliberation is also related to time spent in the other phase. The phase from foreboding to certainty is associated with *less* time given to the phase from certainty to filing ($r = -.25$ for women and $-.45$ for men). Rather than the whole process being slow or swift, then, it seems that haste in one phase is linked with hesitation in another. Duration from foreboding to filing can be considered anticipation time. Women tend to have a longer anticipation period than men (the median is 31 months for women and 18 months for men), although a fifth of both men and women experience the entire dissolution process in 6 months or less. Having children tended to draw out the deliberation period (gamma = .34).

Open discussion about divorce between marital partners can occur at any time in the dissolution process. For half of the men and women involved, the first open discussion occurred *before* the partner was certain that his or her marriage was going to end. For another 40 percent of the partners, the first discussion coincided with their certainty about the end of marriage. The remaining 10 percent did not discuss divorce with their partners until after they were certain about the end of their marriage. About half of these partners timed the discussion between certainty and filing, while the other half never discussed the divorce or waited until after filing.

For some couples, discussion of divorce recurred throughout the marriage as a serious consideration or as a threat. Many couples vacillated painfully. They talked again and again about whether to separate or to try to mend their marriage. The uncertainty was excruciating. A woman, whose husband had filed for divorce but was still living in the house, portrayed the agony of indecision.

> This sounds weird, but he's trying to stay here, but he wants to go away. He's mixed up. . . . Sometimes I think he still loves me. Just that he's *here*. He's sort of clinging to us. He doesn't want to give us up. Why else would he stay? . . . He's afraid to have anything to do with me. He says he doesn't love me, but I think he just does things to get back at me. The love is there, but he wants to hurt me. Sometimes he wants to kiss or hold me I can tell, but I won't. He thinks I've hurt him through the years. I don't know. If I did, I didn't know it.

Other couples had batted around breakup as a threat so often that they failed to recognize the importance of the final discussion:

> She started talking a lot about how maybe the marriage was a mistake and maybe we should separate and get a divorce. At first I didn't think she was very serious, I mean she threw the idea of divorce up every time we had a row right from the first of the marriage, but it was just off the top of her head. She was never serious about it before.

Another man, who admitted that he was not as involved with his wife as she would have wanted, was surprised by their first and only discussion:

> It all happened all of a sudden. Things were just about the same right up till the time she left. We had an argument on a Saturday afternoon. I don't even remember what it was about. Anyway, after the fight, she said that she wanted a divorce and that she wanted half of the money, and that she would leave. I said that that was fine with me, but I really thought she was just bluffing.

It is charitable to call that a discussion; it is more an announcement. For some, there was no discussion and no announcement; the partner just left:

> Nothing made sense to me during those first few months of the separation. I didn't really know what was going on. I kept trying to talk to her and find out what was bothering her, but she wouldn't talk about it. I talked to friends of ours and asked them to find out anything they could. I even asked her mother to find out what was wrong, but nobody would tell me. I found out later that most of them, including her mother, knew about the other man, but nobody would tell me. . . . I was depressed and confused, and I just didn't know what I had done or what to do about it. I figured we could work it out if we tried.

Separation is an event that may occur at any point in the process of martial breakup. The typical pattern is for the man or woman to have thought about the possibility of separation and divorce, discussed the possibility with the partner, reached a level of certainty about the breakup, and finally separated from the partner. Although this is the typical pattern, there is a sizable minority for whom events did not proceed in this way. For example, a quarter of the partners discussed the divorce coincident with the final separation while another 10 percent did not discuss the breakup until after the separation. For 35 percent of the sample, the final separation coincided with their certainty about the end of their marriage. Another 15 percent were not certain until after the final separation. For the most part, these people cited filing as the point of certainty.

More than filing for divorce or the decree, the final separation marks the end of marriage for most people. Those men and women who had a longer deliberation overall (foreboding to filing) were more likely to have a longer period of certainty before the final separation. Those people with the shortest deliberation (0–6 months) were more likely than those with longer anticipation time to be certain that the marriage was ending only when or after someone finally moved out ($X^2 = 41$, df = 9, $p < .01$). In our sample, it was rare (7 percent) for both partners to move out of the house at the final separation, and it was more often the wife who moved out (51 percent) than the husband (42 percent).

For about half of our participants, the final separation was the only separation. Among those with a previous separation, the first separation was, of course, much more ambiguous than the final separation, especially in retrospect. One young woman described the period between her first and final separations:

> See, he never could hold a steady job. Beat me and knocked me around. I had him arrested in May, and he spent three days in jail. He cried, said he'd change and begged me to come back. He loved me and couldn't live without me. The same old story. Well, I went back to him in June and things were fine, really good. He treated me wonderful until October or November, then he started mistreating me again. Forced me to do things I didn't want to do. He'd hit me if I gave him coffee that was too hot. He was insane.

For many of those with more than one separation (4 percent of the men and 27 percent of the women), the first separation was the first time the person had any sense that his or her marriage might break up. A third of the men and women separated the first time with *no* prior discussion of ending the marriage and, in retrospect, the first separation occurred before the partner felt certain about the breakup for the majority of partners. A man married 11 years recalled that things started going badly about a year and a half into his marriage when the first child was born. He described the sequel to his first separation:

> She started calling and said she had made a mistake and wanted the family to get together again. She wanted to come back and try again. At first I wasn't sure, but then I got thinking that I would probably always be wondering if we could have made it. I knew I was still in love with her. So, I said okay and I stopped the divorce proceedings, and she moved back in. Well, within two weeks it became obvious that she was just sitting around moping about the other guy and that she was not serious in really trying to make our lives together work. So, I told her to leave.

Although the marriage had been deteriorating for almost a decade, he was not certain that his marriage was over until he discovered that his wife was seeing someone else. In the highly ambiguous situation of bringing a marriage to a close, the presence of "the other man" or "the other woman" may be necessary to clinch certainty.

In comparing the final separation for those who did and those who did not experience a previous separation, men and women with more than one separation were more likely to have openly discussed and be certain about the end of marriage by the time of the last separation than participants who experienced only one, final separation.

The timing and sequence of the above events are important because they tell us something about the anticipation and ambiguity of ending a marriage. Not only are timing and sequence of dissolution events related to the circumstances of marriage and its demise but also to the emotional impact of the breakup. In subsequent sections and chapters, we use duration of the period from foreboding to certainty, the period from foreboding to final separation, the ordering of certainty with final separation, and the occurrence of a previous separation to understand anticipation and ambiguity in movement toward divorce. By the time of the respondents' interviews with us, there was little question that the marriages were over (only 12 percent of the men and women fostered thoughts of reconciliation) although such certainty was imposed on some of the marriage partners.

Recollection of the partner's role performance in marriage was not related to the length of time required to move toward separation. The only exception was among women and men who were parents. Recalled satisfaction with the partner's parenting performance was associated with a slower movement toward separation than among the more dissatisfied partners.

The majority of women and men approached the final months before separation with an inkling, if not a certainty, that the marriage was over. From the husband's vantage point, the longer period from foreboding to final separation was associated with greater consensus ($r = .23$), but lower companionship ($r = -.22$) in the final months of marriage. Among wives, however, those who had anticipated the breakup for a longer time recalled less harmony in the final months of marriage ($r = .20$) than those who had a shorter time from foreboding to final separation.

In general, with our data we did not find that the degree of disappointment with the partner's role performance as parent, provider, housekeeper, sexual partner, companion, or confidant slowed or hastened the movement toward breakup. We also found only slight indications that the time spent anticipating and deliberating the dissolution was associated with the quality of marriage in its terminal stage. We thought, perhaps, that a longer approach to separation might be linked with a calmer, although more distant, marriage near the end. This is somewhat the case among husbands, but among wives there was greater rancor and conflict with a longer approach to separation than with a shorter approach.

Using an index of the extent to which the partner lived up to the respondent's expectations summed across the several domains, the degree of satisfaction with the spouse was connected to the relative timing of separation and certainty about the end of marriage among wives. Wives who were more satisfied with their husband's performance were more likely than disappointed wives to be uncertain that the marriage was over until the final separation—or even after (gamma = .32). The timing of the separation was not related to evaluations of the partner's performance among husbands. Of the four dimensions of marital quality, only affectional expression in the final months of marriage was related to the timing of separation. Among both men and women, the recollection of sexual and affectional incompatibility in the terminal stage of marriage was related to a longer phase between certainty that the marriage was over and the final separation (gamma = −.34).

Commitment reflects dedication to the continuance of the relationship. It is not surprising that among women the expression of greater commitment in the final months of marriage is connected with disbelief that the marriage was going to end until separation or after; while those women who reported a lag period between certainty about the end of marriage and the final separation were more likely to express less commitment by the final months of marriage (gamma = .34). Among men, commitment in the terminal stage of marriage was unrelated to the timing of certainty and separation.

When does a person finally know that his or her marriage is over? Frederico (1979) says that a person reaches a "point of no return" at which he or she gives up on the idea that the marriage has more emotional gains than costs. At that point, emotional investment in the marriage wanes and can never be recovered. Typically, the marital partner is not aware or is reluctant to accept that the marriage is over. According to Frederico, it is probably only in retrospect that a person can identify the point of no return and recognize his or her strategies for bringing the marriage to a close. The strategies serve to sabotage the marriage and spread out responsibility for its demise, although neither partner may realize what is happening.

The final separation openly declares the end of marriage. Yet a person may reach the point of no return long before the separation. Among both men and women in our sample, sexual and affectional incompatibility in the final months was linked with a longer period between certainty that the marriage is over (the point of no return) and final separation. We cannot say whether certainty led to sexual and affectional upheaval in marriage, or whether such upheaval clinched certainty. Regardless of the causal connection, however, it is clear that sex and affection are at the center of the emotional end of marriage. Women seem to accumulate evidence from realms of marriage other than sex and affection. Their disappointment in their husband's role performance and their own subsiding commitment was linked with their certainty about the end of marriage. Women who were relatively satisfied with their husbands and committed to their marriages more often needed the separation to mark the end of marriage.

## Suggestion and Blame

Marital dissolution by divorce is typically considered a mutual and voluntary decision (Levinger, 1979), but accounts of failed marriages consistently reveal that one partner wants and pushes for the divorce more than the other partner (Cuber and Harroff, 1965; Goode, 1956; Hunt, 1966; Weiss, 1975). Although an admitted oversimplification, the issue is most often reduced to "the leaver" and "the left" (Weiss, 1975) or the "breaker-upper" and the "broken-up-with" (Hill et al., 1979). Hill and his colleagues regard this differentiation as crucial to understanding everything else about ending relationships.

In our sample, 64 percent of the women claim to have first suggested the divorce, 27 percent pointed to the spouse as having first suggested the divorce, and 9 percent saw the divorce as a mutual conclusion. This distribution is almost identical to that reported by Goode's (1956) divorced women over 20 years ago. Among the men in our sample, 34 percent accept responsibility for the initial suggestion to separate or divorce, 47 percent attribute the suggestion to the spouse, and 19 percent recall a mutual conclusion. Women are clearly more likely than men to suggest the final separation or divorce, although there is also a tendency toward self-bias for women and men in such reports (Hill et al., 1979).

Specifying the leaver and the left does not, however, accurately portray the complexity of control over the process and progress of marital dissolution. Goode (1956) speculates that it is actually more often the husband who first wishes to escape the marriage and, by various strategies of withdrawal and conflict, maneuvers the wife into suggesting a divorce out of sheer exasperation. As evidence, Goode reports that the length of deliberation between serious consideration and filing for divorce is much shorter when the husband suggests the divorce than when the wife suggests the divorce; divorce by mutual conclusion takes the most time.

Our data show that regardless of the phase of deliberation addressed, divorce by mutual conclusion involves a longer deliberation time than it does when one spouse unilaterally suggests the dissolution. We found no evidence that the progress of moving toward final separation or filing for divorce was more swift when the husband suggested the breakup than when the wife suggested the breakup. There were, of course, differences in the duration of phases depending on whether the partner was the leaver or the left. Regardless of gender, the anticipation and deliberation period was longer for those partners who suggested the separation or divorce themselves rather than received the suggestion from the spouse. As markers of duration reflect subjective foreboding and certainty, it is sensible that the partner who finally suggests the end of marriage has had more time to anticipate its demise. Among those on the receiving end of the suggestion, only 28 percent of the women and 30 percent of the men reported that they were very or completely surprised by the idea. The majority of partners suspected that their marriages might end even if they themselves did not suggest the breakup.

It seems plausible that differences in who suggested the separation or divorce was associated with differences in the attractiveness of marriage, but this was not the case among the women in our study. Among men, however, who suggested the divorce was related to marital harmony ($X^2 = 8.8$, df = 2, $p < .01$) and commitment to marriage ($X^2 = 9.9$, df = 2, $p < .01$) in the final months. Men were more likely to claim that they first suggested the divorce or that it was a mutual decision if they recalled the final months of marriage as lacking harmony and personal commitment. Attributing the initial suggestion to the wife was associated with recollections of greater harmony in and personal commitment to marriage. Although the pattern did not reach statistical significance, it persisted across several other variables among men: Husbands more often attributed the initial suggestion to their partners when the husbands recalled greater companionship in marriage and felt that their wives had lived up to their expectations as parent, provider, sexual partner, and confidant. They were more likely to report a self- or mutually initiated separation or divorce if they recalled less companionship in the final months of marriage and greater disappointment in their wives' role performance.

Among men, then, memories of a good marriage are linked with attributing the first suggestion to end the marriage to the partner. We can infer that men tend to suggest the divorce themselves or cooperate in a mutual decision when they wish to break out of an unattractive marriage. We cannot draw a similar conclusion about women from our data.

Responsibility for the initial suggestion to separate or divorce and blame for the breakup are two different aspects of control over the process of marital dissolution. The respondents were asked, "If you had to assign blame for the breakup of your marriage, whom would you blame?" Table 2.5 compares the target of blame for the breakup with the source of the initial suggestion to separate or divorce. Very few partners are willing to take the blame for a one-sided breakup (7 percent). Blaming a person outside the relationship is also uncommon (7 percent). Sharing the blame with the spouse is the typical pattern (55 percent), although attributing blame for the breakup solely to the spouse is quite common (31 percent). As a group, husbands are somewhat more likely to blame their wives for the breakup than the other way around.

The source of the first suggestion to breakup and attribution of blame are related, but a different impression of the dissolution emerges from the two approaches. Separation or divorce by mutual conclusion is associated with sharing of blame for the breakup between partners. Among those who recall that the spouse first suggested the separation or divorce, it is equally likely that these men and women will blame the spouse solely or share the blame with their spouse. In the self-suggested

TABLE 2.5
Source of Suggestion to Separate or Divorce
and Target of Blame for Breakup (in percentages)

| Source of Suggestion | Target of Blame | | | | |
|---|---|---|---|---|---|
| | Myself | Spouse | Mutual | Other Person | Total |
| Myself | 9 | 28 | 57 | 6 | 100 |
| Spouse | 7 | 40 | 45 | 8 | 100 |
| Mutual | 0 | 15 | 78 | 7 | 100 |

breakup, the tendency is to share the blame. A good proportion of partners, however, attribute blame for the breakup to their spouses even though they themselves initially suggested the separation or divorce. Among the self-suggested cases, women were more likely to share the blame with their husbands while men tended to place the blame squarely on their wives. There is no evidence in these recollections, then, that it is more often the husband that wants to escape the marriage.

Even more than the source of the initial suggestion to end the marriage, we thought the target of blame for the breakup would be linked with recollections of the marital relationship, but our data did not bear this out. For both women and men, the degree to which their marital partners lived up to their expectations in various role domains and the quality of marriage in the final months were not related to how the respondent partialled out blame for the breakup.

## Summary

Many marital partners were disappointed in their mate's role performance. Husbands and wives expressed the greatest disappointment about the mate as companion and confidant. Across domains, women evaluated their husbands more severely than men judged their wives. Women were particularly disappointed in their husbands as parents and helpers with household tasks. Although wives had unmet expectations of their husbands regarding those roles traditionally assigned to women, husbands did not display similar disappointment in their wives as providers. Disappointment in one's mate, therefore, revolved around affectional involvement and the husband's failure to share roles traditionally assigned to women. As one women said,

> After we were married, I realized all he wanted was a housekeeper, bed partner, and maid. . . . [He wanted] someone to do all the housework, and someone who never got tired. I expected more than I got, that's for sure. . . . I wanted someone who was understanding. I thought I should be able to talk to my husband about my feelings and problems, but I couldn't.

For most people, the final months of marriage were characterized by dissension and withdrawal. Companionship, sex, and affection continued to be at the center of disagreement and involvement. Although most husbands and wives had reduced their involvement in the marriage, they were still tied to their partner and still haggled over their independence. One young woman described the haggling in this way:

> He was always checking up on me, calling, "Where was I?" He didn't want me going out by myself, even when he was at work, didn't want me seeing my friends. He couldn't understand why I'd want to go out to dinner with a male friend who was very close, and I hadn't seen in years. Things like that. Married couples were supposed to do everything together. . . . He was so dependent, needed me so much. . . . I wanted us each to have our own separate lives and one together. . . . According to him I was frigid. He was all touchy-feely. He always wanted me next to him, cuddling. I wasn't supposed to sit across the room from him ever, always next to him on the couch. He said if we couldn't be like husbands and wives were supposed to be, then he wanted to be divorced. I agreed.

Women had a bleaker view of marriage in the final months than men. By the time of the final separation, women felt less affection for their mates than men. The terminal stage of marriage may be more unpleasant for women, but they may also be more prepared for the marriage to end.

Disappointment in the partner's role performance did not hasten or delay the pace of moving toward separation. Only children seemed to make a difference: Among both women and men, having children slowed the progress even more. Among husbands, there was some evidence that a longer approach to separation meant less disagreement and less involvement by the final months—a gradual calm and withdrawal. Among wives, however, there was greater dissension and irritation in the final months if the separation was a long time coming.

Typically, partners thought about the possibility of breakup, discussed the possibility with the partner, reached a level of certainty about the end of marriage, and finally separated. For those who did not experience the breakup in this way, it was likely that the open discussion of the divorce, the actual separation, and certainty that the marriage was over all happened at once. These people tended to have a shorter time between thinking that their marriage might end and believing that it would. For them, there was less anticipation of the end, and the objective events of dissolution—open discussion and actual separation—occurred together and precipitated their certainty about the crumbling of their marriage. For many, an attempted separation preceded the final separation. Particularly among men with more than one separation, the first separation was likely to be the first time they had any sense that the marriage might be breaking up. Afterward, the final separation usually followed the typical pattern described above.

Among both men and women, sexual and affectional incompatibility in the final months was linked with a longer period between certainty that the marriage was over and the final separation. Sex and affection are the emotional battleground in the dissolving marriage: Partners use sex and affection to sabotage or save the marriage. Shifts in sexual and affectional involvement reflect the partners ambivalence about the end of marriage. Partners also use sex and affection to gauge the viability of their marriage. A woman married only two years gave the following account of feelings and messages gone amiss:

> We didn't argue. There wasn't anything specific to argue about. . . . He was so unhappy, and I always wondered if it was me. . . . Sometimes he was just depressed and wouldn't do or say anything. I took it as disinterest, especially in me as a woman. I got really jealous of him, of where he spent his time, of when he wasn't with me. He took that as my trying to trap him and just withdrew more.

For those who were reluctant to admit the end of marriage based on its emotional climate, only a physical separation seemed to convince them that the union was over. Moreover, women seemed to be more sensitive than men to the emotional keel of marriage and attended to a wider range of cues when judging the success of and hope for their marriage.

CHAPTER 3

# Outsiders

No marriage or divorce involves only the man and woman who participated in the marriage ceremony. There are always "outsiders" who have a stake in the marriage and consequently influence its direction. There are also powerful social forces that influence the conduct of marriage and the process of dissolution. Our society's economic, legal, and political systems, for example, may have consequences for a couple. Friends and family may be influential. Extramarital sexual partners sometimes play a role in the dissolution of a marriage. In this chapter we consider the impact on the disintegrating marriage and the partners of such outside influences. We examine how these outside influences provide barriers or inducements to the breakup. Specifically, we consider extramarital sexual partners, children, reactions of family and friends to the disintegrating marriage, economics, legal barriers, and professional help for marriage problems. All these outside forces can either push the husband and wife together or pull them apart.

## Extramarital Sexual Partners

More than a generation ago, many people were surprised by the findings that one-half of American men and one-fourth of American women surveyed by Kinsey and his colleagues had had extramarital coitus by the age of 40 (Kinsey et al., 1948; Kinsey et al., 1953). More recent estimates based on journalistic surveys suggest only a moderate change over the course of a generation. It is likely, however, that to the extent there is change it is undoubtedly on the increase, particularly among women. Yet when Hunt (1974) asked over 2000 respondents whether they would object if their mates were to have an extramarital love affair or have extramarital coitus, 80 to 90 percent of the sample responded that they or their mates would object. Other studies based on national samples report similar data (Glenn and Weaver, 1979; Singh et al., 1976). What we find in America, then, is the existence of a widespread practice that is disapproved of by a substantial majority of the population. It is no wonder, then, that the role of extramarital sexual relations in the termination and aftermath of marriage is interesting.

In this section we examine the role that such relationships played in our sample. Clearly, with or without a spouse's objections or knowledge, extramarital sex is a phenomenon affecting a significant number of married individuals. This activity may directly affect marital quality and, consequently, marital stability (whether or not a marriage remains intact). Extramarital sex may be viewed as either a cause or a consequence of marital problems, or as unrelated to them. Undoubtedly, extramarital sex and divorce both result from many interrelated influences. It is likely that for some individuals extramarital sex and marital problems reciprocally influence each other and culminate in divorce.

Many individuals, including three-fifths of our sample, have not had extramarital sex and therefore do not report extramarital relationships as a factor in the dissolution of the marriage. Thus, it is important to recognize that this phenomenon is an issue in only some cases. When asked about extramarital sex, responses to our case-study interviews ranged from speculations about "what if" to reports of some unusual extramarital arrangements that influenced the marriage, as illustrated by the following comments:

> Not on my part for sure. I think I can say with pretty much safety that she hasn't either. It's funny, but it might have been good if she had; then I would know that she could have those type feelings. Our relationship was just so damned platonic. I know it seems like a paradox, but she could be very warm and sensitive, but just couldn't really give herself wholly to anyone.

Another man revealed the following:

> We got involved in what you might call a group marriage. For about a year another man and I would switch houses for a day or so, swapping wives and kids. After about a year we decided that we should all move in together, and all ten of us formed a group marriage. We had this arrangement for about another year, when we decided to get the divorce.

Why do some married persons engage in extramarital sex whereas others do not step out of the boundaries of marriage? Explanations include the need for sexual variation, retaliation, rebellion, new emotional satisfaction, development of sex from friendship, spousal encouragement, and the aging factor (Bell, 1963); use of alcohol, lack of maturity, and uncooperativeness of the mate (Christensen, 1958); alienation and opportunity factors (Whitehurst, 1969); compensatory measures for a defective marriage, discontinuity of many marriages, and nonacceptance of a monogamous commitment (Cuber, 1969); and inequitable relationships (Walster et al., 1978). One man simply stated, "I guess I just got bored being married. The girl I was running around with was just the opposite of my wife."

A discriminant analysis was performed using the occurrence of extramarital coitus (EMC) as the dependent variable; group 1 consisted of those respondents who did not engage in extramarital coitus, and group 2 consisted of respondents who did (Spanier and Margolis, 1983). The variables used to discriminate the two groups were number of premarital sexual partners, quality of marital sex, length of marriage, religiosity, and physical attractiveness (Spanier and Margolis, 1983). The discriminant function was unable to differentiate between the two groups. Thus, based on the data available in this study, it is not possible to differentiate an individual's participation in extramarital sex among persons who ultimately divorce.

No significant relationship was found between engaging in EMC and religiosity ($X^2 = 5.4$, 2 df, $p > .05$). However, there is a strong association between the number of years after the beginning of marriage that EMC first occurred and religiosity ($X^2 = 9.0$, 2 df, $p < .02$). The less religious the respondent, the earlier in the marriage EMC began (if it began at all). Among those who were very religious, 30 percent experienced extramarital coitus less than four years after the marriage began, whereas 70 percent of the very religious who had EMC first did so more than four years after the marriage began. Among those reported to be somewhat or slightly religious, the statistics were 49 percent and 51 percent respectively; and for those who were in the "not at all" religious category, 83 percent first had EMC less than four years after the marriage began. We conclude that religiosity plays some role in the occurrence of EMC. It does not appear to be a critical determinant of whether or not EMC occurs; however, religiosity seems to influence when in the marriage EMC occurs;

The relationship between engaging in EMC and taking vacations apart from one's spouse was examined and found to be significant ($X^2 = 6.7$, 1 df, $p < .01$). A higher percentage of respondents who reported that they and their spouses took vacations apart from each other (52 percent) engaged in EMC than respondents who did not take vacations apart (32 percent). Taking vacations apart from one's spouse may be viewed as a *weak* indication of the opportunity to engage in EMC. Respondents taking a vacation apart from their spouses may do so with the intention of getting involved in an extramarital relationship. More likely, taking a vacation apart from one's spouse (or having one's spouse go on vacation) may present the opportunity to engage in EMC. Of Whitehurst's (1969) sample 41 percent reported that opportunity was a crucial factor in determining their extramarital involvement.

Finally, no significant relationship was found between engaging in EMC and marital quality during the months *directly preceding* separation ($X^2 = .00$, 1 df, $p > .05$). Thus, respondents who engaged in EMC did not differ significantly in preseparation ratings of marital harmony, companionship, consensus, or affectional expression from respondents who did not engage in EMC. It appears that respondents' extramarital sexual relations had little effect on their perceptions of marital quality compared to respondents who did not engage in EMC.

What do individuals themselves say about their views of extramarital sex during their marriage?

> My opinions changed during the marriage. When I first married, I strongly disapproved. Then later I approved.

> I'm afraid I fall into that category of it depends on the circumstance. . . . That's a double standard and I don't like that. It's like making a judgment for someone else and I don't think I have a right to. The whole moral situation has changed.

As shown in Table 3.1, 39 percent of the men and 38 percent of the women in the sample stated that they engaged in extramarital coitus (EMC) during their marriage and before their separation. (All data presented in this section pertain to this time frame.) It is noteworthy that an almost equal percentage of men and women engaged in EMC in this sample and that the percentages are lower than one might expect in a sample of separated persons. We must be cautious, however, in comparing the frequency of EMC from one sample to another due to

## TABLE 3.1
### Extramarital Sexual Relationships for Men and Women (in percentages)

| Extramarital Relationship Items | Men | Women |
|---|---|---|
| (1) Engaged in extramarital coitus | (n = 91) | (n = 114) |
| yes | 38.5 | 37.8 |
| no | 61.5 | 62.2 |
| (2) Extramarital kissing or petting, but not sexual intercourse with someone | (n = 91) | (n = 114) |
| yes | 31.9 | 25.4 |
| no | 68.1 | 74.6 |
| (3) Number of extramarital coital partners | (n = 35) | (n = 42) |
| 1 | 42.9 | 64.3 |
| 2 | 22.9 | 26.2 |
| 3 | 8.6 | 4.8 |
| more than 3 | 25.7 | 4.8 |
| (4) Extramarital coitus first occurred | (n = 35) | (n = 42) |
| after separation seemed likely | 22.9 | 38.1 |
| shortly before separation seemed likely | 11.4 | 28.6 |
| well before separation seemed likely | 65.7 | 33.3 |
| (5) Number of years after marriage began that extramarital coitus first occurred | (n = 41) | (n = 47) |
| less than or equal to 4 years | 54.3 | 54.5 |
| more than 4 years | 45.7 | 45.5 |
| (6) Last extramarital affair was | (n = 35) | (n = 42) |
| one night stand | 28.6 | 4.8 |
| short-term involvement with little or no emotional attachment | 20.0 | 23.8 |
| involvement with some emotional commitment | 40.0 | 31.0 |
| a more long-term love relationship | 11.4 | 40.5 |
| (7) Last extramarital relationship ended | (n = 35) | (n = 42) |
| before separation | 65.7 | 33.3 |
| after separation, but before divorce | 5.7 | 21.4 |
| after divorce | 8.6 | 11.9 |
| continued to interview | 20.0 | 33.3 |
| (8) Extramarital sexual relations were | (n = 35) | (n = 42) |
| very satisfactory | 34.3 | 57.1 |
| somewhat satisfactory | 54.3 | 26.2 |
| a little unsatisfactory | 8.6 | 7.1 |
| very unsatisfactory | 2.9 | 9.5 |
| (9) Extramarital relations were... | (n = 35) | (n = 42) |
| a cause of marital problems | 2.9 | 9.5 |
| a result of marital problems | 68.6 | 71.4 |
| unrelated to marital problems | 28.6 | 19.0 |

*(continued)*

## TABLE 3.1 (continued)

| | | | |
|---|---|---|---|
| (10) | Having extramarital sex made respondent feel | (n = 35) | (n = 42) |
| | very guilty | 11.4 | 38.1 |
| | somewhat guilty | 22.9 | 21.4 |
| | a little guilty | 20.0 | 14.3 |
| | not at all guilty | 45.7 | 26.2 |
| (11) | Do you think spouse knew about your extramarital relations while you were living together? | (n = 35) | (n = 42) |
| | yes | 60.0 | 61.9 |
| | no | 34.3 | 38.1 |
| | don't know | 5.7 | — |
| (12) | Would you say your (former) spouse | (n = 22) | (n = 26) |
| | strongly disapprove of your extramarital relations | 40.9 | 65.4 |
| | somewhat disapproved of your extramarital relations | 22.7 | 15.4 |
| | neither disapproved nor approved | 31.8 | 11.5 |
| | approved | 4.5 | 7.7 |
| (13) | Did (former) spouse engage in extramarital sex? | (n = 91) | (n = 113) |
| | yes | 52.7 | 52.2 |
| | no | 29.7 | 24.8 |
| | don't know | 17.6 | 23.0 |
| (14) | Did spouse engage in extramarital kissing or petting, but not sexual intercourse with someone? | (n = 91) | (n = 113) |
| | yes | 41.8 | 42.5 |
| | no | 36.3 | 25.7 |
| | don't know | 22.0 | 31.9 |
| (15) | Spouse's extramarital sex first occurred | (n = 48) 9) | (n = 59) |
| | after separation seemed likely | 8.3 | 6.8 |
| | shortly before separation seemed likely | 16.7 | 18.6 |
| | well before separation seemed likely | 75.0 | 74.6 |
| (16) | Number of years after marriage began that spouse's extramarital sex first occurred | (n = 48) | (n = 59) |
| | less than or equal to 4 years | 74.4 | 75.0 |
| | more than 4 years | 25.6 | 25.0 |
| (17) | Spouse's last extramarital affair was | (n = 47) | (n = 59) |
| | one night stand | 10.6 | 10.2 |
| | short-term involvement with little or no emotional attachment | 23.4 | 33.9 |
| | involvement with some emotional commitment | 31.9 | 21.0 |
| | a more long-term love relationship | 34.0 | 33.9 |

**TABLE 3.1 (continued)**

| | | | |
|---|---|---|---|
| (18) | Spouse's last extramarital relationship ended | (n = 47) | (n = 59) |
| | before the separation | 21.3 | 23.7 |
| | after separation, but before divorce | 17.0 | 13.6 |
| | after divorce | 10.6 | 1.7 |
| | continued to interview | 46.8 | 49.2 |
| | don't know | 4.3 | 11.9 |
| (19) | Respondents who found out about spouse's affairs | (n = 48) | (n = 59) |
| | strongly disapproved of spouse's extramarital relations | 66.7 | 64.4 |
| | somewhat disapproved of spouse's extramarital relations | 14.6 | 11.9 |
| | neither disapproved or approved | 12.5 | 15.3 |
| | approved | 6.2 | 8.5 |
| (20) | Spouse's extramarital relations were | (n = 48) | (n = 59) |
| | a cause of marital problems | 52.1 | 45.8 |
| | a result of marital problems | 29.2 | 35.6 |
| | unrelated to marital problems | 18.8 | 18.6 |

the great variability across samples of age, geographic location, social class, length of marriage, and marital status. We could speculate that the relatively rural environment of Central Pennsylvania might account for these figures.

Respondents were asked in a separate item about their participation in sexual relations that involved just kissing or petting but not sexual intercourse. In the total sample, 32 percent of the men and 25 percent of the women reported that they had had extramarital sexual relations that did not culminate in coitus. Further analysis revealed that 71 percent of those who responded that they had ever engaged in relations involving only extramarital kissing or petting had also engaged in extramarital coitus with at least one other individual. Thus, only a minority of all respondents (8 percent) had engaged in extramarital kissing or petting without ever having had extramarital coitus with someone.

Males were found to have had a significantly greater number of extramarital partners than women ($X^2 = 8.0$, 3 df, $p < .05$). For example, 26 percent of the men had more than three partners compared to only 5 percent of the women. Of the females, 64 percent had only one partner compared to 43 percent of the men. The range was 1 to 47 partners. Kinsey and his associates (1953) and Hunt (1974) both found that about 40 percent of the females in their respective samples had engaged in EMC with only one partner.

The majority of our respondents who engaged in EMC (77 percent of the men, 62 percent of the women) reported that they did so "shortly" or "well before" rather than "after" their separation seemed likely. Thus, it appears that most of the respondents did not engage in an extramarital sexual relationship with the knowledge that their marriage might terminate in the near future. A significantly higher percentage of men than women reported that they had EMC well before separation seemed likely ($z = 3.02$, $p < .01$; 2-tailed test).

In our sample, 54 percent of the men and a like percentage of the women who engaged in EMC first did so within four years after marriage. Thus, many respondents who engaged in EMC did so relatively early in their marriages and continued their marriages for many years following their initial participation in EMC. It may be concluded that in many cases EMC is not followed immediately by a separation or divorce.

A significantly higher percentage of women than men reported that their last extramarital relationship was a more long-term love relationship ($z = -3.07$, $p < .01$; 2-tailed test). Fifty-one percent of the men and 72 percent of the women who engaged in EMC reported either that their last extramarital sexual involvement had some emotional commitment or was a more long-term love relationship. This result precludes the idea that sexual satisfaction alone maintains the majority of extramarital relationships.

Of all of the most recent extramarital relationships, 73 percent had ended by the time of the interview. This may suggest a difficulty in concomitantly maintaining a new relationship and going through a separation or divorce with one's spouse; this finding may further imply that such relationships do not, in general, lead to new marital relationships. It must be noted that the most recently formed extramarital relationships were continuing at the time of the interview for only 20 percent of the men and 33 percent of the women, a significantly higher percentage for women than men ($z = -1.34$, $p < .05$; 2-tailed test).

Most of the respondents (86 percent) who had EMC reported that their extramarital sexual relations were somewhat or very satisfactory. A higher percentage of women (57 percent) compared with men (34 percent) reported that their extramarital sexual relations were very satisfactory. A higher percentage of women (38 percent) than men (25 percent) rated the quality of their sex during marriage as very unsatisfactory. This finding is interesting since it suggests that divorced women are more likely than men to find marital sex very unsatisfactory and extramarital sex very satisfactory. This may suggest that sexual satisfaction is more directly related to the quality of a particular relationship for women or perhaps that sexual satisfaction is more prominent among women than among men as a barometer for relationships.

Seventy percent of the respondents (69 percent for men, 71 percent for women) who engaged in EMC reported that their extramarital relations were a result of marital problems; 34 percent of the men and 59 percent of the women reported that they felt either somewhat or very guilty after engaging in extramarital sex. A higher percentage of men (46 percent) than women (26 percent) reported feeling no guilt for engaging in EMC. A nearly equal percentage of men and women (60 percent and 62 percent, respectively) reported that they thought their spouse knew about their extramarital relations; 65 percent of the women compared with 41 percent of the men reported that their spouses strongly disapproved.

We also questioned respondents about their spouses' extramarital relationships: 53 percent of the men and 52 percent of the women responded that their spouse had engaged in EMC. It is interesting to note that these percentages are higher than the percentages of respondents reporting that they engaged in EMC. Of both men and women respondents 42 percent reported that their spouses had engaged in extramarital kissing or petting that did not lead to intercourse. Again, these percentages are higher than the percentage of respondents reporting extramarital kissing or petting.

There is not necessarily a correspondence between respondents' and spouses' extramarital activity. It should be noted that 58 percent of the respondents who reported engaging in EMC also reported that their spouses did, whereas 49 percent of those reporting that they did *not* engage in EMC reported that their spouses did. Three-fourths of the respondents reported that their spouses' EMC first occurred well before separation seemed likely. Similarly, three-fourths of both the men and women reported that their spouses' EMC first occurred within four years of marriage.

Of the respondents who reported that their spouses had engaged in EMC, 60 percent stated that their spouses' extramarital relationships had some emotional commitment or were a more long-term love relationships. This percentage is concordant with the percentage of respondents who reported that their extramarital relationships had either some emotional commitment or were more long-term. However, 11 percent of the men reported that their wive's extramarital affairs were more long-term love relationships, whereas 34 percent of the women reported that their husbands' extramarital relationships were long-term love involvements. This may suggest a differential perception between men and women of the intensity of relationships. Perhaps women label relationships with a greater intensity than do men.

It was reported by 48 percent of the respondents that their spouses' extramarital relationship continued up to the date of the interview compared with 27 percent of the respondents who reported this for their own extramarital relationship. Although most of the respondents who had been involved in an extramarital relationship went through the separation and/or divorce period without being involved in a new relationship, it appears that many of the respondents' spouses had such relationships during the period of separation. Of course, misperceptions of the spouse make such comparisons potentially unreliable.

Of those who knew of their spouses' extramarital relationships, 80 percent of the men and 75 percent of the women reported either that they strongly or somewhat disapproved of it. This can be compared with 63 percent of the men respondents and 81 percent of the women respondents who thought either that their spouses strongly or somewhat disapproved of their extramarital relationships. It must be noted that the first set of percentages (80 percent and 75 percent) represents the respondents' attitudes toward their spouses' extramarital relationship. These figures corroborate Hunt's (1974) conclusion that men and women disapprove equally of their spouses' extramarital relations. The latter set of percentages represent the respondents' perceptions of their spouses' attitudes toward extramarital relations. This discordance between the two sets of frequencies suggests that men may think that their wives will be less disapproving than they actually are. One man, for example, said "the fact that another woman finds me attractive makes me more attractive to [my wife] also." It would be interesting to know the wife's views.

Finally, 52 percent of the men respondents and 46 percent of the women respondents reported that their spouses' extramarital relations were a cause of marital problems; only 6 percent of the respondents reported that their own extramarital relations were a cause of marital problems. It seems that when an individual has had an extramarital relationship, he or she does not think that it caused marital problems. However, when one's *spouse* has engaged in extramarital sex it is seen as causing marital problems. This striking finding is not unexpected, as it is common for individuals to assign blame to others more often than to assign blame to themselves; the magnitude of the difference between respondent and spouse in the assignment of blame is, however, dramatic. This one bit of data provides a powerful indication, it seems to us, that there is little objective reality to the circumstances of marital separation and its evaluation. Respondents construct their own views of marriage and accounts of its dissolution, and these views may have little relationship to each other.

Discrepant views between partners may be explained partially by the process of attribution in close relationships (Kelley, 1979). A husband or wife is not likely to have as much information about the nature of the spouse's extramarital affair as about his or her own, especially as extramarital relationships tend to be taboo. This lack of information may lead to speculation about motivations and consequences—and ultimately to negative judgments about the spouse and the marriage. Also, it is likely that individuals experiencing the breakup of a marriage will explain their own behavior as circumstantial while the spouse's behavior is explained as basic to that person's character.

There are many reports in our qualitative data that focus on the role that the spouse's extramarital relationship had in the dissolution of the marriage.

> The worst thing was . . . the period when I didn't know what was going on. I was depressed and confused, and I just didn't know what I had done or what to do about it. . . . After I learned what the real story was [wife had left him for another man], I was actually relieved. I wasn't happy about it or anything, but I was relieved because everything fell into place and started to make sense.

Another man who learned suddenly and unexpectedly that his wife was leaving him after being involved with another man, put it this way:

> I was at first extremely distraught. I think that I was in a suicidal state for a while. I contemplated suicide at one time. After this period I just kind of went into a state of shock that lasted [a couple of months]. After that I just felt hurt that all of it had happened.

There are a few reports of individuals who acknowledge the role their own extramarital relationships had in the marital breakup. These reports tend to be much more matter-of-fact in tone and lack the emotional content of the reports above.

> I did have some [extramarital relationships], and I think she knew about it; but we never discussed it, and we never had any fights about it.

> Well, I started a relationship with a female colleague of mine about eight or nine years ago. My wife found out about it after the first few years. . . . After my wife found out about the affair, the four of us, my wife, me, the other woman, and her husband got into a four-way sex thing.

> So she [wife] finally asked me if I was running around. I didn't lie, I just told the truth.

Finally, we may note that for many individuals the notions of guilt and blame are difficult to articulate. As one respondent put it, "Part of me strongly approved and part of me didn't."

The relationship between the assignment of blame for the breakup of the marriage and participation in EMC is presented in Table 3.2. Among women, the relationship is significant; among men, however, the relationship is not significant. Men who have participated in EMC are about as likely to blame their spouse for the breakup of the marriage (34 percent) as men who have not had EMC (32 percent). About half of the respondents in the study blame themselves and their spouses (i.e., "both") for the breakup of their marriages. Further inspection of Table 3.2 reveals that both men and women respondents who engaged in EMC were more likely to blame themselves for the breakup of their marriage than respondents who did not engage in EMC ($z = 2.37$, $p < .05$; 2-tailed test).

Given the disposition of respondents to cite their spouses' extramarital relations as a cause of marital problems, we thought that the spouses' participation in EMC would surely be connected with assignment of blame for the breakup. As the bottom half of Table 3.2 demonstrates, this is not the case. Although separated men and women view their spouses' extramarital experiences as contributing to marital problems, they do not blame their spouses' sexual behavior for the final demise of their marriage. In general they are more sensitive to their own

### TABLE 3.2
### Assignment of Blame for the Breakup of the Marriage and Participation in Extramarital Coitus (in percentages)

| | Participated in Extramarital Coitus | | | |
|---|---|---|---|---|
| | Men [a] | | Women [b] | |
| Assignment of Blame for Breakup of Marriage | Yes (n = 35) | No (n = 56) | Yes (n = 42) | No (n = 69) |
| Spouse | 34.3 | 39.3 | 11.9 | 31.9 |
| Both | 45.7 | 42.9 | 61.9 | 42.0 |
| Self | 8.6 | 3.6 | 16.7 | 2.9 |
| Neither | 8.6 | 8.9 | 7.1 | 10.1 |
| Other person | 2.9 | 5.4 | 2.4 | 13.0 |
| Total | 100.0 | 100.0 | 100.0 | 100.0 |

| | Spouse Participated in Extramarital Coitus | | | |
|---|---|---|---|---|
| | Men [c] | | Women [d] | |
| Assignment of Blame for Breakup of Marriage | Yes (n = 48) | No (n = 43) | Yes (n = 59) | No (n = 54) |
| Spouse | 39.6 | 34.9 | 27.1 | 22.2 |
| Both | 41.7 | 46.5 | 52.5 | 46.3 |
| Self | 4.2 | 7.0 | 5.1 | 11.1 |
| Neither | 8.3 | 9.3 | 5.1 | 13.0 |
| Other Person | 6.3 | 2.3 | 10.2 | 7.4 |
| Total | 100.0 | 100.0 | 100.0 | 100.0 |

a. $X^2(4) = 1.47$, $p > .05$
b. $X^2(4) = 16.02$, $p < .01$
c. $X^2(4) = 1.40$, $p > .05$
d. $X^2(4) = 4.00$, $p < .05$

guilt and culpability than to their spouses'. Frederico (1979) also suggests that extramarital relationships are not so much a cause of marital dissolution as they are a part of the escalation of discord and the process of distancing oneself from the marriage as it ends.

Guilt can temper the pleasure of an extramarital relationship. We found a significant relationship between satisfaction with extramarital sexual relations and level of guilt after participating ($X^2 = 11.2$, 4 df, $p < .03$). The lower the level of guilt after engaging in EMC, the higher the satisfaction with EMC. Of those who felt very guilty after engaging in EMC, 35 percent rated their extramarital sex as little or not at all satisfactory, whereas only 7 percent of those who felt no guilt after participating rated their extramarital sex this way. Among those who reported extramarital sex to be somewhat satisfactory, 20 percent felt very guilty about the involvement as compared to 41 percent who did not feel at all guilty; a "very satisfactory" evaluation was provided by 45 percent of those who said they felt very guilty about having participated in extramarital coitus, whereas 52 percent reported that they felt not at all guilty.

The previous discussion ought to dispel the notion that much marital breakup is related to the lure of a specific third party. It is fairest to say that when a marriage is in trouble, it becomes especially vulnerable to external influences, including romantic—or purely sexual—involvements with partners outside of the marriage. It is rarely the case that the marriage falls apart because the husband or wife in a relatively healthy marriage falls in love with someone else. Nevertheless, we must acknowledge the numerous reports of separated or divorced men and women who perceive a third party as responsible for the demise of the marriage.

> I can't explain to you what it feels like. I trusted him for 21 years, and then all of a sudden your whole life tumbles down. I don't have a life now. You have to go through it to realize. I could accept him coming home around midnight and working long hours, but I can't share my husband. I don't know, maybe I gave him too much freedom.

## Children

In virtually every marriage with children, divorce takes on different meaning from marriages where there are no children. Concerns about children are very close to home. Children can become catalysts for the transformations tied to ending a marriage; they may also be immensely helpful to a mother or father in coping with the difficulties of separation. Among the major adjustment problems reported by separating parents are worrying about the effects of the separation on the children, deciding who should have custody and, for those without custody, feelings of loneliness or guilt. This section deals with children as a barrier to breakup, the involvement of children in the process of ending a marriage, consequences of breakup for parent-child relationships, custody, and problems for parents with and without custody.

To gauge the influence of children as outsiders in the parents' decision to divorce, we inquired about whether the separation or divorce was postponed because of the child(ren). Approximately half of the respondents with children indicated it was. As we reported in Chapter 2, parents deliberated longer about separation and divorce than marital partners without children. There are several facets to the presence of children as a barrier to marital separation: concern about damage to the children, concern about loss of parenting rewards and any detrimental effects on parent-child relationships, and the greater reluctance of others to approve the separation when children are involved (Levinger, 1979; Spanier and Casto, 1979).

A man who was separated but had not yet filed for divorce told us how his daughter fit into his decision to end the marriage:

> If I lose my daughter, it won't be very good. I love her very much and have very deep feelings about her. I don't know how I will take that loss.

A 47-year-old man who divorced only after his two children had reached adulthood reported this:

> I would rather we had never gotten married. But I wouldn't have wanted to separate before the children were raised. I mean I guess a lot of years of my life were wasted in some ways, but at least I'm glad I fulfilled my obligations to the kids. I don't believe in shirking responsibility, and I did provide a home and things for them until they were grown. I mean we were never rich, but I always made sure we had food and clothes and a place to live.

Most of the parents interviewed seemed to be trying to work together to minimize the effects of separation and to settle custody in the best interests of the children. One father's words seemed to represent the attitude of many of these parents:

> We wanted there to be as little disruption as possible for the kids. Because both of the kids were loved very much by both of us and because of our agreement to share custody, I feel they suffered only minimally. . . . Now they don't have to compete with the

other parent for attention, and they don't have to live with constant quarreling.

In general the respondents said they were making an effort not to let their marital difficulties affect their children's relationships with the other parent. However, this is not always easy. As one mother put it after describing her anger against her husband,

> It was so hard to tell them [the children] your daddy loves you when you want to say something so different.

Another mother said her daughter had told her she was "always accusing daddy with [her] tone of voice."

We did find several notable cases, however, where it seemed that children were used either to punish the other spouse or to get a better settlement. When we were told about the children being thus used, these tactics were attributed to the spouse not interviewed. For example, a mother of three—with two girls from a previous marriage and a boy from the marriage in question—stated that the hardest part of the divorce is

> the way he treats the boy. I have to really avoid him. [If I meet him around town] he's so bad he just ignores the boy and [son] will get so upset and cry for his daddy. . . . He [husband] takes it out on the little boy. He whips him for no reason when he has him. He'll tell [son] he doesn't love him, that he never did. And the poor boy gets so upset. . . . He told the girls he doesn't want them calling him daddy anymore and things like that. He's really turned them against him.

Two respondents, one man and one woman, stated that their spouses continually threatened to cut them off from the children if they would contest either the divorce or any part of the settlement. Both respondents yielded because they said they could not take the chance of losing their children.

One mother later regretted trying to turn her children against their father:

> The pain of the children being torn is the hardest. . . . I worry about my kids being alienated and about what I've said to them about their father. I stopped that. It was only when I was so angry. But I wonder what damage this has done.

Were the parents' fears of the consequences of the breakup for children and parent-child relationships realized? We did not examine the effects of separation and divorce on child development and well-being (see Hetherington et al., 1978; Wallerstein and Kelly, 1980). We did consider, however, several aspects of parent-child relationships.

Apart from the complexities that decisions about custody, visitation, and child support pose for the couple, there are more hidden emotional issues that many individuals sometimes find difficult to confront. For example, we asked our respondents how close they and their spouses were to their children before the separation and how this degree of closeness has changed. Respondents, both men and women, tended to claim that they were closer to their children than their spouses were and that their degree of closeness had increased since the separation, but the spouses' degree of closeness was not as likely to have increased. Such a response pattern, summarized for the whole sample in Table 3.3, is undoubtedly an accurate reflection of perceptions of those interviewed but must certainly conceal the reality. If anything, it shows us that when children are involved it is difficult to be objective about emotions, closeness, and possessiveness. A similar bias is found in response to questions about the amount of time respondents report they and their spouses spent with the children before the separation and changes in time spent since separation.

The results in Table 3.3 combine the responses of men and women to illustrate the comparison between self-reports of closeness and percep-

**TABLE 3.3**
**Reports of Closeness to Children and Changes in Closeness (in percentages)**

|  | Before Separation | | Since Separation | |
|---|---|---|---|---|
|  | Your Closeness | Spouse's Closeness | Your Closeness | Spouse's Closeness |
| Very close | 75.0 | 37.8 | | |
| Somewhat close | 20.3 | 36.2 | | |
| Not very close | 4.7 | 26.0 | | |
| Total | 100.0 | 100.0 | | |
| Increased | | | 51.6 | 29.3 |
| Stayed the same | | | 35.2 | 35.0 |
| Decreased | | | 13.3 | 35.8 |
| Total | | | 100.0 | 100.0 |

NOTE: n = 128 (respondents with children)

tion of spouse's closeness to children. As might be expected, however, there were dramatic differences between men and women in reports of changes in closeness since separation. Of the fathers, 20 percent—as compared with only 7 percent of the mothers—felt that closeness to their children had dwindled since separation. Many more mothers than fathers (63 percent and 38 percent, respectively) felt closer to their children now than before separation. About a third of the parents (41 percent of men and 30 percent of the women) experienced no change in closeness.

A similar gender disparity exists with regard to satisfaction with time spent with children. Four in five fathers would like to spend more time with their children; 38 percent of the mothers desire more time. No father in the study wished to spend less time with his children, yet 1 in 10 mothers indicated they desired less time. This can best be interpreted in relation to the responses of mothers and fathers on the question of how the amount of time actually spent with one's children has changed since separation. Mothers are nearly equally divided between spending more, the same amount, or less time with their children. Among fathers, however, more than two in three report that they are actually spending less time with their children; only 16 percent are spending more time with their children, the same as the percentage of fathers reporting no change in the time spent with children. The loss of close ties to children is the bane of separation and divorce for many fathers.

Nearly half of our respondents without custody report that they see their children at least once a week; about 7 in 10 respondents without custody indicate that they see their child at least once a month. This contrasts with findings from a national study (Furstenberg et al., 1983) that suggest visitation by noncustodial parents to be more rare. The more rural nature of the sample may account in part for this difference, as well as the fact that our respondents have only been separated, on the average, for about one year with virtually all respondents separated less than two years. When viewed in this light, it is perhaps surprising that as many as 3 in 10 noncustodial parents are already seeing their children less than once a month. In our sample, 5 respondents do not see their children at all.

We again find discrepancies between respondent reports of their own visitation with respondent reports of spouses' visitation. Because we did not systematically interview both men and women from the same couple, strictly speaking, we cannot determine how discrepant the reports of former spouses are. But our data do indicate that one may be inclined to overestimate his or her own contact with children and underestimate the spouse's contact with children. Half of the respondents, for example, report that their former spouses see the children once a month or less, with one in six reporting that the spouse never sees the child. This can be contrasted with the data presented above, which suggest somewhat more contact.

The majority of parents acknowledge that they and their former spouse agree on matters of how to raise the children only sometimes or never. This might be expected, of course, given that by the time of separation couples report their levels of disagreement to be rather high on several dimensions of the marriage. It is also expected given the disparate perceptions of one's own and the partner's relationship with children. A parent who believes he or she is closer and has more contact with the children than the spouse is likely to feel entitled to a greater say-so in child rearing.

Undoubtedly contributing to some of the problems in subsequent child rearing are the circumstances surrounding the initial custody decision. Respondents report that custody was determined by mutual agreement in about two-thirds of the cases. Courts made the decision in about one in five cases; the children themselves made the decision in 7 percent of the cases; and a small number of custody determinations were reported to have been made in other ways (3 percent).

Nearly three-fourths of our respondents report that the wife has custody of all the children. Husbands have custody of all the children in 8 percent of the cases where there are children. Joint custody was reported by 6 percent of the respondents and split custody by 5 percent of the respondents. We defined joint custody to be an arrangement whereby both parents have custodial rights and responsibilities for the child. Split custody refers to situations where the husband has custody of one or more of the children and the wife has custody of one or more of the children. Finally, 9 percent of our sample reported that neither the husband nor wife had custody of the children. These statistics are rather similar to national data (Spanier and Glick, 1981).

It is noteworthy that the differences between men and women in satisfaction with custody arrangements are quite substantial. Whereas 7 in 10 women report that they are very satisfied with the custody arrangement, fewer than one-third of the men report that they are very satisfied. While 4 in 10 men are somewhat or very dissatisfied, only 14 percent of the women report this level of dissatisfaction. Given the loss of closeness and time with children experienced by so many fathers, it is not surprising that men are more dissatisfied with the custody arrangement than are women.

Of our 77 respondents who have custody or joint custody, nearly two-thirds report that they are glad they have custody and that it has not been a problem. Although glad to have custody, one-third of the sample reports it has been a burden or that the responsibility is difficult to handle. Two respondents were unsure about their ability to continue with the responsibility. One respondent who did not have custody reported, "I was bitter about losing my son, but on the other hand I was glad not to have him because of the hassles involving him."

Guilt is reported by many parents, particularly parents without custody. One woman with four children, two of whom were in the father's custody, said,

> I was feeling really sad about the two children who weren't with me. I felt I had nothing to give.

Whether or not they received child custody, all parents reported the necessity of major adjustments. Parents with principal custody as well as those without custody experienced adjustment problems related to their children. Some parents who do not have custody change residences to be near the children. One man reported, "Well, the children are the principal reason why I moved back here, so I could be close." Fathers with custody reported the same problems as mothers with custody, and mothers without custody similar problems to fathers without custody. The only sex difference we found was that mothers who did not get custody reported more public censure than did fathers without custody. One mother who had split the custody of their four children with the father reported this:

> Everybody seems horrified that we had split the children—like "How could you do such a thing?" . . . [My attorney] laid a real guilt trip on me about giving up the two children. He was always asking me, "Are you *sure* you want it this way? How could you?"

The parent who receives principal custody now must fulfill alone roles previously performed jointly by two parents. It is hard to get time away from the children and this creates problems with work, dating, and social life in general. Parents with custody report feeling much more responsibility and a greater sense of being trapped by the children.

One mother, thinking back about her major problem after an earlier divorce, stated,

> [My major problem was] knowing I had four children on my *own* to be responsible for—trying to keep us together, raising two boys to be boys. That was hard.

Another mother described her current situation as follows:

> I hate feeling totally responsible for the kids. They're mine completely. At least when I was married, I could mentally not feel responsible at times. . . . It gets lonely with the kids in bed by 8:00. It's an ambiguous role. [I want to go out but] I don't want the kids to be stuck with a babysitter three or four nights a week.

A father with custody of his children expressed the same sense of consuming responsibility:

> I was doing a tremendous job with the kids, but I needed to do something for myself. I needed to start thinking about me and setting up my own new life. I haven't thought about that much, but I guess that will be important for me to do. Nothing really comes easy. You always find yourself second guessing yourself, wondering if you can handle everything, sometimes wishing there was still someone to share the responsibility and talk to about it.

One complaint many custodial parents have is that the other parent, who only sees the children occasionally, does not have to deal with discipline and, therefore, may be more attractive to the child. A father with principal custody put it this way:

> One big problem that aggravates me a lot is that now my wife sees the kids during all the nice and fun times, and I have to be the one who makes them clean their rooms and do their homework, etc. I have to be the disciplinarian. I know I can't let that alter the way I treat them because they do need discipline, but sometimes I don't think it's fair. . . . Too often when I say something they'll say, "but mother said the opposite."

While there are hardships in having principal custody, most who have custody are glad that they do. Many of them cited their children as a major source of support during their separation or divorce.

Parents without custody must adjust to being with their children less often, which most see as a serious deprivation. They miss their children greatly. Several parents stated that the main thing, or in some cases the only thing, they regretted was losing the children.

Many parents report feeling guilty about "deserting" their children and being dissatisfied with the limitations of their relationships. The mother who had split the custody of her four children with her husband said,

> The most I could do was be their friend, so I worked really hard at that. And I saved for Christmas because that has always been very important to me. But it was so tight, and by Christmas I had so little, I was really depressed.

Another woman with a split custody arrangement worried about her son's care:

> I worry he's not getting the attention he needs. They go out a lot, and I think the children are neglected. But I don't know what to do about it. I feel so powerless. . . . My heart aches for them more than myself.

Parents without custody also tended to find their children to be sources of support through the divorce process. One father of three older children (one married, two living with mother) said this:

> One of the pluses of this experience has been my relationship with my children. Their behavior has been admirable. They have been available, supportive, and caring towards both their mother and me without intruding in our marital problems and without being judgmental. Their adjustment and maturity in handling their own lives during this time has been very freeing for both of us.

Children as a source of support are considered in more depth in Chapter 6.

## Reactions of Family and Friends

Divorce is such a critical life event that it is inevitable that significant others such as relatives and close friends will become involved in the event at least indirectly, if not directly. Chapter 6 will consider the role of friends and relatives more fully, but here we shall briefly highlight the reactions of others to the breakup.

Even if a marriage is conspicuously unhappy and dissentious, family and friends of the couple may disapprove of and discourage the dissolution. We asked our respondents what their parents and in-laws did after learning that separation or divorce was planned. One in five parents and one in six in-laws were reported to have encouraged the respondents to go through with the breakup. Only 11 percent of the parents, contrasted with 24 percent of the in-laws, encouraged the individuals in our sample not to go through with it. A few parents and in-laws didn't know about the dissolution of the marriage. The majority of both parents and in-laws, however, were reported to have "pretty much stayed out of it."

The disapproval of family and friends is among the anticipated or experienced costs of marital breakup. About 60 percent of the women in Goode's (1956) sample of divorced mothers reported mild or strong approval of the divorce from family and friends. Similarly, half of the women in this study judge their mothers' and fathers' initial reaction to the separation to be some degree of approval. The men lag somewhat behind the women with about 35 percent perceiving parental approval. Somewhat less than a third of the women and somewhat more than a third of the men experience disapproval of the separation by their mothers and fathers. The remainder suppose their parents to be neutral to the breakup. Parents-in-law are perceived as particularly censorious, with well over half the men and women judging that their spouse's parents disapprove of the separation.

Overall, women perceive their in-laws as more disapproving than men while the opposite is true of their own parents. Friends are the least judgmental; in fact, almost half of the men suppose their friends to feel neutral about the separation. Only a quarter of the women feel this. Of the women, 88 percent perceive approval from their friends, while only 36 percent of the men experience such acceptance. As in Goode's (1956) sample of divorced mothers, families are perceived as more disapproving than friends; and the partner's family is perceived as more disapproving than one's own family. Many have noted historical decline in the social restraints holding marriage together, including the sanctions against divorce employed by family and friends (Levinger, 1979; Weiss, 1975). Yet, although 30 years separate the Goode study from this one, the proportion of women whose family and friends approve or disapprove of the divorce is surprisingly similar.

Family and friend networks respond differentially to the news of the separation and divorce. This is illustrated in Table 3.4. Different sets of roles govern these networks. The investment, commitments, and values involved in family relationships make it more likely that family members would disapprove and intervene in a dissolving marriage than friends (Goode, 1956; Weiss, 1975). More often than not, outsiders are

**TABLE 3.4**
**Reactions of Family and Friends to Separation (in percentages)**

|  | Men | Women |
|---|---|---|
| **Mother** | | |
| strongly disapprove | 27.8 | 16.3 |
| mildly disapprove | 10.1 | 13.5 |
| feel neutral | 25.3 | 19.2 |
| mildly approve | 20.3 | 21.2 |
| strongly approve | 16.1 | 29.8 |
| **Father** | | |
| strongly disapprove | 25.0 | 17.1 |
| mildly disapprove | 6.3 | 14.8 |
| feel neutral | 35.9 | 19.3 |
| mildly approve | 12.5 | 22.7 |
| strongly approve | 20.3 | 26.1 |
| **Mother-in-Law** | | |
| strongly disapprove | 29.2 | 49.0 |
| mildly disapprove | 26.4 | 19.6 |
| feel neutral | 18.0 | 12.7 |
| mildly approve | 9.7 | 10.8 |
| strongly approve | 16.7 | 7.9 |
| **Father-in-Law** | | |
| strongly disapprove | 32.2 | 43.5 |
| mildly disapprove | 20.3 | 15.9 |
| feel neutral | 27.1 | 29.0 |
| mildly approve | 8.5 | 5.8 |
| strongly approve | 11.9 | 5.8 |
| **Friends** | | |
| strongly disapprove | 7.7 | 6.1 |
| mildly disapprove | 12.1 | 10.5 |
| feel neutral | 44.0 | 25.4 |
| mildly approve | 22.0 | 22.8 |
| strongly approve | 14.3 | 35.1 |

unaware of the troubles that are rupturing a couple (Weiss, 1975). Goode (1956) offers a convincing reason for the differential response of family and friends based on this awareness. He speculates that the trouble brewing in and breaking up a marriage can be placed along a continuum of social knowledge. There is behavior that is mainly observable only by the husband and wife, behavior observable by and known only to the couple and very close friends and kin, and behavior that can't be hidden from anyone. Goode further suggests that friends may be closer to the conflict than parental families and may be more understanding of why the separation is justifiable.

A perusal of intercorrelations among dimensions of the marital relationship and various sources of disapproval by others, shown in Table 3.5, provides some insight. Among men, the correlations between disapproval of the separation by friends and the dimensions of the marital relationship are considerably more substantial than those between family disapproval (measured by the combined score for parents) and marital dimensions. The disapproval of friends is associated notably with marital consensus, compatibility, harmony, and commitment. A substantial correlation (.47) links the disapproval of friends with marital harmony. Of the factors tapping marital behavior, discord may be most open to public knowledge within the network. Friends are probably more apt to approve of divorce in a marriage they know is acrimonious.

Among women, the pattern is more equivocal. There is a substantial correlation (.43) between the disapproval of friends and affectional compatibility. It would be expected that among all the dimensions of

**TABLE 3.5**
**Correlations Between Dimensions of Marital Quality and Sources of Disapproval by Others**

| | Source of Disapproval | | |
|---|---|---|---|
| Dimension of Marital Quality | Parents | In-Laws | Friends |
| Consensus | .23(.19) | .07(.23) | .21(.23) |
| Companionship | .23(.06) | .15(− 0.5) | .18(.15) |
| Affectional compatibility | .15(−.20) | .13(−.01) | .43(−.20) |
| Marital harmony | −.03(−.24) | .20(.08) | .16(.47) |
| Commitment to marriage | .05(.10) | .24(.04) | .24(.22) |

NOTES: n = 91 (males)
n = 114 (females)

marital behavior, affectional compatibility—agreement about demonstrations of affection and sex relations—would be the *least* readily observable or known within the network. Perhaps women confide in their friends about the affectional aspects of marriage, and discontent with this aspect of marriage is judged by their friends as adequate grounds for approval of the separation and divorce. The disapproval of friends is associated marginally with consensus and commitment among women, but the various dimensions of the marital relationship are related also to the disapproval of divorce by parents and spouse's parents. It is likely that women are closer to the family network than are men, making observance and knowledge of marital behavior more accessible (Anspach, 1976; Weiss, 1975). The reports of disapproval are retrospective perceptions. The pattern of associations among variables simply may reflect a tendency to revise and recall what occurred in the manner that is most comfortable to live with (Weiss, 1975).

A highly conspicuous factor in marriage is the presence of children. We found the presence or absence of children to be unrelated to the disapproval of the separation or divorce by others although we made no distinction about age, number, and living arrangement of children.

## Economics

One often hears that sex and money are the two greatest problems in marriage today. Although this is certainly an oversimplification, there can be no doubt that these are two important dimensions. Economics has not been studied very much in relation to divorce (much less than sex has), yet our qualitative interviews revealed over and over again the importance of economics in the dissolution of marriages. For example, a 24-year-old woman, when asked to say what went wrong in her marriage, told the interviewer the following:

> We didn't argue. . . . It wasn't other women. . . . It was just that he was in his later 20s already and didn't know at all what he wanted to do. He always seemed to be floundering. . . . He quit working as soon as we got married. . . . But he always felt guilty about not working. . . . We hardly talked to each other. Everything just fell apart completely.

Stability of the husband's employment is more important to marital stability than actual income (Cherlin, 1979). As Cherlin reports (p. 164), "How regularly a husband brings home a paycheck may matter more than how much he makes." Others reported that spending money was the issue moreso than unemployment. For example, a 25-year-old woman with no children who had been married for three years complained,

> He wouldn't even let me spend the money I earned. He wanted someone to do all the housework. And someone who never got tired. I expected more than I got, that's for sure. I wanted an equal share in the money, especially. He had to see a list every time I bought groceries. I wanted someone who was understanding.

Many women appreciate the control over money that comes with separation, even if their actual income is drastically reduced (Kohen et al., 1979). Some women, however, find financial control after divorce a burden—particularly those who had been married to affluent men (Kohen et al., 1979). A 27-year-old woman with two children was asked "What was the most difficult adjustment for you?" Her answer follows:

> Organizing the money and paying bills. It annoys me. Taking care of all the day-to-day things bugs me. He was very practical, realistic, and well organized. He accused me of being a dreamer.

The theme of economic stability in the stability of marriage and in the transition from marriage to divorce is recurrent. By economic stability we refer not to the absolute economic level of the individual but rather to the continuity of security he or she enjoys through the transition from marriage to divorce. At all socioeconomic levels, stability emerges as being the more critical element. Economic adjustments are also revealed as important if one listens to the respondents' recollections. One woman, for example, who said she was "excited" when she first realized she was getting a divorce and "viewed it as an adventure I was looking forward to" was very depressed at the time of our interview:

> The lack of financial stability is the worst part. It creates all sorts of fears and anxiety. The kids don't understand why I'm still so messed up. . . . If only I could earn some money, maybe I could relax and pull myself together. Somehow I'm supposed to come out

of this a whole human being, but I'm not sure how. . . . The worst part of the divorce has been the job problems and the financial insecurity.

Her plight reveals an important dimension to the economics of divorce—namely, that there are important sex differences. Few men reported major economic problems caused by the divorce. Most men had full-time jobs before the separation and either continued in that job or obtained another comparable one. For women, the opposite tends to be true. Many report that they are substantially worse off. In our sample 21 percent of the women compared to 12 percent of the men reported that they returned to work, after a period away, since the separation. With regard to economic stability, men are more likely than women to report that they are very stable after separation (62 percent versus 45 percent).

Many women not working before the separation or only working part-time find it difficult to get a job. At the time of the interview 27 percent of the women, compared with 12 percent of the men, were unemployed. Only four women reported that they were not working by choice. For some, economic adjustments affect their whole recovery. Some women have been out of the labor market for a long time or had never been in it; some have few marketable skills. The presence of young children makes it particularly hard to find work, and babysitters' wages often cut deeply into earnings. In our study, 13 women—but no men—were not working because of child-care responsibilities.

Several women reported discrimination against separated and divorced women in addition to discrimination against women in general. Some also reported discrimination in housing, and many (54 percent)

**TABLE 3.6**
**Experienced Discrimination Because Separated/Divorced (in percentages)**

|  | Men | | Women | |
| --- | --- | --- | --- | --- |
|  | Yes | No | Yes | No |
| In social groups | 37 | 63 | 40 | 60 |
| In getting housing | 11 | 89 | 21 | 79 |
| In getting a job | 19 | 81 | 18 | 82 |
| In getting credit | 18 | 82 | 54 | 46 |

found it difficult to get credit because of their separations. (See Table 3.6.)

Quite a few women and some men also objected to being asked to indicate "divorced" or "separated" on job applications. One young woman currently looking for a job said,

> I was thinking about the social stigma. My friends and I were talking about filling out job applications and about how I should fill out marital status. They were making me uneasy about it. I wish you didn't have to answer that on applications. I'm afraid it might hurt my chances.

A common area of concern reported by older women married for many years was being cut out of their husband's social security and insurance programs even though most of his benefits had been accumulated during their marriages. Even among older women with good jobs there was much concern about what they would do after retirement.

Economic issues are cited by respondents as being points of conflict in the marriage in a remarkably high proportion of cases. This is demonstrated in Table 3.7 where between 18 percent and 56 percent of the respondents reported that various economic issues had been troublesome before the separation.

Our respondents did not say very much about economic insecurity as a barrier to divorce, but we suspect that behind much of the reluctance to separate is the fear, particularly among women, of having to be financially independent and self-supporting following divorce. Women who have been out of the work force especially face the challenge of achieving economic stability. Cherlin (1979) found that wives whose

**TABLE 3.7**
**Economic Issues that Were Points of Conflict (in percentages)**

|  | Yes | No |
|---|---|---|
| You or your spouse's working hours | 54.1 | 45.9 |
| The amount of work-related traveling | 18.0 | 82.0 |
| Time away from home because of a job | 40.0 | 60.0 |
| The amount of money you had | 55.6 | 44.4 |
| The kind of job you or your spouse had | 39.0 | 61.0 |
| The people with whom you or your spouse worked | 34.6 | 65.4 |

potential wages compared favorably with the wages of their husbands had a greater likelihood of ending their marriages. Alternative sources of earnings enhance the independence of wives from their husbands. We suspect that it was not often mentioned by our respondents because those who divorce must have in some way grappled with the issues and come to some resolution or at least have reduced any dissonance they had. Undoubtedly we would find more open expression of this phenomenon if we talked to women who were married but unhappy.

At the time of our interview, there was considerable diversity in the employment situations of our respondents. Although 88 percent of the men and 73 percent of the women were employed, there are many difficulties for those who are not. One woman told us the following:

> I feel like I'm groping around trying to find out what I'm doing, who I am. I wish there was more help with jobs available, job rehabilitation. I need all the help I can get.

Another woman, 44, divorced after 17 years of marriage, spoke bitterly about her views:

> I thought I was going to have an emotional collapse. It was the fear of financial problems, of poverty. I have a great disdain for married women who work because they don't have anything else to do. They take jobs away from people like me who really need the money. . . . I've thought of suicide at least once a month.

Respondents reported problems such as being laid off, sick, or unable to get a job (30 percent of those who are unemployed). One respondent cited pregnancy to account for her lack of employment; two men and three women were in school. Only one in nine respondents reported that the reason that best explains why they are not working is "not working by choice." Of course, this distribution of circumstances can be considered particular to the region, the respondents, or the time of data collection. Thus, no conclusion should be drawn. The data, however, are instructive of some of the frustrations that can be coincident with separation and divorce—and consequently must be negotiated simultaneously with it—if not caused by or directly related to the separation.

Perhaps most revealing in understanding the economic adjustments required following divorce is the summary presented in Table 3.8 of changes in work situation that often follow separation or divorce. Although a larger number of respondents—men and women equally—

## TABLE 3.8
### Changes in Work Situations Since Separation (in percentages)

|  | Yes | No |
|---|---|---|
| Started work for the first time | 5.4 | 94.6 |
| Been promoted | 24.9 | 75.1 |
| Changed to a more responsible job | 33.7 | 66.3 |
| Been demoted | 2.0 | 98.0 |
| Changed to a less responsible job | 5.9 | 94.1 |
| Been laid off or fired | 8.8 | 91.2 |
| Expanded business | 15.7 | 84.3 |
| Returned to work after a period away | 17.1 | 82.9 |
| Had a business fail | 1.0 | 99.0 |

have been promoted or changed to a more responsible job, and whereas nearly one-fourth of the men and one-tenth of the women have expanded a business, a small but important number of respondents have had such problems as being demoted, laid off, fired, or having a business fail. Again, it is not possible to know the extent to which a comparable sample of married men and women might have experienced similar circumstances, but it is likely that any such complications shortly after a marital separation constitute an unusual degree of stress and frustration.

It is prudent to point out, however, that many men and women don't have a clear idea themselves of the causal connection between work and their social-psychological states. It is difficult to judge how the two are tied together, as reflected in the answer of a man to the question of whether separation affected his work:

> No, I don't think so. It's hard to judge your own work. I got two commendations and two raises during that time. I may have worked harder to keep my mind off of the problems. It was the off-hours that were difficult.

Looking to the future, we asked our respondents how stable they thought their future financial situations would be. Most were optimistic, with men (62 percent) more likely than women (45 percent) to say they thought they would be very stable financially. We also asked how well their future incomes were expected to meet their needs. The contrast between men and women is more striking here, with 43 percent of the men and only 20 percent of the women thinking that they would have more than enough income. Just under one half (45 percent) of the men and just over half (56 percent) of the women thought they would have just enough. However, women (24 percent) were twice as likely as men (12 percent) to say they thought they would have not quite enough or not at all enough.

Depending upon one's viewpoint, there is cause for both optimism and pessimism in viewing data on economic adjustments following separation and divorce. Although a range of problems can emerge following the separation, one must recall the even greater proportion of respondents reporting economic problems before the marriage. When viewed in relation to each other, reports of financial strain during the marriage and after the marriage dissolved provide some basis for optimism. Table 3.9 illustrates a shift in the direction of less financial strain for the sample as a whole. Although the data do not address the question directly, one can speculate that it is not necessarily the amount of money one has which is important but rather the peace of mind one has in making decisions about the money one does have.

## The Legal System

Marriage and divorce laws are one means by which the government seeks to regulate sexual relations, childbearing, child rearing, and economic support among its citizens. A survey of opinion on the recent trend in divorce law reform has revealed uncertainty as to the impact of strict or liberal divorce laws on the incidence of divorce. Some claim that strict laws have failed to restrict the increasing divorce rate because

**TABLE 3.9**
**Financial Strain During the Marriage and After (in percentages)**

| | During the Marriage | | At Present | |
|---|---|---|---|---|
| Level of Financial Strain | Men | Women | Men | Women |
| A lot of financial strain | 35 | 49 | 21 | 12 |
| Some financial strain | 34 | 34 | 27 | 21 |
| Very little financial strain | 19 | 13 | 34 | 41 |
| No financial strain at all | 12 | 4 | 19 | 25 |
| Total | 100 | 100 | 100 | 100 |

those seeking a divorce have been able to manipulate the laws and the legal system (Blake, 1962). Rheinstein (1971) argued that perjury, falsification of evidence, and undue animosity and hardship have resulted from the present adversary divorce system still found in some states. However, making divorce laws more restrictive or more liberal has appeared to have little impact on the trend toward divorce (Abel, 1973; Wright and Stetson, 1978). Earlier studies have found little relationship between statutory grounds for divorce and the actual causes of marital breakup (Harmsworth and Minnis, 1955; Mowrer, 1924; Stetson and Wright, 1975).

In this section we focus on how the legal system affects the process of breaking up and adjustment to marital separation. Contact with the legal system usually begins well before a divorce is decreed. Once an individual has made the decision to file for a divorce or establish a custody, support, or separation agreement, one of the first contacts is with a lawyer who may represent the individual in the divorce proceedings and related matters. Therefore, interaction with the legal system may be the first of many new experiences with which the separated person must cope.

At the time of data collection Pennsylvania was one of only three states without any no-fault divorce provisions. The majority of those interviewed expressed strong dislike of the legal system. Most of these individuals expressed resentment at what they were forced to say about the partner under an adversary arrangement. Typical comments were: "It was just terrible, all the listing of indignities, and placing blame and fault," or "You have to make him look rotten. I didn't like making him look worse than he really was." There are two key questions about an adversary divorce procedure: (1) Do such procedures help to keep marriages intact? (2) What are the effects of the laws on the people who are going through the divorce process? Our study provides no insight as to whether the Pennsylvania adversary system initially discouraged people from separation or divorce. We did, however, find evidence that once in the process, the system made it very difficult for spouses to reconcile. In response to a follow-up question about how the system was "forcing us further apart," one woman replied,

> I think it could work out. Ours could. But to help myself, I have to go there and tell things that are husband and wife business, and he has to do the same. I don't want to hurt him. I want to be fair.

The legal system appears to encourage couples to become adversaries to a greater degree than they already are. It encourages them to lie about each other and to use "dirty tricks" to get the best of the other.

> We had to decide who would divorce who. I just couldn't do the lying, so he did. It really got to me—all the dirty little games you have to play. Having to tell all those twisted half-truths.

Some respondents stated that their lawyers "beefed up" the charges without consulting them until after the charges had been filed. Some expressed fears of being charged with perjury:

> I really resented saying all those mean things. . . . I had to swear I was telling the truth, and I had visions of being convicted of perjury.

Other respondents seemed to view the legal system in a matter-of-fact way:

> We both just looked at the divorce as a legal requirement. I hate the word "divorce." There ought to be a better one in our case.

Regarding the effects of the system on individuals who do get a divorce, we found that not only does it often aggravate relations with the spouse, it also upsets and humiliates people who must openly discuss their intimate marital problems. We found that the legal system offers little support for people going through a separation or divorce.

Many of the respondents who dealt with attorneys found them understanding and helpful, while one-third had negative feelings toward their lawyers. Many felt that they received no real support, and reported that the lawyers seemed to be in it only for the money.

One woman who had been involved in a long fight over both child custody and the property settlement and who had consulted a total of four lawyers stated this:

> I was beginning to feel bitter about the legal process. Most lawyers are just making money. They really take advantage of people when they are vulnerable.

Another younger woman, who was pregnant and in need of welfare when she separated, presented the opposite viewpoint:

> My lawyer is a doll. Really helped me out. Got me a doctor and mother's assistance right away. . . . He only charged me $90 for the work that he did. He helped me get my name changed for free.

Several respondents felt their lawyers or their spouses' lawyers used delaying tactics and other "dirty tricks" to prolong the process and increase the fees. One man said that he thought it was all "a game to the lawyers" and gave a variety of anecdotes to illustrate his opinion. He claimed that after months of costly fighting, the final settlement was essentially the same as he had first proposed and blamed his wife's attorney for having given her very unrealistic expectations in order to prolong the proceedings.

A number of women reported that they had suffered humiliation and emotional distress in the hands of their lawyers. One woman involved in a lengthy property dispute described the following tactics which were almost identical to those described by several other female respondents:

> His lawyer tried to make me crack. I don't know how they live with their conscience. . . . [He] broke me down in stages. I just gave up for peace and serenity. After we started the court case he [husband] wouldn't let me charge anything and would let checks bounce that I wrote. We never finished the case. He told lies. I felt deflated. It was all part of his lawyer's tactics. They work. . . . He [attorney] knew it was tearing me up. I know [it was the lawyer] because other people who have used him told me.

In the present sample, 55 percent of the respondents indicated that they were dissatisfied with the entire legal process of divorce (including the laws, judges, masters, domestic relations office, and lawyers). Seventy percent of our sample strongly disagreed and 14 percent mildly disagreed with the statement that "divorce laws should require that one spouse be held responsible for the failure of the marriage." A striking 84 percent agreed that the Pennsylvania laws should make it legal for persons who are incompatible to dissolve a marriage (something which has since become possible), while 60 percent of our sample disagreed that strict divorce laws lower divorce rates. Of the respondents, 26 percent agreed that Pennsylvania laws prevented them from obtaining a divorce as soon as they wanted to.

We asked our respondents about their overall impressions of the legal system. In response to an interviewer who asked, "After going through all this do you have any general feelings about the whole legal process in terms of getting a divorce?" one man responded,

> Well, I think they make it too easy to get married and too hard to get divorced. The automatic waiting period of twenty days here and thirty days there, etc. . . . really drags it out and makes for some problems because until it's final it's hard to really get your life reorganized.

A woman, commenting on the same question, said,

> Well, I think the whole legal process is a problem. I mean it takes so long and costs so much, but they don't do anything during that time to help the marriage.

The grounds available for a divorce in Pennsylvania at the time of the study included impotency, bigamy, adultery, desertion, cruel and barbarous treatment, indignities, fraud, sentence to imprisonment for two years or more, or consanguinity. Indignities was the most commonly cited ground. In the present sample, four-fifths of the respondents used indignities as a ground. Many of the respondents stated that indignities had been used because it was sufficiently nebulous and did not place specific blame on one spouse.

In terms of personal experience in the legal sphere, 84 percent of the respondents had hired or consulted an attorney and 38 percent of the sample had consulted more than one. Satisfaction with the job their lawyer did concerning legal matters was indicated by 74 percent. Ratings of lawyer helpfulness with nonlegal matters were somewhat less favorable. Although 30 percent of the sample regarded their lawyers as extremely helpful and 38 percent regarded their lawyers as somewhat helpful, 32 percent regarded them as not at all helpful. Moreover, 16 percent believed their legal fees were outrageous for the amount of work done, and an additional 36 percent believed the fees were too high. Nearly 73 percent of the respondents reported that they had been informed of the legal fees after the first appointment with their lawyer. Finally, 6 percent reported that their attorneys used delaying tactics to increase their fees, and 27 percent believed their spouses' attorneys had used delaying tactics to slow down the divorce process.

Advice to exaggerate marital problems during the process of divorce was not an uncommon occurrence. More specifically, 20 percent of the respondents maintained that their lawyers encouraged them to make a bigger issue of the separation or divorce than they wanted to. For 37 percent it was considered necessary to exaggerate problems in the marriage to obtain a separation agreement or divorce. In addition, 26 percent admitted that they or their spouses had lied or trumped up statements in the hearing to help ensure the desired outcome. The system often encourages couples to become greater adversaries than they already are. Another noteworthy finding was that 29 percent of the sample reported that they had been advised by their lawyers to do things that might aggravate their spouses. Specific advice from attorneys for dealing with estranged spouses, according to respondent reports, included not paying bills (13 percent), not talking to the other person (20 percent), taking money out of the savings (15 percent), and moving out of the house (13 percent).

A range of feelings was found concerning lawyers. The reported effect on the marital relationship of dealings with lawyers seems sometimes to have been adverse. Of the sample 26 percent reported that involvement with attorneys worsened the relationship with the spouse; only 6 percent cited improvement, and 69 percent believed there was no effect whatsoever. A lawyer had been consulted jointly with their spouses by 21 percent of the respondents, and 28 percent mutually had decided in advance with their spouses the grounds for the divorce.

Respondents sometimes focused their frustrations with the legal system directly on the attorneys. As one woman stated it,

> I really detest the divorce laws in this state. It seems like people could just decide that they don't want to be together anymore, without having to go through all this accusation thing. It seems like a racket for lawyers to me.

A man who didn't think much of attorneys said,

> Well, most of the time I didn't really need an attorney except to file for the court order. . . . I don't want to waste all my money on an attorney the way my wife has. I think her attorney is the only one who has really gotten anything out of this whole mess.

In an earlier analysis (Spanier and Anderson, 1979), we used both cross-tabular and multivariate analyses to assess the impact of the legal system on the adjustment to marital separation. We found that satisfaction with the legal process explained only a trivial amount of variance in adjustment to marital separation. Thus, although individuals who have gone through a divorce report numerous problems with the legal system, there is no evidence to suggest that such problems later influence their social-psychological adjustment.

The data in the present study indicate quite clearly that the legal system is burdensome for individuals in many ways. Over half of the respondents reported dissatisfaction with the legal process, and the overwhelming majority of the respondents felt that the divorce laws of Pennsylvania should be changed. The data suggest that divorce statutes based on an adversary model encourage collusion and dishonesty. Not only do significant numbers of the respondents report that they lied in hearings or trumped up statements that were to their advantage, many indicated that their attorneys suggested to them that they do these things.

The data should not be interpreted as critical of attorneys. The attorney's role is that of an advocate for his or her client, and under an adversary divorce statute the best interests of the client perhaps may be served by advice that is not wholly consistent with the procedures specified by the law. Anecdotal evidence we have collected suggests that judges also bend the law when necessary to expedite a divorce decree that is assumed to benefit all parties involved. Defenses that could be used against a petition to divorce, such as collusion, condonation, or recrimination, are sometimes overlooked, for example, if the divorce is not formally contested. Attorneys, masters, and judges often attempt to facilitate a divorce that is wanted by both spouses even when a justifiable defense exists.

If attorneys and judges are performing in the best interests of those involved and yet a great deal of frustration is still produced by the system for those who must negotiate a divorce, then one must inquire into the source of the frustration. If we look beyond the data to why attorneys and other actors in the legal system contribute to interpersonal discord or dishonesty among separated or divorced persons, we are led to a consideration of the adversary divorce statutes.

Such statutes do not reflect the reality of the marriage and divorce experience nor are they sensitive to social and psychological needs. Collusion, condonation, and recrimination are widespread. Marriages rarely fail as a result of the wrongdoings of one spouse (Lewis and Spanier, 1979). Furthermore, there is serious doubt about whether the adversary system encourages reconciliation. The respondents often reported being given advice and conducting themselves in ways that reduce the possibility of reconciliation.

Spanier and Casto (1979) found no evidence that individuals are inclined to avoid or postpone divorce or to attempt reconciliation as a result of the current adversary statute. Whereas the present data do not allow for fault and no-fault divorce law comparisons, we were able to conclude that the adversary legal procedures were cumbersome and disruptive for a significant portion of the sample.

## Seeking Help

Where do persons who are approaching separation turn for help when faced with marital problems? As we reported earlier, family, friends, and coworkers are a source of much nonprofessional help. But we also wanted to ascertain the extent of professional help sought and how effective it was judged to be. Table 3.10 suggests that men and women approaching a divorce do seek professional help in rather large numbers. Of our respondents, 70 percent sought professional help from at least one source. More than a third of the sample had consulted a clergyman. A third had sought the services of a marriage and family counselor, and more than one in four respondents, women more often than men, had spoken to their physicians specifically about the problem. Nearly one respondent in five obtained the help of a psychologist and a similar proportion saw a psychiatrist. The data also reveal that many of those who sought professional help consulted more than one source.

We also asked how helpful these professionals were. These are, of course, subjective reports at a time of great stress in the lives of the men and women we studied. Despite the fact that all of the marriages under study eventually terminated, it is perhaps surprising—or reassuring— that 30 percent of the respondents reported that the professionals were extremely helpful. Another 51 percent indicated that the service was somewhat helpful. Only 19 percent indicated that the professionals were not at all helpful.

Among the 30 percent of the sample who did not seek professional help, nearly two-thirds of the respondents indicated that the idea was suggested (and presumably rejected) by one of the partners. Only about one in nine respondents in the study never even considered seeking help.

The reports of the success of the counseling or therapy were mixed, of course, when the respondents described to us what they felt was accomplished. Many of the stories we heard suggested that the therapy

**TABLE 3.10**
**Sources of Professional Help During Marriage (in percentages)**

| Sources of Help | Seeking Help | | |
|---|---|---|---|
| | Men | Women | Total |
| Clergyman, priest, or rabbi | 28.6 | 40.4 | 35.1 |
| Psychiatrist | 14.3 | 21.1 | 18.0 |
| Physician | 18.7 | 33.3 | 26.8 |
| Marriage and family counselor | 37.4 | 31.6 | 34.1 |
| Psychologist | 17.6 | 20.2 | 19.0 |
| Social worker | 9.9 | 7.0 | 8.3 |
| Public health nurse or other nurse | 1.1 | 2.6 | 2.0 |

or advice was sought after it was too late to make a difference. Other problems frequently encountered centered around the lack of motivation of one of the partners for using the therapy to facilitate changes in the relationship. In the most typical case, it is fair to say that the therapy was found to be useful overall, but did not accomplish the ultimate goal that brought most individuals or couples for help—namely, to "save the marriage."

One woman summarized it as follows:

> I insisted that we go see a counselor, that things should change. The way it was then we each saw the counselor separately and that wasn't really [effective]. We'd each come out having said our mind, but the other person wasn't there, so they wouldn't really know. Then we each went to an encounter group separately, but at the end we went to see the counselors who led them together. I think it was a good thing. What I got out of it was that [my husband] had to stop hitting, but I had to stop feeling victimized. I had to stand up for myself.

A man who was very positive about his counseling experience nevertheless reported that a three-month trial separation, which the counselor discouraged, turned into six months, and finally divorce. The couple was married 27 years.

> [We received help] from a pastoral counseling center that the church runs. It is staffed with clinical psychologists and not just

clergymen. For the most part, this counseling dealt with me and my personal problems and not with the marital relationship. I went once a week [for 8 months]. . . . We went [a few times together] and then we stopped going. My wife suggested a trial separation and the counselor discouraged that idea, and she wasn't happy about that so we quit going. Finally, after consulting with some friends we set up a three-month separation. . . . I agreed to be the one to move out.

Finally, we investigated whether seeking help was related to any of several factors pertaining to the circumstances of the breakup. We found help-seeking unrelated to length of deliberation about the divorce, marital quality in the final months, or response to the breakup, including acceptance, guilt, or anger at partner.

## Summary

Divorce, like all of life's more critical events, does not operate in a vacuum. The social context, including economic and legal influences, exerts some influence. In the case of divorce, economic and legal influences may be especially relevant. In addition, we examined the role of children in the decision to divorce, the subsequent timing of divorce, and the influence of significant others beyond the children. In particular, we considered the special case of extramarital sexual partners. We learn from all of this that divorce is not simply an event that follows from low marital quality; rather, the decision to divorce, the subsequent timing of the separation, and the aftermath are all altered by external influences that may operate differently for each individual or couple.

Our exploration of extramarital sexual involvements revealed that marriages that are candidates for dissolution can be especially vulnerable to the romantic or sexual influences of third parties. However, it seems to be rarely the case that marriages fall apart primarily because the husband or wife becomes involved in another relationship. Although our data do not allow for an assessment of causality, we are inclined to conclude that the relationship between marital dissolution and extramarital affairs is reciprocal, most often originating when the husband or wife perceives that important needs are not being met in the marriage. This may lead to a response to opportunities for extramarital involvement that did not occur earlier in the marriage. When extramarital affairs finally occur, they can often become a wedge between the husband and wife that further pulls the marriage apart.

Many outside involvements first occur, however, after the marriage is in trouble and separation is contemplated. In this situation, extramarital sexual relations become part of the process of coping, seeking support from intimates in the adjustment, and one way of enhancing one's self-concept. Regardless of the causal mechanisms involved or the timing of such relationships, both our qualitative and quantitative data reveal that extramarital affairs are prominently mentioned by men and women as factors involved in the breakup. In divorces where extramarital relationships exist, they often become the focus of explanations of what went wrong and what led to the divorce. It is particularly noteworthy that the spouse's outside involvements are reported to be much more of a factor in the demise of the marriage than one's own outside relationships.

Although children are not a primary focus of our study, we did learn much from our respondents about their own views of the role children played in their lives following the breakup. We found that divorce is often postponed because of the children. Once separated, children can become a source of great satisfaction for the parents—helping ease the difficulties of the adjustment—or they can become pawns in fierce psychological or legal battles between parents. It is difficult, however, to offer clear reports of the role children play in marital separation as parents' statements on this topic tend to be emotional and undoubtedly quite biased.

Our respondents without custody reported a relatively high frequency of contact with children following separation compared to a national sample, but it is still striking how contact with children tends to drop off when one does not live in the same household. By the time we interviewed them, 3 in 10 noncustodial parents were already seeing their children less than once a month. Issues of custody continue to plague some couples for months or years after the separation, and disagreements about child rearing sometimes exist. It is reasonable to expect that men and women who reported high levels of disagreement on numerous matters of importance during the marriage would similarly have disagreements about custody or child rearing after the marriage ended.

Family and friends are outsiders of a different sort. Separated men and women often turn to their families for support, and they are likely to receive it. Sometimes, however, such support is mixed with disapproval of the separation or divorce. This may not facilitate adjustment to the separation. Friends, on the other hand, are the least judgmental about marital dissolution. There is some evidence that friends are most approving when the circumstances associated with the breakup are most negative, particularly among women.

Economic and legal institutions play a key role in the aftermath of marital separation. Our data illustrate that one's financial stability can affect the timing of divorce as well as social and psychological adjustments after the divorce. Economics undoubtedly also relates to the probability that divorce will occur, although we were not able to study this.

The legal system in Pennsylvania at the time of the study was based on an adversary model. This led to substantial numbers of reports of advice and behaviors that would be unlikely to facilitate reconciliation. It can fairly be said that our sample on the whole had little good to say about the legal system. A majority indicated that they were dissatisfied with the entire legal process although a significant minority of the sample rated their lawyers as extremely helpful. Despite an impression of great struggle with the legal system, however, our data reveal no significant relationships between such experiences and postseparation adjustment.

Finally, we discovered that men and women are active in their search for help from nonintimates, with 70 percent of the sample seeking help from at least one professional source. Marriage and family counselors and clergymen are most often consulted. Such help-seeking from professionals as well as that from family, friends, and children suggests that the transition from marriage to divorce may not be as lonely as one might expect. Even with lots of help, of course, there is much about the transition that can go wrong. We explore some of the many aspects of this transition in the chapters to come.

In the next chapter, we alter our focus from the more global perspective to the more personal, considering the personal relief or distress that accompanies marital separation.

CHAPTER 4
# Relief and Distress

Researchers have characterized the aftermath of marital breakup in a variety of ways. Across the characterizations the change in accustomed life patterns—stress, trauma, disorganization—is recognized, although there is great diversity among individuals in the focus, degree, and duration of disruption experienced after marital dissolution. Life is unstable after the breakup. Life falls apart or falls in place, or both in turn. Some men and women are devastated by the event; others are mildly distressed; still others experience relief.

In this chapter, we describe the emotional disorganization that follows marital breakup. Later in the chapter, we examine the circumstances leading to and surrounding the breakup to understand better the emotional consequences of the end of marriage.

## Reactions to the End of Marriage

Adjustment to the end of marriage is characterized by a stable and resilient pattern of life, separate from the previous marriage and partner and based on anticipation rather than memory (Goode, 1956; Hetherington et al., 1978; Hunt, 1966; Spanier and Casto, 1979; Weiss, 1975). This anticipation was expressed by one woman in this way: "I'm relieved. It has been a long road, and I wouldn't want to go back. I've got a lot of plans for the future, and I'm feeling a great deal of confidence." Many men and women told us that they wanted the breakup to be over with so they could make "a new life." The process of leaving behind the old and beginning the new is vulnerable to relapses, however. A young woman whose marriage was short-lived and troubled from the start told us this:

> I was really high when I decided to actually do it, but really low when I started to confront what I was going to do with my life. But I tried really hard to go about what I wanted to do. But

there's a danger there. You tell yourself you're over it, that it doesn't bother you, and you ignore warning signs that it's still there. It takes longer than you'd like.

Another woman, married over 20 years, described the pain of being unable to forsake the past and take on the future:

I have one foot in each world. It's like living in two worlds—his and mine. You can't believe how I feel. I just feel so empty. I talked to his sister on the phone before you came. It helps to talk to someone. That way sometimes I can get motivated to get up and do something. His sister just can't understand him. No one in the family can. My girlfriend tells me to be an individual, to get going and get myself a job. It's gonna take time. It's so hard to start again. All those years wasted. I helped him build this house and gave him the children. Now look. I don't have a life.

Reactions to the end of marriage reflect this process of adjustment. We look at acceptance, anger, guilt, and loneliness as indicators of a person's efforts to separate himself or herself from the former partner and the experience of breaking up. Thoughts and attempts of suicide are an indication that anticipation of the future holds little appeal for the separated or divorced person. Emotional, physical, and behavioral shifts are reactions to the uncertainty and upheaval of ending a marriage. Taken together, the reactions help us comprehend the emotional experience of dissolving a marriage.

## ACCEPTANCE, ANGER, GUILT, AND LONELINESS

We define acceptance as the extent to which a person accepts separation and divorce as an inevitable decision that is correct rather than as a regretful mistake. The concept encompasses detachment of self from the former spouse, obsessive review and preoccupation with the event, and a sense of regret about having done the wrong thing. The scale we used to measure acceptance (Thompson and Spanier, 1983) includes a range of feelings about the end of marriage—disbelief, regret, preoccupation with the former partner, relief, sense of tragedy. A disbelieving woman said, "In some ways it hardly seems like it happened, like the marriage and everything was a dream." For some, the disbelief was a protective dream; for others it was a nightmare: "I've started having nightmares about my marriage. Isn't that funny? I hardly think about it at all during the day, but at night I have nightmares." One man called the breakup "a terrible waste," while another man told us he was "relieved, just relieved." Several of the separated described their feelings of loss. A woman, fighting back tears, said, "It's like part of my life has been taken away." Many wondered if they had done the right thing:

> I really miss family life. I hate coming home to an empty house. We'd been married for 28 years. Things were really desolate for a while. I kept wondering if I did what was right. I had a lot of mixed feelings. . . . I had to do it, though, to prove to myself that I could do it.

Others were sure:

> I feel stronger. It's been a lot of work. I haven't done any wavering since my decision. I feel I did all I could. I know it's better for all concerned.

Most distressing were those people who could not figure out what had happened. A middle-aged woman described her perplexity and preoccupation in this way:

> I can't put my finger on what went wrong. . . . Maybe I should have given him more. I've thought about a lot of things. I lay on that bed in there all day and think and cry. I'd try to get up and do things I should do, but I can't.

In our sample, separated 26 months or less, men and women generally were accepting of marital termination. "Not at all" was the least intense of the four response choices offered for the acceptance items. At least half of the men and women characterized themselves with this response when asked about spending a lot of time thinking about the former spouse, wondering what the former spouse is doing, finding it difficult to believe that the divorce occurred, feeling pressed into the divorce or dumped, regretting that they didn't try longer to make the marriage succeed, or feeling that the divorce is a horrible mistake which they will never get over. Over half of the men and women reported that they are very much relieved and glad that the break was finally made. Almost 30 percent of the men and women, however, felt very much that divorce is one of the most tragic things that can happen to a person; almost 40 percent did not at all have this sense of tragedy, while the remaining others displayed more moderate responses. Few of the men and women participating in the study (less than 10 percent) appear to be unable to accept the end of marriage and the final separation from spouse.

Although researchers have observed (Weiss, 1975) or speculated (Goode, 1956) that marital separation and divorce are as likely to be emotionally distressing for men as for women, other studies (Chiriboga et al., 1978; Hill et al., 1979; Nager et al., 1977) have shown men to be less emotionally accepting of relationship breakup than are women. The men in this study were less accepting of marital termination, but the difference in group means was small.

Anger is probably a distinct reaction to the end of marriage. In factor analyses, the anger and guilt items did not cluster with other emotional reactions to separation. Half of the men and women reported that they were not at all angry at their partner, and only 9 percent of the respondents reported that anger very much described their current feelings. There were no gender differences in expressions of anger. A middle-aged woman who recalled a good marriage for 26 years and suspected there was another woman said, "I'm a vengeful person. . . . The resentment and anger keep me going." Some of the separated find the experience of anger novel and bothersome. One man came home from a business trip and found a note from his wife saying the kids were with a babysitter, she had left him, and she had never loved him. He later found out there was another man. He expressed the burden of his anger in this way:

> I'm a very easygoing, friendly person who is usually happy, and feeling disgust and hate is a new experience for me. It's often very hard for me to cope with. I don't think of myself as a vindictive person, but this whole situation is almost making me one, and that scares me.

In a later section, we report that, among men, being left and blaming the partner or an outsider for the breakup are related to anger.

Weiss (1975) notes two forms of response to the end of marriage. The first, regret and rejection, is implied by the acceptance scale. The other response is guilt and remorse. Guilt and remorse were more common feelings among our respondents than regret, rejection, or anger. About half of the men and women said that they very much felt guilty about the separation and divorce. We found no differences between men and women in the reported experience of guilt. Women as a group, however, were more likely than men to report that the separation and divorce hurt the spouse very badly: 18 percent of the men and 36 percent of the women felt very much that this is true in their situation, and this pattern continues through response categories. These results suggest that women are more apt than men to inflict pain during the divorce process or, alternatively, to be more apt to perceive the pain experienced by the partner. Women acknowledged their partner's pain in the following ways: "It was like he was losing the only thing he had." "I was very worried about him and felt I'd abandoned him." Another woman said simply, "He feels bad; he's hurting." In Chapter 5, we offer evidence that it is the continuing affection and sympathy between partners rather than culpability that allows awareness of each other's hurt.

We asked our respondents whether they thought separation and divorce are harder on men or women. With only a small bias toward thinking that breakup was more difficult for one's own gender, both men and women thought that women are harder hit by the end of marriage. No such self or gender-bias emerged when people thought about their own situation. Reporting that getting used to the breakup was harder for themselves was no more likely than reporting that the breakup was harder for their partner.

Loneliness is the bane of marital breakup. Most often, separated men and women expressed their loneliness in painful, simple statements: "I just have this overwhelming lack of a sense of belonging." "I really dread being alone. There's no one to share things with, no one to talk to." "I feel pretty lonely now." Table 4.1 shows the degree, timing, and source of loneliness for the men and women in our study. Few escaped loneliness since their separation. Mild episodes of loneliness was the most common experience, but bouts of severe loneliness were experienced by about 30 percent of the separated people. Among both men and women, the period just after the separation was usually the most lonely, while the least lonely period usually occurred sometime after the separation. The timing of loneliness was somewhat different for men and women. Men were more likely than women to find the final months of marriage least lonely, while women were more likely than men to find the final months of marriage most lonely. A young woman told us, "I'd been lonely since the beginning (of the marriage). I've always missed having someone to talk to, having friends, some warmth."

Others had the chance to get accustomed to loneliness long before the separation. One man whose wife "spent the whole day with her mother until late evening" put it this way:

> I just usually stay home here, but like I said, that gets lonely after a while, and I guess that's what bothers me the most. Being alone. Of course, that wasn't as sudden as it might have been because my wife wasn't around much during the last months anyway.

Loneliness implies social solitude and separation, but the source of loneliness may differ across people. Weiss (1975) refers to emotional and social loneliness. Emotional loneliness results from lack of intimacy; social loneliness from lack of contact and activity. For many, marital breakup means the loss of one's most intimate relationship, regardless of how woeful the tie was by the final months. The pattern of social life also is disrupted by the breakup. We asked our respondents why they felt lonely, whether loneliness was linked to a particular sense of longing or isolation. The results in Table 4.2 show that longing for the former spouse was a common source of loneliness, but not as common as some other sources. Longing for an opposite-sex friend other than the former partner was a familiar feeling to most men and women. Women were somewhat more likely than men to long for the

TABLE 4.1
Loneliness (in percentages)

|  | Women | Men |
|---|---|---|
| Felt lonely at times since separation or divorce: | | |
| very lonely | 26 | 32 |
| somewhat lonely | 55 | 54 |
| not at all lonely | 19 | 14 |
| total | 100 | 100 |
| Felt most lonely: | | |
| before the decision to separate | 31 | 23 |
| just after you separated | 40 | 55 |
| sometime after you separated | 29 | 22 |
| total | 100 | 100 |
| Felt least lonely: | | |
| before the decision to separate | 18 | 38 |
| just after you separated | 24 | 13 |
| sometime after you separated | 58 | 49 |
| total | 100 | 100 |

**TABLE 4.2
Reasons for Loneliness**

|  | Percentage Answering "Yes" | |
| --- | --- | --- |
|  | Women | Men |
| Felt lonely because |  |  |
| bored | 45 | 43 |
| longing for former spouse | 33 | 40 |
| longing for same-sex friend | 35 | 24 |
| longing for opposite-sex friend | 56 | 69 |
| longing for children | 20 | 54 |
| isolated from social life | 60 | 40 |

company of a same-sex friend and to feel isolated from social life. Men keenly felt the separation from their children. Even boredom—weariness from social tedium and dullness—was experienced more commonly than longing for the old partner. It was often difficult, however, for participants to single out a particular form of loneliness. One woman whose husband worked nights and often did not come home even on his days off put it this way:

> I really get depressed in the evenings, after the kids are in bed. I just sit. I haven't kept up the house or anything. It's funny because I never saw him in the evenings before. . . . But I was never lonely in the evenings before. I don't know if I really care for him or if I'm just afraid to be alone. I don't want to be alone.

## SUICIDE

The desolation and dullness of loneliness and the regret and remorse of a marriage gone awry make thoughts of suicide understandable. A man, who fought with his wife throughout their three-year marriage but was still very attached to her, described his distress in this way:

> At first I was pissed off, hurt, mad. I felt like I wanted to kill someone. I was really in bad shape. I really got depressed, to the point of having suicidal thoughts. . . . I would forget to do things I was supposed to. I just generally couldn't function. I'm just now getting to where I don't mind getting up in the morning to face a new day.

A middle-aged woman said,

> Somehow I'm supposed to come out of this a whole human being, but I'm not sure how. I've thought about suicide at least once a month. I'd never thought of it before; it's frightening. I'm not used to being alone. I was much more dependent than I realized.

Table 4.3 shows that women were more likely than men to seriously consider, plan, and attempt suicide. One-fifth of the women seriously considered taking their own life. Most of these women made plans, although less than half made an actual attempt. Thoughts of suicide were quite common among both men and women, although most realized they would never go through with it. Some saw suicide as a way out. When we asked one man how he thought things would be for him a year from now, this was his reply:

> I might be dead. That's always an option if other things don't work out. I really think that I will be happier, but you never know what will happen. . . . I know now that one minute I will feel good and free and the next I will be alone and depressed.

A tendency toward suicide was associated negatively with acceptance of the end of marriage ($r = -.22$ for women and $-.25$ for men) and with loneliness ($r = -.38$ for women and $-.25$ for men). Thoughts, plans, and attempts of suicide were not related to guilt, remorse, anger, or the specific sources of loneliness.

**TABLE 4.3**
**Thoughts of and Attempts at Suicide Since Separation**

| | Percentage Answering "Yes" | |
|---|---|---|
| | Women | Men |
| Thought about doing it even if would not really do it | 44 | 39 |
| Seriously considered taking your life | 20 | 9 |
| Made plans | 16 | 7 |
| Made an attempt | 8 | 2 |

NOTE: Reproducibility coefficient for Guttman scale = .98.

## RELIEF AND DISTRESS

Few men and women who experience the breakup of a marriage get away without suffering some upheaval. Separation and divorce are highly disruptive events (Holmes and Rahe, 1967). The motif of stress, trauma, change and disorganization has characterized the study of separation and divorce since Goode's (1956) classic study. Although the time frame varies across studies, the practice of characterizing the reaction to the divorce process by a global assessment of behavioral and emotional well-being or distress is almost traditional. The inclusion of relief in this range of responses is recent. Researchers gradually have accrued evidence that it is possible to have positive reactions to the end of marriage: Dissolution can actually be a relief after a stressful marriage and provide opportunities for growth and development (Brown, 1974; Chiriboga and Cutler, 1977; Cuber and Harroff, 1965; Kitson and Sussman, 1982; Kraus, 1979).

One man described metaphorically the upheaval in his life:

> It's just that everything is so unsettled, and things seem to change so abruptly from one minute to the next, the way I feel and what's happening and everything. It's sort of like I'm a very little boat on the ocean with the big waves, being tossed up and down, up and down.

Another woman recounted the first months after she had left her abusive husband:

> My nerves were bad, and I'd get so sick that I'd have to sleep. I wouldn't be able to do anything. . . . I was so depressed. You know how it is. You don't really know what's going on, you just eat and sleep. . . . I felt so terrible I even started drinking, and I'd never done that before. Everything was shattered. I didn't care about anything.

Many of the separated expressed the same distress. One person would say "My nerves were getting the best of me. I couldn't sleep; I'd just sit in the living room in the dark." Another person would echo, "I was a wreck. . . . I was nervous, always shaking inside, very unsure." The litany was repeated again and again: tension, listlessness, apathy, sleeplessness, and irritability. A mother described how her dark moods involved her son: "Detached, I'd go through periods of ignoring Hank.

Then I'd spank him and holler. Real extremes." For most, the emotional and behavioral distress subsided with time. For many, escaping the estranged marriage brought immediate relief. One woman said, "The divorce doesn't bother me. In fact, I have more peace of mind." Another woman told us she felt "relief that the deadly day-to-day contact has ended." A man married over 15 years described a different aspect of relief: "After the divorce from my wife I felt freedom, a sense of starting over emotionally, of having a less complicated life." With the same theme, a woman said, "I felt relieved once I was out on my own." While some feared independence and being alone, others saw freedom as a beacon. For some, the relief turned to distress and the sense of freedom went sour:

> When I first realized I was going to be divorced, I was really excited, viewed it as an adventure. I was actually looking forward to it. I was going to be free, not have to answer to anyone. But I've been separated a year and a half and I can't see any advantages to being divorced, none at all. I don't feel good about the divorce, or about myself. . . . I feel like I'm groping around trying to find out what I'm doing, who I am. I'm lonely and unhappy.

Distress and relief, in our case, are defined as change in subjective symptoms since marital separation. The reaction is the extent to which the respondent perceives that symptoms sensitive to emotional and physical disturbance intensified, stayed the same, or diminished since separation. Four common symptoms were used to assess reaction to marital separation—sleeplessness, nervousness, tiredness, and moody spells. Using an unrestricted latent structure analysis, we found that three classes accounted for individual differences in subjective patterns of change in the symptoms after separation: relief, no change, and distress (Spanier and Thompson, 1983).

In the sample as a whole, the relief and no change groups were about equal in size, while the distress group was somewhat smaller. Only about one-quarter of the sample, overall, experienced distress after marital separation. Women were much more likely than men, however, to be in the distress and relief groups, while men were more likely than women to maintain an even keel after separation and be in the no change group ($X^2 = 9.8$, df = 2, $p < .01$). A third of the women, as compared to 19 percent of the men, can be said to have experienced substantial symptomatic distress. Almost half of the men and somewhat over a quarter of the women were stable after separation, while 35 percent and 41 percent of the men and women, respectively, experienced relief after marital separation.

The results indicate that women are more likely to experience distress after marital separation than men, but they are also somewhat more likely than men to experience relief. Both distress and relief reflect disruption in the life pattern after marital separation, although in different directions. Only the no-change category reflects stability in the experience of separation and divorce. We can conclude that women's emotional lives are more changeable during marital disruption and dissolution than men's lives, and that women are more likely to experience distress or relief rather than steadiness after marital separation than are men.

Relief and distress coincided with other reactions to the end of marriage. Among both men and women, those in the distress group were least accepting of the breakup, those in the relief group were most accepting, and the steady group was in the middle (F values for group differences: 3.87, 2 and 87 df, $p < .02$ for men; 14.21, 2 and 110 df, $p < .01$ for women). The same pattern emerged for loneliness: The distress group was most lonely, the relief group was least lonely, and those people that maintained an even keel were in the middle (F values were 6.29, 2 and 88 df, $p < .01$ for men; 7.67, 2 and 111 df, $p < .01$ for women). Among the men, symptomatic shifts were not related to anger, guilt, specific sources of loneliness, or thoughts of suicide. Among distressed women, however, an increase in symptoms was accompanied by a longing for the former partner ($F = 8.76$, 2 and 110 df, $p < .01$) and feelings of social isolation ($F = 5.19$, 2 and 110 df, $p < .01$). Although relief and distress were not related to anger, guilt, and thoughts of suicide among women, changes in symptoms were related to feelings of having hurt the partner badly. Those women who *most* strongly felt that they had hurt their partner were likely to be in the *relief* group; those in the distress group were least likely to feel that they had hurt their partner badly; and the even keel group lay in the middle ($F = 3.53$, 2 and 110 df, $p < .05$).

## SUMMARY OF REACTIONS

After separation, a person is left to mourn and account for the past and to build the future. The most common feelings experienced after separation by the participants in our study were relief, guilt, and loneliness.

In mourning the marriage, guilt and remorse were the most common responses; but feelings of regret and rejection had more severe consequences. Although only a small proportion of men and women were unable to accept the end of marriage, difficulty accepting the breakup was connected with thoughts of suicide and symptomatic distress after separation. Feelings of anger, guilt, and remorse did not appear to have such severe consequences.

The process of pining for the past overlaps with putting together a new life. Loneliness is a common and painful reaction to the end of marriage, with the period right after the separation being the most painful. Longing for the old partner is part of pining for the past. Most men and women, however, experienced their loneliness as a current longing—as part of the process of putting together a new life. Longing for an opposite-sex friend, a new attachment, and boredom were more likely to be reported by people after separation than longing for the old mate. Severity of loneliness after separation was connected with thoughts of suicide and distress.

In most cases, men and women tended to have similar reactions to the end of marriage. Acceptance of the breakup, anger, guilt, and loneliness were much the same for men and women. There were some gender differences in the timing and source of loneliness: Women were more likely than men to remember the final months of marriage as the most painful. Women felt more socially isolated after separation than men, although men more often bore the pain of being separated from their children. Women were more likely than men to contemplate seriously and attempt suicide. Women were also more likely to experience shifts in emotional and behavioral symptoms after separation. While most men maintained an even keel after separation, women tended to experience either symptomatic relief or distress. Regardless of gender, however, loneliness and wrestling with feelings of regret and rejection were associated with thoughts of suicide and distress after separation.[1]

## Circumstances of the Breakup and Reactions to the End of Marriage

Although the period right after the final separation is especially traumatic for most people, the terminal stage of marriage—that period before the final separation—also represents a traumatic peak in the dissolution process (Chiriboga and Cutler, 1977; Frederico, 1979). The marital and social circumstances of the final months of marriage were discussed in Chapters 2 and 3. The purpose of this section is to explore conditions in the terminal stage of marriage that contribute to individual differences in reactions to the end of marriage. The notion that the events leading to the marital breakup have consequences in the aftermath has been discussed repeatedly in qualitative and quantitative reports (Chiriboga and Thurnher, 1980; Cuber and Harroff, 1965; Goode, 1956; Hetherington et al., 1978; Hunt, 1966; Kitson and Sussman, 1982; Weiss, 1975). It is likely that what is experienced in the final months of marriage is associated with emotional response, relief, and distress after the separation.

The circumstances surrounding the end of marriage include attractions in the marriage, external pressures to remain married, and alternative attractions (Lewis and Spanier, 1979; Levinger, 1965, 1979). Attraction to marriage is viewed as the balance of rewards and costs of marital interaction. Consensus, companionship, affectional compatibility, and marital harmony measure the attractiveness of marriage in its final months. Commitment to marriage represents an overall evaluation of the individual's attraction to the marriage and dedication to the continuation of the relationship (Dean and Spanier, 1974).

The social structure in which partners live or which they have created for themselves gives rise to external pressures to remain married. Such pressures include the normative costs of breaking a social and legal commitment, as well as the emotional costs to others for which an individual feels responsible. Religious constraints, obligation toward children, legal barriers, and the disapproval of family and friends are examples of pressures, aside from the marital relationship itself, that keep the marriage intact. External pressures help bind the partners together in marriage and make escape from marriage more troublesome. Many individuals continue in a dissatisfying marriage because they find the cost of termination too high. Who finally suggests the separation or divorce reveals, in part, which partner considers the cost of termination preferable to continuation in a dissatisfying marriage.

Alternative attractions are sources of reward outside of the marriage that make marital termination more attractive or feasible—inducements to leave the marriage or forces that temper termination costs. An alternative partner, separate kin and friend affiliations, and educational alternatives are the attractions outside of marriage considered in this section. These alternatives provide material and affectional gratifications that may compete with those provided by the marital relationship. The existence of real or anticipated alternative mates who are preferred to the present spouse can be a strong inducement to the end of a moribund marriage (Cuber and Harroff, 1965; Goode, 1956; Levinger, 1979). In a comparative study of cultures, Ackerman (1963) found that societies in which husband and wife have separate networks of kin and friends are more divorce-prone than those in which partners share a common network. He suggested that competing primary affiliations splinter spousal loyalties outside of the marriage and erode conjugal solidarity. Although Ackerman's work was at the level of societies, many believe that the principle is applicable to couples and their affiliations (Levinger, 1979).

Previous research suggests that the final months of marriage bequeath something to the separated man or woman. In the following discussion, we explore whether the costs incurred and escaped when a marriage is surrendered are related to subsequent reactions to the end of marriage.[2] In Table 4.4, we offer the correlations between circumstances of the breakup and acceptance and loneliness after separation. We consider other reactions—anger, guilt, relief and distress, and thoughts of suicide—as well.

## THE MARRIAGE

Among both men and women, personal commitment to marriage in the final months substantially detracts from later acceptance of the breakup. The more the person was willing to invest in marriage and the more hope he or she held for the marriage, the more difficult it was to accept that the breakup had occurred. A man married only a couple of years told us that he and his wife married because they had a good time together, then they fought all the time. He said, "The main reason why I think the marriage didn't work and the separation has been so easy for us is neither of us took the marriage serious enough to get that upset

### TABLE 4.4
### Correlations Between Circumstances of the Breakup and Acceptance and Loneliness After Separation

|  | Acceptance | | Loneliness | |
| --- | --- | --- | --- | --- |
|  | Women | Men | Women | Men |
| **The Marriage** | | | | |
| Consensus | ns | ns | ns | ns |
| Companionship | −.18 | −.29 | ns | .21 |
| Affectional Compatibility | −.42 | ns | ns | ns |
| Marital harmony | −.30 | −.42 | .21 | .21 |
| Commitment to marriage | −.41 | −.43 | .23 | .19 |
| **External Pressures** | | | | |
| Religious constraints | −.19 | ns | .19 | ns |
| Obligation toward children: | | | | |
|   postpone separation | ns | ns | ns | ns |
|   didn't postpone separation | ns | ns | ns | ns |
| Legal barriers: | | | | |
|   lawyer encouraged bigger issue | ns | ns | ns | ns |
|   lawyer advised aggravation | ns | ns | ns | ns |
|   lied or trumped-up statement | −.34 | ns | ns | −.26 |
| Parental disapproval | −.16 | −.30 | ns | ns |
| In-law disapproval | −.17 | ns | ns | ns |
| Sibling disapproval | −.29 | −.43 | ns | ns |
| Friend disapproval | −.45 | −.30 | 26 | 23 |
| Suggested divorce: | | | | |
|   self | .24 | .28 | −.22 | −.22 |
|   spouse | −.31 | −.50 | .23 | .21 |
| **Alternatives** | | | | |
| Alternative dating partner | ns | .19 | −.18 | ns |
| Shared kin affiliation | ns | −.23 | ns | ns |
| Shared friend affiliation | −.24 | ns | ns | ns |
| Years of education | .27 | ns | −.21 | ns |

NOTE: Correlations based on 114 women and 91 men. Only those significant at p < .05 are reported; others are nonsignificant (ns).

when it ended." On the other side of commitment was a woman married over 20 years who centered her life on her husband and marriage:

> It's a low-down feeling. I can hardly describe how it feels to lose someone you don't want to lose. I never had anyone else sexually either. He was the only one, and now it's down the drain.

The people still committed to marriage by its final months were also more lonely after separation than those who had given up on their marriages. Loneliness was experienced especially as a longing for the former partner (correlations with commitment were −.38 for women and −.37 for men).

Escaping contention and discord by leaving the marriage was associated with greater acceptance of the separation and less loneliness than was relinquishing a harmonious marital relationship. Among men, lack of harmony in the final months of marriage also was related to relief after separation ($F = 3.1$, $df = 2, 88$, $p < .05$). Kitson and Sussman (1982) found the recollection of miscommunication and conflict in marriage to be related to positive affect after divorce. The participants in Weiss's (1975) seminars describe the discomfort and pain of the end of marriage. They chronicle the disparaging remarks, betrayals, confrontations, recriminations, and hostilities. It is little wonder that men and women emerging from a marriage stormy with dissension should be more accepting of the breakup and, for men, experience symptomatic relief after separation.

For some people, however, the tension of the final months piled up, leaving the person depleted at separation. One woman who fought with her husband right up until leave-taking put it this way:

> I've never been so depressed. I had thought the worst was that last year before he moved out, but I guess not. . . . I just feel like I've got to get my feet back on the ground. I got through that whole year when Alan was here, and I was beautiful. I stayed on top of things, I didn't cry except now and then. Now it's all over, I should be calmer, and I end up on tranquilizers.

Weiss's participants also recount the silences and withdrawal of the final months. As we described in Chapter 2, many couples have reduced drastically their emotional and behavioral involvement by the final months of marriage. We thought that leading separate lives before the actual separation would soften the impact of the breakup (Chiriboga and Thurnher, 1980). As one man put it, "I had adjusted mostly during the marriage, while we were growing apart." Companionship, however, was not related to relief and distress after separation. Greater companionship in the final months was associated with more severe loneliness after separation among men and more difficulty in accepting the breakup among both men and women. The associations were not striking (see Table 4.4). Sexual and affectional compatibility in the final months of marriage was a strong inhibitor of acceptance of the breakup among women. Although affectional compatibility was not related to global loneliness among women, it was related to longing for the former partner ($r = -.34$). Not surprisingly, the more agreement women recalled about sexual relations and demonstrations of affection and love, the more adverse their reaction was to the separation. Among the men in our sample, affectional compatibility in the final months of marriage was not connected with the aftermath of separation.

Overall, the quality of marriage in the final months was unrelated to relief and distress, feelings of anger and guilt, or thoughts of suicide after separation. Calm and involvement at the end of marriage was more likely to leave the person feeling regretful, lonely, and longing for the old partner. Harmony, personal commitment to marriage and, to a lesser extent, companionship preceded lack of acceptance and loneliness for men. General bickering and irritation also tended to make separation a relief for men. For women, affectional compatibility, commitment to marriage, and to some extent harmony portended a difficult acceptance of the end of marriage.

Accepting the breakup was especially difficult for those who still loved their mate at separation. Any other feelings for the partner— liking, hate, ambivalence, and the absence of feeling—were associated with greater acceptance ($X^2 = 17.2$, 4 df, $p < .01$ for men; $X^2 = 16.8$, 4 df, $p < .01$ for women). Loving the partner at separation also was connected with greater loneliness than any of the other feelings ($X^2 = 26.6$, 8 df, $p < .01$ for total sample). There was not a single person who said they still loved their partner who also said that they were "not at all lonely" since separation. The pattern was the same for men and women. Men and women who expressed love or a combination of hate and love were more likely to report longing for their former partner than those who said they liked, hated, or felt nothing for their partner by the time of separation ($X^2 = 44.4$, 4 df, $p < .01$ for total sample). Feelings for the partner at separation were not related to anger, guilt, or remorse among men. Women who reported love, hate, or a combination of love and hate also reported more anger at their partner ($X^2 = 10.7$, 4 df, $p < .05$) and less recognition that the separation hurt the partner badly ($X^2 = 14.2$, 4 df, $p < .01$) than women who reported liking or feeling nothing for their husband at separation.

Goode (1956) says that liking or feeling nothing for the old mate is least traumatic; strong feelings, either positive or negative, enhance the pain and disruptiveness of ending a marriage. Our data support Goode's conclusion. Strong feelings at separation, especially love, foretell a difficult emotional aftermath.[3]

## EXTERNAL PRESSURES

The perceived approval or disapproval of the separation and divorce by people outside of the marriage is crucial to understanding the aftermath of the breakup (Goode, 1956). The results in Table 4.4 indicate that the disapproval of friends is particularly painful and renders the person more lonely and less accepting after the separation than if friends approve of the breakup. Although the disapproval of friends was not related to symptomatic relief and distress after separation among women, disapproval marked the distress group among men ($F = 5.1$, 2 and 88 df, $p < .01$). Men in the even keel group perceived less disapproval than those in the distress group, while the men in the relief group typically perceived that their friends approved of the divorce. Disapproval of the dissolution by brothers and sisters had greater consequences than parental disapproval, especially among men. In addition to its association with difficulty in accepting the breakup, the disapproval of brothers and sisters was related to symptomatic distress among men ($F = 5.4$, 2 and 79 df, $p < .01$). The pattern of sibling disapproval across relief and distress groups was the same as for friend disapproval. Although in Chapter 3 we reported that women perceive more disapproval than men, it appears that the consequences of disapproval are more severe for men than for women.

The disapproval of parents and parents-in-law was related to difficulty accepting the end of marriage, but the connection was not strong. Family disapproval was unrelated to loneliness or relief and distress after separation. The intercorrelations of mother and father disapproval for natural parental pairs and in-law pairs hovered around .8, making a combined parental score appropriate. In almost all cases, the association between mother and father disapproval and reactions to the breakup were alike. The only exception was the feeling among men that the divorce had hurt their partner badly. Although acknowledgment of the wife's pain was unrelated to the disapproval of mothers or mothers-in-law, it was connected to both the disapproval of fathers ($r = .38$) and fathers-in-law ($r = .34$). Except for this singular association, the disapproval of others—friends, brothers and sisters, parents, and in-laws—was not related to feelings of guilt and anger about the breakup or recognition of the partner's distress.

Goode suggests that the approval of others has two dimensions: Approval may mean that (1) the act of ending the marriage is approved, or (2) there is an understanding of why the dissolution is justified. Parents, in-laws, brothers and sisters, and friends may mean very different things with their approval, and the implications of approval may be very different. Family and friends may push for reconciliation, encourage a separation, feel personally threatened, or display other responses to divorce. We do not know the exact nature and timing of outsider involvement in the divorce deliberation of our respondents.

As we might expect, the perceived disapproval of others was linked with who suggested the separation or divorce. Both men and women perceived others as more approving of the breakup if they themselves first suggested it than if their partner suggested it. Such is the self-protective nature of perceptions.

Weiss (1975) differentiated between the response to separation of the leaver and the left. The leaver feels guilt and remorse; the left feels regret and rejection. Other researchers have reported the greater emotional upheaval of the partner left behind (Goode, 1956; Hill et al., 1979). For the correlational results in Table 4.4, we created dummy variables from the suggestion categories, using the shared suggestion as the reference category. We also examined contingency tables to understand better the patterns of association. The important distinction appears to be whether or not the person is in the broken-up-with position, the left. Whenever there was a connection between the source of the initial suggestions to divorce and reactions to the breakup, the spouse-initiated suggestions contrasted with the other two categories—the self-initiated and the mutual suggestions. Among both men and women, being on the receiving end of the suggestion to separate was related to difficulty accepting the breakup, loneliness, and longing for the old partner ($X^2 = 6.4$ for men and 7.0 for women, 2 df, $p < .05$). Among men, being left was also connected with feelings of anger ($X^2 = 7.5$, 2 df, $p < .02$). A young woman recalled that her husband suddenly became distant and said he needed to get away. He never returned, and she only talked with him once after that. She described what it was like when her husband left her:

> I lost 20 pounds. I had to talk—to my father, brothers, to friends at work, to anyone who would listen. I kept trying to figure out

what went wrong. . . . I kept asking myself, "Why? Why? Why?" When I realized what was happening, I wondered, when is the hurt going away?

According to Weiss, the leaver is vulnerable to feelings of guilt and remorse. In our sample, who suggested the breakup was not related to guilt. Among women, however, acknowledgment that the breakup hurt the partner badly was more typical of women who themselves suggested the separation than of those who received or shared the suggestion to end the marriage ($X^2 = 7.4$, 2 df, $p < .02$). The pattern was the same among men, but did not reach significance. Among both men and women there was a tendency for the leaver to experience symptomatic relief after separation, but again the link was not statistically significant.

The reactions to the end of marriage included in our study portray well the experience of the person left behind. The qualitatively unique distress of the leaver, however, is not so finely portrayed. Control over the process and progress of dissolution is much more complex than merely the concept of a leaver and a left (Frederico, 1979; Goode, 1956). Our other attempts to capture this complexity—anticipation time and the timing of separation with certainty about the end of marriage—were not related to reactions to the breakup.

Placement of blame for the breakup was connected with the aftermath. Blaming the spouse or an outsider rather than sharing the blame or blaming oneself was the important distinction. Women who blamed their partner or an outsider were characterized by low acceptance ($X^2 = 12.8$, 3 df, $p < .01$), longing for the old partner ($X^2 = 13.2$, 3 df, $p < .01$), and denial that the breakup hurt the partner badly ($X^2 = 9.9$, 3 df, $p < .05$). Men showed similar patterns regarding acceptance and the partner's distress, but the connections with blame did not reach significance. Among men, blaming the spouse or an outsider was characterized by anger after the breakup ($X^2 = 8.3$, 3 df, $p < .05$). Women also tended to experience greater anger after separation when they blamed their partner or an outsider than if they accepted some of the blame themselves, but the connection was not statistically significant. The target of blame was not related to guilt about the breakup.

With some exception, reactions to the end of marriage were not related to religious constraints, obligations toward children (as evidenced by postponing the breakup for their sake), or legal barriers.[4] Women who felt pressure from their church or from their own personal religious beliefs not to break up the marriage had somewhat more difficulty accepting the divorce and were more lonely afterward than women who did not experience religious constraints. Telling lies or making trumped-up statements to be sure the divorce hearing turned out right was related to difficulty accepting the divorce among women and subsequent loneliness among men. Overall, the disapproval of others and not participating in the initial suggestion to end the marriage were the most consequential features of the final months outside of characteristics of the marriage itself.

## Alternatives

Most of the alternative sources of gratification outside of marriage that we consider are social. We looked at whether or not the respondent was planning on dating a particular person after separation and the extent to which the respondent shared a common network of friends and kin with the mate during marriage. We also considered educational alternatives.

The presence of an alternative partner could ease the transition to singlehood. In Goode's (1956) sample of divorced women, however, he found that being in love with someone else does not necessarily ease the dissolution or its aftermath, because feelings of guilt may counteract the benefits of an alternative source of gratification. As Table 4.4 indicates, the presence of an alternative dating partner was related marginally to acceptance of the breakup among men and less loneliness after separation among women. There was some evidence that having another person waiting was connected with guilt among men ($r = .18$) and recognition of the spouse's pain ($r = .21$) but reduced anger ($r = -.17$) among women. Our measure of alternative partner in this study referred only to an anticipated dating partner; it did not imply the nature of involvement with or preference for the alternative. Goode observes that early daters lose their initial advantage quickly because most people begin to date after divorce and catch up.

To explore further the connection between romantic and sexual gratifications outside of marriage and reactions to the breakup, we looked at extramarital sexual involvement (see Table 4.5). Among women, whether or not they had extramarital sexual relations had little effect on their reactions to the end of marriage. For those who had extramarital sexual relations, however, the circumstances of their

## TABLE 4.5
### Correlations Between Extramarital Sexual Involvement and Reactions to the End of Marriage

| | | Reactions to the End of Marriage | | | | | |
|---|---|---|---|---|---|---|---|
| | n | Acceptance | Anger | Guilt | Hurt Partner | Loneliness | Suicide |
| **Women** | | | | | | | |
| Extramarital coitus | 114* | ns | ns | ns | ns | ns | ns |
| Involvement with last partner | 42** | ns | -.28 | ns | .28 | -.31 | ns |
| Continuation | 42 | ns | ns | ns | ns | -.27 | ns |
| Satisfaction | 42 | ns | ns | ns | .28 | ns | ns |
| Spouse's approval | 26*** | ns | ns | -.40 | -.32 | ns | -.32 |
| Guilt | 42 | ns | ns | ns | ns | ns | ns |
| **Men** | | | | | | | |
| Extramarital coitus | 91* | .30 | ns | ns | ns | -.25 | ns |
| Involvement with last partner | 35** | .32 | .31 | ns | ns | -.50 | -.29 |
| Continuation | 35 | .32 | .34 | ns | ns | -.36 | -.28 |
| Satisfaction | 35 | .49 | ns | ns | ns | -.30 | -.35 |
| Spouse's approval | 22*** | .32 | ns | ns | -.36 | ns | -.37 |
| Guilt | 35 | -.33 | ns | ns | ns | ns | ns |

\* includes all respondents
\*\* includes those respondents who have had extramarital coitus
\*\*\*includes those respondents whose spouse knew of extramarital coitus
NOTE: Only those correlations significant at $p < .05$ are reported; others are nonsignificant (ns).

involvement were related to the emotional aftermath of separation. The more involved they were with the last partner, the less anger and loneliness they experienced after separation; but they also had a greater recognition that the breakup had hurt the spouse badly. Continuation of the relationship past separation reduced loneliness as well. Satisfaction with the last sexual liaison was related to acknowledging the spouse's pain. The perception that the spouse approved of the involvement served to temper the perception that the breakup hurt the spouse and guilt about the breakup. The spouse's approval also reduced thoughts and attempts of suicide among women whose spouses knew of their sexual activities outside of marriage. Guilt about extramarital sexual activity, however, was not related to the emotional aftermath of separation.

Men tended to be more accepting of the end of marriage and less lonely after separation if they had been involved sexually outside of marriage than if they had no extramarital sexual experience. Among those men who were involved sexually outside of marriage, it was found that the more emotionally involved they were with the last partner, the more accepting they were of the breakup, the less lonely they were after separation, and the less prone they were to thoughts and attempts of suicide. They were also, however, more angry about the breakup if they were emotionally involved with the last sexual partner. If the relationship continued past separation, men were more accepting, less lonely, and less prone to suicide than if the affair did not continue. Again, they were also more angry at their wife if their extramarital relations persisted past separation. Except for the enhancement of anger, satisfaction with the last extramarital sexual liaison mirrored the pattern of associations found for emotional and continued involvement with the partner—greater acceptance, less loneliness, and less propensity to suicide. As with women, the more spousal approval men perceived, the less they felt that the breakup had hurt the spouse badly and the less likely they were to think about and attempt suicide. Among men whose wives knew of their extramarital sexual activity, spousal approval was also related to acceptance of the breakup. Guilt about extramarital sexual activity detracted from acceptance among men but was otherwise unrelated to emotional reactions to the end of marriage.

We also examined the extent to which respondents shared a common network of kin and friends with the spouse during the last year or two of marriage. The sharing of friends and family reflects the social interdependence of marital partners and may result in difficulty sorting out loyalties after separation. We measured shared friend affiliation by whether partners had mostly separate friends, some separate and some shared, or mostly shared friends. Sharing friends with the husband during marriage was related marginally to difficulty accepting the breakup among women. We measured shared kin affiliation by whether or not the respondent named a member of the spouse's family as one of the three people he or she felt closest to during the last year or two of marriage. Sharing kin in such a way was related to difficulty accepting the breakup among men. This is surprising as it is usually women rather than men who think of their in-laws as family and friends (Anspach, 1976; Weiss, 1975). In our sample, however, 20 percent of the men and 25 percent of the women named a member of the spouse's family as a close friend. Sharing family or friends with the partner during marriage was not related to loneliness after separation for either men or women.

Finally, we looked at educational alternatives. Education can be viewed as a source of satisfaction and income outside of marriage. The wife's independent social and economic status is a force that makes life outside of marriage more feasible—perhaps even more attractive (Levinger, 1979; Nye, 1979). Years of education was associated with greater acceptance of the breakup and less loneliness after separation among women. The relative lack of education also characterized the symptomatic distress group among women ($F = 5.5$, 2 and 111 df, $p < .01$). Education was unrelated to acceptance, loneliness, or relief and distress among men. The economic and occupational independence afforded by education does not shift with marital status for men as it does for women. Again and again, women expressed their fear of not having any money and no marketable skills. One woman said, "I was so frightened. I thought, what'll I do now. I'm middle-aged and untrained. . . . [I have] a vague fear about money when I'm old." Another middle-aged woman described the plight she shared with many other women:

> I thought I was going to have an emotional collapse. It was the fear of financial problems, of poverty. I have a great disdain for married women who work because they don't have anything else to do. They take jobs away from people like me who really need the money. If only I could earn some money, maybe I could relax and put myself back together. . . . If I was educated, or at least seemed to be very competent and professional. If only I knew what I was doing.

None of the alternatives outside of marriage surveyed in our study dramatically influenced emotional reactions to the end of marriage. Among men, extramarital sexual relations and the depth and persistence of that involvement eased the transition to singlehood. Among women, the alternatives linked with education made separation less difficult.

## Summary

We wanted to know how the circumstances surrounding the breakup related to the emotional aftermath of separation. We began the chapter by describing reactions to the end of marriage. Guilt, remorse, and loneliness were more common feelings than regret and rejection. Difficulty accepting the breakup—with feelings of regret, rejection, obsessive review, and preoccupation with the partner—and loneliness after separation had the most severe consequences in the aftermath. Both reactions were associated with thoughts and attempts of suicide and symptomatic distress. Difficulty accepting the end of marriage is pining for the past, while loneliness is suffering the present. We discovered that acceptance of the breakup and loneliness also were the reactions tied most closely to the circumstances in the final stage of marriage.

For men and women, difficulty accepting the end of marriage and loneliness after separation were linked with the following circumstances in the final months of marriage: Marital calm rather than conflict and irritation, personal commitment to marriage, love for the partner, and disapproval of the breakup by friends. The disapproval of family members—parents, brothers, and sisters—also meant a more difficult time accepting the divorce, especially among men.

Among men, the disapproval of friends and siblings was linked with symptomatic distress after separation as well as to troubled acceptance and loneliness. Men appear to be more vulnerable than women to the approval and disapproval of others. There was other evidence that social ties outside of marriage eased or worsened the breakup for men. Men who were planning on dating a particular other person after separation or who were involved sexually outside of marriage before separation were more accepting of the end of marriage than men who did not have such alternatives. Men with extramarital sexual experience were also less lonely after the breakup. Among husbands with sexual experience outside of marriage, it was the circumstances of the experience that most influenced subsequent reactions to the end of marriage. The following circumstances were linked with greater acceptance of the breakup, less loneliness, and even a lesser tendency toward suicide: emotional involvement in and satisfaction with the sexual liaison, continuation of the relationship past separation, and the wife's approval of the involvement. Planning on dating a particular person after separation was related to guilt about the breakup and acknowledgment of the wife's distress. Although these associations were small, having a prospective dating partner was the only circumstance in the final months of marriage and breakup that was related to guilt and remorse among men. Anger among men was connected with the position of being left by the wife and blaming the wife or an outsider for the breakup.

Sexual and affectional compatibility with the husband, even in the final months of marriage, meant that women had more difficulty accepting the end of their marriage. Women also had more trouble accepting the end if they blamed their husband or an outsider for the breakup rather than assuming at least some of the blame themselves. Women also were hesitant to recognize that the breakup hurt their husband badly if they blamed the husband, reported that the husband first suggested the breakup, and still felt strongly about the husband—either love, hate, or a combination—at separation. Such strong feelings also enhanced their anger at their husband. None of the circumstances of the final break were linked with guilt about the separation and divorce for women. Women who had a potential dating partner were somewhat less lonely after separation than those without someone waiting. For those with sexual experience outside of marriage, the depth and persistence of their involvement also eased the loneliness of separation. Most striking among women, however, was the connection between education and the aftermath of separation. The more years of education a woman had, the more she accepted the breakup, the less lonely she was after separation, and the less likely she was to experience symptomatic distress.

So what have the final months of marriage and the breakup bequeathed the separated man or woman? Men seemed to be sensitive particularly to the bickering and irritation of the final months of marriage and the approval of others. These circumstances and the possibility of another partner tempered the pain and distress of ending a marriage for men. For men, as well as women, being in the position of being left, loving the marriage partner until the end, and holding out hope for the marriage foretold a troubled aftermath to separation. Women also responded to the dissension of the final months and the dissapproval of others, but not as much as men. Women were sensitive particularly to the sexual and affectional quality of the last stage of marriage and to the placement of blame for the breakup. While for men, social approval and alternatives eased the transition to singlehood, for women, the financial and occupational alternatives provided by education made the difference.

## Notes

1. Researchers have found that time since separation is an important dimension in the response to breakup (Goode, 1956; Hetherington et al., 1978). In our cross-sectional sample, time since separation was not related to any of the reactions to the end of marriage.

2. Multivariate analyses of the relationship between the end of marriage and reactions to the breakup appear in Thompson and Spanier (1983) and Spanier and Thompson (1983).

3. Length of marriage was not related to any of the reactions to the end of marriage.

4. Note that not having any children was used as the reference category when creating the dummy variables for postponing the separation for the sake of the children. The lack of association, then, means that the presence or absence of children in marriage was not related to the emotional aftermath of separation as we measured it.

CHAPTER 5

# The Partners After Marriage

During an interview, a man married 20 years told us, "Divorce doesn't really end anything.... A piece of paper can't end all the years together or the problems or the commitment." Just as the process of withdrawal may begin long before the actual separation, the entanglement between marital partners may persist long after separation. Lives cannot be connected one day and separate the next. Feelings shift from day to day; and although the day of separation is significant, it is only one day of many. Even though the marriage is supposed to be over, partners may still hanker for each other. Even though they know they have done the right thing, partners may be drawn to each other for contact, conversation, and solace. In the emotional confusion, partners may feel anger, resentment, and regret right alongside the longing.

In this chapter, we describe the partnership after marriage. We explore contact, conversation, feelings, preoccupation, and pining. In later sections, we examine circumstances connected with the partnership after marriage: time since separation, children, memories of the final months of marriage, and social opportunities outside of the partnership.

## The Partners After Marriage

### CONTACT AND CONVERSATION

When we asked respondents how they felt about keeping in touch with their former marital partner, about half of the men and women said they preferred some contact, but only when necessary. The other half was split about equally between desires of close contact and no contact at all. Those who want no contact with the former partner are often adamant: "I just don't want another thing to do with him.... I'm very bitter now. I can't bring myself to talk to him." Table 5.1 displays the mode of contact between former spouses. About a third of the men and women would make an effort to avoid seeing the old partner. A woman married almost 30 years who had been provoked into asking for a divorce by her husband said, "I don't go to parties when I know Ted will be there. I don't want to avoid him, but I have to for my own sanity."

At least half of the separated had spoken to their partner, either by phone or in person, in the past few weeks. About a third had heard news of their partner through family or friends. Letters, dates, and sex were more unlikely between former partners. Many separated men and women still think about sex with their former partner, but don't act on their thoughts. A woman who still professed love for her former husband but thought it was "not worth the effort to live with him" said,

> He still comes over Saturday or Sunday. There are times I'd like to have him stay, but I don't ask him. I wish he would offer. He hasn't made any advances, but I wouldn't want it. It's just not a good thing to get involved.

Like many others, she wants him; but, then again, she doesn't.

We created a Guttman scale of contact to be used in further analysis. Contact ranged from speaking with the former partner, through hearing about the partner from others and going out with the partner, to having sex with the partner (coefficient of reproducibility = .89). Asking or hearing about the partner through other people, then, emerged in the scaling procedure as a higher form of contact than speaking to the

**TABLE 5.1**
**Contact with Former Spouse in the Past Few Weeks**

| Nature of Contact | Percentage in Contact | |
|---|---|---|
| | Yes | No |
| Made effort to avoid seeing spouse | 35.6 | 64.4 |
| Seen spouse but not talked to | 19.0 | 81.0 |
| Heard from spouse by letter | 10.2 | 89.8 |
| Written to spouse | 7.3 | 92.7 |
| Spoken to spouse by phone | 59.5 | 40.5 |
| Spoken to spouse in person | 49.8 | 50.2 |
| Heard about spouse through family | 32.2 | 67.8 |
| Heard about spouse through friends | 36.6 | 63.4 |
| Gone out with spouse | 10.2 | 89.8 |
| Had sex with spouse | 4.4 | 95.6 |

partner directly. This is consistent with Goode's (1956) research in which finding out about the husband fell in between seeing and dating the former husband.

When asked who usually initiates contact, respondents demonstrated a bias away from admitting that they initiated contact. Only about 20 percent took responsibility for making contact while twice as many named their partner as making the effort. The remaining 40 percent shared the responsibility with the partner. Respondents most likely believe that the appropriate connection with a former marital partner is polite indifference (Goetting, 1979). Any bias in reporting is probably toward passivity and apathy (Goode, 1956). Initiation of contact may be hard to determine, however. One man whose wife lives in Canada wryly reported,

> She still calls regularly. Actually, she manages to call when I'm not home so I have to return the calls, and I've had to pay for most of them.

For some, contact is tied to services former partners render one another. Usually the services are common to one gender or the other, skills not acquired because the other partner always did them. Women do laundry or provide a meal, while men take care of the car or do repairs. A man in his early forties who had ended a traditional marriage reported this:

> We have dinner together once in a while. I go over to her house and do some repairs, and help her with her car that's hard to keep tuned right. I probably see her on the average of about once a week.

Some people provide services grudgingly, even resentfully. One young woman with two children endured a shortage of money throughout her marriage. In spite of dire financial straits, her husband was a spendthrift and would not allow her to work. Now, he doesn't pay his support. In tears, she told us the following:

> He sold his car; he's in debt again, so he comes over to use mine. I let him, but I resent it. It's hard on us, but we're trying to make ends meet. He's not even trying. . . . Here he is using my car, and not contributing anything.

It's difficult for many partners to quell their sense of rights and responsibilities.

What do the former marital partners have to talk about together? Tables 5.2 and 5.3 show the content of conversations—topics discussed and topics avoided. Among most couples with children, the children provide a ready and unavoidable topic of conversation. Similar to other people, the mundane aspects of life (daily happenings and practical problems) were usual topics of discussion. Personal problems were more difficult to talk about and were avoided by over one third of the sample. About a quarter of the men and women typically discussed their relationship, while half considered the marriage taboo in conversation. As a topic of conversation to be avoided, new relationships and dating were at the top of the list. There are some former partners who see one another but do not speak: "I see him when he comes to pick up the children, but he doesn't talk to me. It's like I'm not even there." The distributions for conversational content and contact were almost identical for men and women, supporting our claim that disparity in the subjective reports of men and women reflect real gender differences.

We also created a Guttman scale for topics discussed and topics avoided. Topics discussed ranged from the mundane, through personal problems, to discussions of the relationship with the partner (coefficient of reproducibility = .90). Prohibited topics ranged from the marriage, through problems adjusting to separation, to new relationships and dating (coefficient of reproducibility = .87). The two scales were

**TABLE 5.2**
**Topics of Conversation Usually Discussed with Former Spouse**

| Topic of Conversation | | Percentage Discussing Topic | |
|---|---|---|---|
| | n | Yes | No |
| Relationship with spouse | 191* | 24.1 | 75.9 |
| Personal problems | 191 | 30.9 | 69.1 |
| Daily happenings | 191 | 48.2 | 51.8 |
| Practical problems (such as home repair) | 191 | 45.0 | 55.0 |
| Children | 142** | 76.8 | 23.2 |
| Child support | 142 | 28.1 | 71.9 |

*does not include those who had no contact with spouse in past few weeks (7% of sample)

**does not include those without children

### TABLE 5.3
### Topics of Conversation Usually Avoided with Former Spouse

| | | Percentage Avoiding Topic | |
|---|---|---|---|
| Topic of Conversation | n | Yes | No |
| New relationships and dating | 191* | 59.3 | 40.7 |
| Marriage with spouse | 191 | 49.0 | 51.0 |
| Spouse's problems with separation | 191 | 38.0 | 62.0 |
| Own problems with separation | 191 | 43.8 | 56.3 |
| Children | 142** | 12.9 | 87.1 |

\* does not include those who had no contact with spouse in the past few weeks (7% of sample)

\*\* does not include those without children

correlated moderately ($r = .33$). Many of the couples were able to discuss personal matters well after separation. When we asked them when it was easiest to discuss personal matters, about a quarter of the men and women said it was easier before the separation and another quarter thought it was easier after the separation. The other half of the men and women did not perceive any change in rapport since separation. One woman explained the emergent ease in her relations with her former husband in this way:

> [We] went out one night and were more open than ever before. I guess we were more free to talk and be open. Before, I think, we were afraid to say things. I think we were afraid of hurting each other and being alone.

When former marital partners discuss their relationship, they may consider getting back together. One or both partners may want to start over again. Pleas, tears, promises, and threats are common in such instances. The following episode was recounted by a young woman whose divorce was already final:

> We saw each other quite a bit. He was hassling me a lot, calling at all hours, pleading with me to come back, crying. I had a hard time with that. It was worse than it had ever been. I was tense and upset. He'd call me at work, was following me around. I never

knew where I'd see him. He'd get mad if I'd made plans or just didn't want to see him. He even threatened to beat up the guys I saw.

Eventually, relations calmed down in this couple. Now they have a standing date once a week. They go out, talk, and sometimes make love. They both see other people, and neither wants to reclaim their marriage. Other couples are less explosive, but just as confused. A woman whose husband had been insecure and unstable told us the following:

> We still talk about getting back together. But he has to prove to me that things have changed . . . I feel so unsure of him. There's no way of knowing whether or not we'd end up back where we were. He seems more settled now and I still feel a lot for him. I wish I knew what to do. It's been driving me crazy.

In this case, the divorce was final and the perplexed woman was living with another man.

About 70 percent of the respondents reported that their relationships with the former marital partner had become less tense since separation, while about 20 percent saw no change, and 10 percent noted an increase in tension. The increase in tension was related to avoiding certain topics of conversation ($r = .31$) and keeping the discussions more mundane ($r = -.16$) among women, but was unrelated to the content of conversation among men. Actual contact was not connected to shifts in tension, although women were more likely to report making an effort to avoid seeing the partner if they felt the tension had gotten worse or had not relented since separation ($r = .32$). Among both men and women, making an effort to avoid seeing the old partner was related to having to avoid certain topics of conversation when they did meet ($r = .40$). The desire for close contact was linked with the discussion of personal topics ($r = .46$) and not having to avoid certain topics ($r = -.25$). Actual contact was related to topics of conversation ($r = .28$) but not to avoidance of topics.

With no daily confrontations, partners often enjoy each other more and get along better after separation than they did during the final months of marriage (Hetherington et al., 1978; Weiss, 1975). As one woman explained, "We get along better now because there's no tension or demands. . . . We don't have expectations for each other." Couples may be able to talk more easily about personal concerns when the strain of bringing the marriage to an end has subsided. Avoiding potentially painful and explosive topics of conversation (the erstwhile marriage, problems with separation, and intimate relations with others) does not enhance the desire for contact. Rather, it is the continuing sympathy and rapport between former marital partners that makes them still want to see each other and maintain contact after separation. There is a danger, however. Harmony after separation may sustain and even enhance affection for and attachment to the partner of old (Hetherington, et al., 1978; Weiss, 1975).

## AFFECTION, APATHY, AND ANIMOSITY

Although many of the separated men and women shared personal problems and insights with their former partner, few reported that they were dependent on their partner for emotional support. Over 85 percent of the respondents said that they were not at all emotionally dependent on the old partner. Emotional involvement is more than emotional support, however. There are lingering feelings for and thoughts about the partner. In interviewing, the separated openly expressed their persistent love. They would say simply, "I still love him" or "In some ways, I still love her." Milder affection was evident when partners referred to good feelings, sentiment, and concern. Or as one woman said, "I always liked him and still do." Apathy was glaring in short, crisp remarks such as "I don't care" or "I don't feel anything." Animosity was often blatant as well: "To be quite frank with you, I hate his guts." Hate can be insidious, however: "I look in the paper at the reports of accidents, and I hope it's Jack. That's really bad."

Some partners acknowledge their ambivalence. For instance, one man began a lengthy description of his passions with "my feelings toward her are quite hostile" and ended with "I guess I still love her a lot." Table 5.4 presents the current feelings toward the partner and changes in feelings since separation.

At both final separation (see Table 3.2) and the time of the interview, the percentage with moderate feelings toward the partner (like or have no feelings at all for the partner) were about the same among men as among women. It was the distribution of strong feelings (love, hate, or love and hate) that differed for men and women. At the time of the separation men were more likely to report love while women were more evenly spread out across love, hate, and love/hate. The combination of love and hate was the most common strong feeling among women at

**TABLE 5.4**
**Change in Feelings Toward Partner Since Separation (in percentages)**

| | Current Feelings | | | | | |
|---|---|---|---|---|---|---|
| Feelings at Separation | Love | Like, but Not Love | Feel Nothing | Hate | Love and Hate | Total |
| **Women** | | | | | | |
| Love | 40 | 20 | 15 | 10 | 15 | 100 |
| Like, but not love | 0 | 75 | 25 | 0 | 0 | 100 |
| Feel nothing | 5 | 15 | 65 | 5 | 10 | 100 |
| Hate | 14 | 24 | 29 | 14 | 19 | 100 |
| Love and hate | 11 | 21 | 43 | 0 | 25 | 100 |
| Total: Current feelings | 13 | 32 | 36 | 5 | 14 | 100 |
| **Men** | | | | | | |
| Love | 38 | 31 | 22 | 3 | 6 | 100 |
| Like, but not love | 7 | 36 | 50 | 7 | 0 | 100 |
| Feel nothing | 8 | 32 | 56 | 4 | 0 | 100 |
| Hate | 25 | 0 | 50 | 25 | 0 | 100 |
| Love and hate | 19 | 13 | 50 | 0 | 19 | 100 |
| Total: Current feelings | 21 | 27 | 42 | 4 | 6 | 100 |

separation. Feelings at the time of the interview show that men were still somewhat more likely to profess love for the partner and women were still more likely to combine love with hate. At the time of the interview, one-fifth of the men still loved their former wives. At separation, about 40 percent of the men and women reported friendliness or indifference toward the partner. By the time of the interview, almost 70 percent were friendly or indifferent.

Goode (1956) also documents this migration of strong positive and negative feelings to friendliness or apathy. He suggests that the important distinction is the strength of feelings rather than whether they are positive or negative. According to Goode, any strong feeling (love, hate, or their combination) shows a continuing emotional involvement with the partner, while liking and indifference reflect less emotional involvement. In analysis, however, we often found that collapsing feelings into strong versus moderate categories often distorted the connection of feelings with other components of postmarital relations.

When feelings for the partner changed over time, they moved from strong feelings toward friendliness and indifference (32 percent). Shifts in feelings from moderate to strong were rare (4 percent). Twenty-eight percent of the men and women maintained strong feelings for the partner over the months or years since separation; love was the most persistent strong feeling. Those men and women whose feelings of friendliness or apathy persisted from separation on made up 36 percent of the sample.[1]

We asked our respondents to speculate about how their feelings might change in the future. Over 75 percent thought that their feelings would not change; some (17 percent) thought they would improve, and a few (8 percent) thought that they would get worse. Understandably, projections were related to current feelings ($X^2 = 24.0$, 8 df, $p < .01$ for total sample). Those men and women who liked or had no feelings for their partner thought their feelings would probably stay the same, with a small number of people thinking things would change for the better or worse. Feelings of love or ambivalence were associated with projections of improved or persistent feelings. No one who hated his or her partner thought that their feelings would improve. Some thought the hatred would endure, while others could even imagine feelings worsening from hatred.

Current feelings toward the partner were also connected with the desire for contact, actual contact, and content of conversations. In most cases, the associations were the same among men and women. Men and women who still loved the partner were more likely to want to maintain close contact than those who did not love the partner; those who liked or felt ambivalent about the partner tended to prefer some contact, only when necessary; hate and apathy were associated with a desire for no contact whatsoever ($X^2 = 73.7$, 8 df, $p < .01$ for total sample). Men and women who loved or liked their partners were more likely to discuss personal topics with them than those who professed no feeling, hate, or ambivalence ($X^2 = 25.8$, 4 df, $p < .01$ for total sample). In the same pattern, men and women who loved or liked their partners were less likely to avoid certain topics of conversation than those who had no or some negative feelings ($X^2 = 10.9$, 4 df, $p < .05$ for the total sample). Positive feelings for the old partner, then, appear to be maintained by open and continued discussion of personal matters, including personal problems, dating, current relations with the partner, and the foregone marriage.

Actual contact, however, was related to current feelings among women ($X^2 = 15.0$, 4 df, $p < .01$) but not among men. For former wives, feelings of love were associated with high contact while feelings of hate and indifference were linked with low contact. There were no differences in contact between women who expressed feelings of friendliness or ambivalence. Speaking to the former partner, either in person or on the phone, was the most important mode of contact in maintaining love for women. Also, of the five women who had been sexually involved with the former husband in the past few weeks, four were still in love with their husbands; the other woman was indifferent. Among men, there was no connection between contact and feelings.

## ATTACHMENT

Attachment is emotional dependence on a specific person, a preference for the person relative to others, and a need for access or physical closeness to the person (Bowlby, 1969; Lerner and Ryff, 1978). As Weiss (1975: 40) says, attachment is a "sense that home is where the other is." The feelings of ease in the presence of the partner and discomfort when separated persist after separation, in spite of irritation, anger, and hurt. Several scholars link the distress of marital breakup with the loss of an attachment figure (Brown et al., 1980; Kitson, 1982; Weiss, 1975).

The theme of attachment ran through our interviews with separated men and women. One man, separated from his wife by time and several states, described his attachment in this way:

> I think about her every day of my life. I wonder who she is with, if she's working, how she's treating my daughter, and lots of other things. I still love her quite a lot.

A young woman put it this way;

> I still think about him. Knowing that he won't come home for dinner is sad. Dinner is the hardest time. We still talk and I wonder how he's doing . . . [there are other] memories, like him cooking breakfast on Sunday mornings. And the family at home at Christmas. It's hard seeing his car downtown and thinking about he and I apart.

Others showed little or no attachment to the former partner. They would remark, "I very seldom think of her." or "I don't miss him." A few would confess, "I like being away from him."

Our scale of acceptance of breakup (Chapter 4) included many of the feelings of loss, including disbelief and a sense of tragedy. In this and subsequent sections, we will draw out two of the acceptance items ("I find myself spending a lot of time thinking about my former spouse" and "I find myself wondering what my former spouse is doing") to indicate attachment. The items reflect preoccupation with and pining for the former partner and were the best markers in Kitson's (1982) attachment scale developed through factor analysis. As an alternative measure of attachment, we use a single item that asked whether or not the respondent experienced loneliness as a longing for the former partner.

What qualities of the current relationship with the partner of old sustain attachment? The desire for close contact with the partner was connected strongly with attachment among former husbands. Those who preferred to maintain close contact also tended to spend a lot of time thinking and wondering about their wives ($r = .50$) and were more likely to feel loneliness as a longing for the old partner ($r = .40$). The connections between desire for close contact and preoccupation ($r = .18$) and longing for the partner ($r = .00$) were more tenuous among wives. Men may be more foolhardy and women more cautious about acting on their hankering for the partner of old.

Actual contact between former spouses could enhance or ease attachment. Seeing or hearing about an old love can call forth buried feelings and set off a bout of preoccupation, even longing. Rather than rekindle affection, contact may bolster the belief that one is better off out of the marriage. As one woman said, "I [had] been thinking things out about Mark. Could it be worked out? But when I saw him, I knew it couldn't." Because separation distress breeds on inaccessibility of the once-loved partner, contact actually may subdue pining for the partner. For instance, a woman who had a difficult marriage and was having an even more difficult separation told us the following:

> For a while I hated him, I was very angry. Then it turned into love; I believed he'd come back. . . . It had been a romantic thing for a while. The less he came around, the more I cared for him, the more I thought about him.

Using our scale of contact, thinking and wondering about the partner was related to contact among women ($r = .29$) but not among men. The experience of loneliness as a longing for the former partner was related to contact among women ($r = .20$) and men ($r = .29$). Brown and her colleagues (1980) also found attachment related to contact.

We looked more closely at the mode of contact and attachment. Among former husbands, speaking to their wives either by phone or in person was linked with longing. It is difficult to say whether longing causes the husband to call or see his former wife or if speaking with her sets off the longing and worsens this specific form of loneliness. We can say, however, that husbands who longed for their wives were more likely to initiate contact themselves, while husbands who did not pine reported that contact was initiated by their wives or by mutual arrangement ($X^2 = 6.7$, 2 df, $p < .05$). As with desire for contact, women did not show evidence of acting on their longings for the partner. Among wives, it was hearing about the former husband through friends that was connected most strongly with thinking and wondering about and longing for him. There could be several explanations for this. Because women do not tend to act on their attachment feelings by seeking or desiring direct contact with their former husbands, they may ask about them from friends instead. Or it may be that hearing about the husband without direct contact aggravates separation distress.

Among men and women, marital partners who continued to discuss personal matters after separation also persisted in their attachment. Using our scale of conversational topics, discussion of personal matters was related to thinking and wondering about the partner of old ($r = .42$ for women and .27 for men) and longing for the partner ($r = .29$ for women and .30 for men). Avoiding personal topics, however, was not related to attachment. Again, we cannot say whether rapport is necessary to the sustenance of attachment or whether attachment motivates reaching out for the other. Both are probably true.

Researchers studying attachment, particularly Weiss (1975), stress that it is the persistence of attachment in contradiction to eroded love that makes marital separation so ambivalent and painful. We looked at the connection between attachment and current feelings toward the erstwhile partner. We found that love or the combination of love and hate characterized men and women who were more highly attached to their partner, while indifference, liking, or hate characterized the less attached (total sample $X^2 = 61.3$, 4 df, $p < .01$ for longing). The pattern was clear and consistent across the two measures of attachment and across gender. The only divergence was liking the former partner. Among men, liking the wife was connected with thinking and wondering about her, while there was little difference in this type of preoccupation among women who liked their husbands. In this sample, then, it is the persistence of love, even if love is tinged with hate, that sustains preoccupation with and pining for the partner of old.

## ANGER, AWARENESS OF PARTNER'S PAIN, AND GUILT

In Chapter 4, we considered the reactions to the breakup that may affect the relationship with the former marital partner: anger at the partner, awareness that the breakup hurt the partner badly, and guilt about the breakup. Anger at the partner was associated with similar relationship conditions for former husbands and wives. Anger was more intense if the couple avoided personal matters in conversation ($r = .24$ for total sample), especially discussion of the foregone marriage or new social opportunities. Discussion of personal matters, then, seemed to temper anger ($r = -.25$ for total sample). Angry husbands and wives were more likely to avoid seeing the former spouse than those who harbored less resentment ($r = .29$ for the total sample). Anger was unrelated, however, to actual contact with the partner.

Feelings of hate and hate linked with love were characteristic of angry people, while friendliness characterized people who expressed little resentment toward the partner; feelings of love or apathy did not distinguish between levels of anger ($X^2 = 28.2$, 4 df, $p < .01$). This is a somewhat different pattern than feelings at separation and current anger. Among men, feelings toward their wives at the time of separation was not connected with anger. Among women, anger was connected with memories of love at separation as well as with forms of hate.

We noted previously that women were more likely than men to acknowledge that the breakup hurt the partner badly. Feelings for the wife were not related to awareness of her pain among men. Among women, awareness of the partner's pain was connected with positive affection for the partner, either love or liking, while feelings of hate or hate with love clouded this awareness ($X^2 = 17.0$, 4 df, $p < .01$). There was other evidence that awareness of the partner's pain was based on sympathy rather than culpability. Awareness was connected with the desire for closer contact among husbands ($r = .20$) and wives ($r = .29$). Although unrelated to actual contact, awareness of the partner's distress was related to continued conversation about personal matters (r = .34 for men and .24 for women).

Culpability is measured more directly by feelings of guilt about the separation and divorce. Those men and women who held any positive affection for their former partner (love, liking, love with hate) expressed less guilt than those who were indifferent toward or hated their partner ($X^2 = 26.4$, 4 df, p < .01). Feelings of guilt were not related to any other relationship conditions among husbands. Among wives, however, guilty women desired closer contact (r = .18) and were more likely to initiate contact ($X^2 = 8.2$, 2 df, p < .02) than women who were less guilty about the breakup. In spite of this, there was less actual contact (r = −.21) and more mundane conversation (r = −.23) with higher levels of guilt. Although these women made some attempt at penance, it did little to improve the quality of their bond with the erstwhile husband.

## TIME SINCE SEPARATION

The tie with the former partner changes over time (Goode, 1956; Hetherington et al., 1978; Kitson, 1982). Gradual disengagement with relapses is the classic pattern. When asked if rapport, tension, and feelings had changed since separation, respondents could make such judgments easily. Narrative (Weiss, 1975) and longitudinal (Hetherington et al., 1978) reports also capture shifts in the interdependence of partners after separation. In our cross-sectional data, however, time since separation did not emerge as a momentous condition for the former partner relationship.

Among wives, the longer they had been separated, the less contact they wanted (r = −.17) and the less contact they had (r = −.27). Conversation was also less personal (r = −.25), and wives spent less time thinking and wondering about the partner (r = −.35) as time went on. These associations with time since separation were negligible among former husbands. The men and women in our study had been separated 26 months or less, but time is an artificial marker of what goes on between former marital partners.[2] Because of relapses of affection and attachment, change is probably not linear and continuous, moving from shared to separate lives. There may be gender differences in the pattern of change after separation. Women, who seem more resolved and less romantic than men, may disentangle themselves steadily from their husbands. Men may succumb more readily to swings in desire for connection with their wives.

To examine the link between feelings for the partner and time since separation, we divided time into both six-month and year intervals. In neither case was there a pattern between time and feelings. Love and love joined with hate were as likely after a year as before a year of separation. Of the 10 men and women who said they hated their former partner, not a single person had been separated for less than a year. The resistance of strong affection and animosity to the passage of time is striking.

## Factors Related to the Partnership After Marriage

### CHILDREN

The study of the aftermath of marital breakup is often limited to those couples who share children (Goode, 1956; Hetherington et al., 1978). Childless couples are often excluded because they have fewer stresses and represent a different family system than couples with children (Brown et al., 1980) or, as Goetting (1979: 395) says, "without children, there is typically no reason for the couple to remain in contact, so no relationship persists after the divorce." Without doubt, family organization and strategies for handling closeness and tension in divorce are much different in families with and without children (Beal, 1979). We cannot address these subtleties with our data. We can, however, address Goetting's assumption.

On the whole, we were struck by the similarity between partners who shared children and those who did not. There was no difference between the groups in the desire for close contact, efforts to avoid seeing the former partner, feelings for the partner, or attachment. This was true among men and women.

Table 5.5 shows a comparison of contact and conversation between former couples who have children and those without children. Speaking to the partner either by phone or in person was more common among couples with children, but was by no means rare among couples without children. Other modes of contact did not differ between couples with and without children. Contact persisted, therefore, for many former marital partners, even if there were no children. Moreover, couples without children were more likely to discuss personal matters and not shy away from sensitive topics than were former couples with children. Childless partners seemed to have a greater rapport than partners who

**TABLE 5.5**
**Comparison of Contact and Conversation Between Couples With and Without Children**

| | Percentage Answering Yes | | |
| --- | --- | --- | --- |
| | With Children | Without Children | Significance * |
| Contact: | | | |
| Spoken to by phone | 69.5 | 42.9 | $p < .01$ |
| Spoken to in person | 58.6 | 35.1 | $p < .01$ |
| Heard about through family | 32.8 | 31.2 | ns |
| Heard about through friends | 33.6 | 41.6 | ns |
| Gone out | 8.6 | 13.0 | ns |
| Had sex | 5.5 | 2.6 | ns |
| Topics usually discuss: | | | |
| Relationship with spouse | 21.7 | 28.2 | ns |
| Personal problems | 40.0 | 62.0 | $p < .01$ |
| Daily happenings | 22.5 | 45.1 | $p < .01$ |
| Practical problems | 45.8 | 43.7 | ns |
| Topics avoid discussing: | | | |
| New relationships and dating | 56.6 | 36.1 | $p < .01$ |
| Marriage with spouse | 63.9 | 51.4 | ns |
| Spouse's problems with separation | 43.4 | 28.6 | $p < .05$ |
| Own problems with separation | 48.4 | 35.7 | ns |

\* results of Chi-square with 1 degree of freedom; ns = nonsignificant

shared children. As Table 5.2 demonstrates, children provided the most conspicuous and least avoided focus of conversation among those with children. Those former partners without children have to find other ways to maintain contact and other things to talk about. Yet, childless couples manage to sustain social and emotional involvement comparable to couples with children.

Among those with children, only about 16 percent ever saw their former partner because of arrangements made by the children. Goode (1956) speculates that child support is the only current condition connected to affection or animosity toward the husband after separation. We found no association between whether or not there were child support payments, satisfaction with support payments and the relationship with the former husband or wife. There was also no connection between satisfaction with the custody arrangement and relationship with the former partner. We did find among mothers, however, that whether or not the couple talked about the children was related to the woman's feelings for her former husband ($X^2 = 20.7$, 4 df, p < .01). Most conspicuous was that all five mothers who hated their husband did not discuss the children with him.

We also asked parents how often they disagreed with the partner on how to raise the children and if they would like to spend more or less time with the children. Among mothers, greater disagreement over childbearing meant mothers desired less contact with their husbands (r = .22). Among fathers, greater actual contact was connected with more frequent disagreement about how to raise the children (r = .31). For mothers, those who would prefer more time with their children were also more likely to want close contact with their former husbands (r = .27), were less likely to make an effort to avoid seeing their husbands (r = −.34), and were more likely to discuss personal matters with their husbands (r = .24) than mothers who were satisfied with the amount of time spent with their children. For fathers, there was no connection between desired contact with children and relationship with former wife, but there was little variation since over 80 percent of the fathers wanted more time with their children. Brown and her colleagues (1980) suggest that fathers' attachment to the former wife is related to being separated from their children as well. We found no connection between preoccupation, pining, and longing for the wife and longing for children among fathers.

Children are a complicating factor in the continuing partnership of former husbands and wives. In an extreme situation, a young woman describes her former husband's treatment of their preschool son in the following way:

> He'll come and get him once a week. That's what really hurts. He'll tell Gary he doesn't love him, that he never did. And the poor boy gets so upset. He'll start crying and tell me his Daddy doesn't love him. It's made him so insecure. I've told Bob that if that's the way he's going to treat Gary, he can't see him anymore.

Couples without children may have a discretionary bond as they prefer, but parents are obligated to maintain at least polite association with each other, regardless of their desires. The tie between former partners, nevertheless, is very similar for parents and nonparents. Even among parental couples, the major issues regarding children—support, time with children, and child rearing (Goetting, 1979; Hetherington et al., 1978)—have only slight impact on the marital pair.

## END OF MARRIAGE AND CIRCUMSTANCES OF SEPARATION

Weiss (1975) speaks of an "account" of the failed marriage. The account is the separated person's explanation of what went wrong. Through the account, the person concentrates on certain weaknesses in the marriage or in the partner, allocates blame, and imposes sense on an otherwise inexplicable experience. After separation, the person worries over the account, weaving the tale together with new insights that may appear as trivial changes in the story to an outsider (Harvey et al., 1978). Because accounts are personally constructed, husbands and wives are likely to have very different versions of what went wrong. Accounts are recollections that may have little similarity to what "really" happened, but they have an importance of their own. Recollections of marriage and the final separation affect the emotional aftermath of divorce (Chapter 4) and, most likely, relations with the former partner after the marriage ends.

As we suspected, recollections of marital quality in the final months were connected with how the former partners were getting along currently. Among former wives, the desire for close contact was related to recollections of greater consensus ($r = .16$), companionship ($r = .30$), and harmony ($r = .16$). Among former husbands, the desire for closer contact was related to memories of greater affectional and sexual compatibility ($r = .24$), companionship ($r = .23$), and harmony ($r = .31$). Personal commitment to the marriage in its final months was not connected to current preferences for contact with the partner. There were no associations between marital quality and actual contact among men. Among women, however, actual contact in the past few weeks was associated with affectional and sexual compatibility ($r = .21$), companionship ($r = .22$), satisfaction with sexual relations ($r = .22$), and commitment to marriage in its final months ($r = .27$).

Similarly, marital quality in the final months was related only marginally to the discussion or avoidance of certain conversational topics among men after separation. Memories of companionship were linked with the discussion of personal matters ($r = .22$); personal matters tended not to be avoided ($r = -.20$). Companionship in the final months included the sharing of feelings as well as activities. The tendency to confide in the partner persisted beyond separation. Among men, memories of relative tranquility in the final months also was related to the discussion (r = .18) and nonavoidance (r = −.17) of personal matters after separation.

The pattern was much more striking among women; every dimension of marital quality in the final months was connected with the level of rapport after separation. Among wives, the discussion of more personal matters was related to greater consensus (r = .31), affectional and sexual relations (r = .32), companionship (r = .36), harmony (r = .32), and commitment to the marriage in its last months (r = .22). As with husbands, avoidance of sensitive topics was linked with recollections of less marital companionship (r = −.16) and harmony (r = −.17). Women, therefore, have greater continuity in their perceptions of relationship quality than men. Their memories of the final months of marriage and their present rapport with the erstwhile husband are more of whole cloth than the perceptions of men.

While women seemed to make a stronger connection between the quality of the relationship with the partner during and after marriage, men were more apt to connect the memories of marriage with personal desires and feelings after separation. Just as the desire for close contact was related to recollections of affection, companionship, and calm in marriage, current feelings for the wife were connected with recalled marital quality among former husbands. Persistent love for the wife was tied particularly to memories of affectional and sexual compatibility ($X^2 = 13.5$, 4 df, $p < .01$) and commitment to marriage ($X^2 = 16.9$, 4 df, $p < .01$). All feelings besides love were tied to lower affectional compatibility and commitment among husbands. Affection—either liking or loving—after separation was connected with equanimity in the final months of marriage. Men who recalled greater consensus with their wives at the end were more likely to have some affection for their partners after separation than those who recalled dissension ($X^2 = 12.6$, 4 df, $p < .01$).

Among both men and women, memories of harmony were related to feelings of affection for the partner, while memories of tension and irritation were related to current feelings of animosity or apathy ($X^2 = 16.2$, 4 df, $p < .01$). Only companionship in the final months of marriage was unrelated to husbands' present affection for their wives. Among wives, however, the memory of sharing feelings and activities with their husbands was tied to affection (either loving or liking) after separation ($X^2 = 10.9$, 4 df, $p < .01$).

In Chapter 4, we reported the connection between recollections of marital quality and acceptance of the breakup, with thinking and wondering about the partner as part of a difficult acceptance. We also reported the link between longing for the former partner and memories of the final months of marriage. The pattern of associations was consistent across the two measures of attachment. Memories of commitment to marriage in its final months were related to thinking and wondering about the partner ($r = .38$ for women and .23 for men) and longing for the partner ($r = .38$ for women and .37 for men) after separation. Among women, recollections of affectional and sexual compatibility were connected with preoccupation ($r = .25$) and longing ($r = .34$). Among men, and to a lesser extent women, recollections of calm and ease in the final months of marriage were connected with preoccupation ($r = .30$ for men and .16 for women) and longing ($r = .30$ for men and .21 for women) after separation. Consensus in the final months was unrelated to attachment, and related to companionship only marginally.[3]

The anticipation time from thinking that the marriage might end to separation, the timing of separation, and previous separations were not related to the current relationship with the former partner. Other researchers, however, have found attachment to be related negatively to the length of time the divorce was considered (Brown et al., 1980; Kitson, 1982). We do not know what they used as a beginning marker for decision time.

The important circumstances of the breakup were the source of the initial suggestion and placement of blame. These conditions are related mostly to desires and feelings after separation, not to actual contact and conversation. Those men and women in the position of being left by their partners were more attached to their partners after separation (thinking and wondering about, longing for) than those who participated in the decision to separate (Brown et al., 1980; Kitson, 1982) Even at the time of the interview, men who had been broken up with were more likely to have strong feelings for their wives (love and/or hate) than men who first suggested the breakup or shared the suggestion with the partner ($X^2 = 9.5$, 2 df, $p < .01$). Current feelings were not connected with who suggested the breakup among women. Husbands who were left were also somewhat more likely to want to maintain close contact with their wives than husbands who had a part in suggesting the breakup ($X^2 = 8.3$, 4 df, $p < .08$).

Among wives, the overriding tendency to prefer some contact only when necessary was strayed from only by those women who themselves suggested the separation. Wives who first suggested the breakup were just as likely to want close or no contact with their husbands as some contact ($X^2 = 11.8$, 4 df, p < .02). As we have noted before, the breakup suggested by the wife does not mean necessarily that she is in the position of the leaver. Women are much more likely to finally suggest separation, but it may be in response to the husband's provocation or passivity. When men suggest ending the marriage, it is more likely that they really want out.

Allocation of blame for the marital breakup is an important part of the account (Harvey et al., 1978; Weiss, 1975). Whether the blame is externalized to the marital partner or an outsider or is at least partially taken on oneself appears to be the important distinction. Men and women who blamed someone other than themselves for the divorce were more likely to still have strong feelings of love and/or hate toward their former partner than those who were willing to accept some blame for the breakup ($X^2 = 14.6$, 4 df, p < .01). This was the only connection between blame and the relationship with the former partner among husbands. Among wives, blaming their husbands or an outsider meant they wanted less contact with their partners ($r = -.23$), would make an effort to avoid seeing them ($r = -.24$), would avoid sensitive conversational topics ($r = -.25$), but would long for them nevertheless ($r = -.33$).

A woman in her forties who dedicated herself to preserving her marriage described her feelings this way:

> It's extremely painful when I see him. I wanted to work it out on a friendly basis but the longer it goes the worse it gets. I get violent when I see him, I could kill him. Because it's more his fault. I was trying to keep things on an even keel, but you can't do that without help.

Many women echoed this sentiment: "I resent him for the fact that I feel those years of my life were wasted. It's partly his fault that I didn't leave sooner." As in Chapter 4, the consequences of blaming are more marked for women than for men.

We do not know whether current association with and feelings for the partner color recollections of the breakup or if remembrance of the end of marriage shapes prevailing relations. Both processes are likely. The data show clearly that the nature of the account and the details of memory are connected to the ongoing partnership of former husbands and wives.

## SOCIAL OPPORTUNITIES DURING MARRIAGE

In the following sections, we consider social opportunities outside of the marital pair and the connection between opportunities and the continuing relationship of former partners. In this section, we examine extramarital sexual and romantic ties during marriage and around the time of the separation. In the subsequent section, we look at dating and remarriage since separation.

Husbands' romantic and sexual opportunities outside of marriage had no connection with the relationship with their wives after separation. We considered whether they were planning to date someone special after separation, whether they had extramarital sexual experience, how long the liaison lasted, and how emotionally involved they were. These social opportunities up to the time of separation were unrelated to husbands' desire for contact, actual contact, efforts to avoid seeing their wives, conversation, current feelings, or attachment.

The pattern was different among wives. Having a particular dating partner waiting was related to wanting closer contact with the husband ($r = .26$), not making an effort to avoid seeing the husband ($r = -.31$), and discussion of personal matters in conversations with the husband ($r = -.24$). An alternative dating or sexual partner was not connected with actual contact with the former husband, feelings, or attachment after separation.

We created categorical variables of extramarital sexual experience. One variable was a simple dichotomy of experience versus no experience. Another variable had three categories: no sexual relations outside of marriage, sexual liaison that ended before separation, and sexual liaison that lasted beyond separation. The final variable also had three categories: no experience, extramarital experience with emotional involvement, and experience without emotional involvement.

The persistence of and depth of involvement in extramarital sexual relations were important in the emotional aftermath of breakup (Chapter 4), so we thought they might also be important to the continuing tie with the former partner. Persistence to separation and emotional involvement, however, did not seem to make much difference. The results consistently broke down into those who had experienced extramarital sexual relations and those who had not. Among wives, then, extramarital sexual experience was associated with a desire for closer contact with the husband ($r = .19$) and no effort to avoid seeing the husband ($r = -.29$). Among women with sexual experience outside of marriage, those who were more emotionally involved with the alternative partner were also less angry at their husbands after separation (see Chapter 4).

The connection between wives' social opportunities during marriage and their bond with their former husbands after separation was slight but consistent. Those women with an alternative partner actually had a more affable partnership with their husbands than those women who did not have an alternative partner. Husbands' social opportunities during marriage were not connected to the continuing tie to their wives. In Chapter 4, we reported that the experience, emotional nature, and persistence of extramarital sexual relations were related to acceptance of the breakup, less loneliness, and fewer thoughts of suicide among husbands. For husbands, then, alternative partners during marriage help to predict their emotional response to and resolution of the breakup but do not predict their continuing relations with their former wives.

The spouse's social opportunities outside of marriage were another story. Husbands were more likely to avoid seeing their former wives if they had a dating partner lined up after separation ($r = .23$) or if they had extramarital sexual experience ($r = .24$). Among both men and women, the former partner's sexual experience outside of marriage was connected with discussing more mundane rather than personal matters when the partners met ($r = -.23$ for women and $-.20$ for men). Unlike one's own social opportunities during marriage, therefore, the former spouse's opportunities stifled the marital pair's relations after separation.

## CURRENT SOCIAL OPPORTUNITIES

Social opportunities after separation will be discussed fully in Chapter 7. In this section, we consider the connection between a new involvement and relations between former marital partners. Remarriage of either partner is the most unmistakable sign of a new involvement. In our study, only 16 percent of the respondents and 25 percent of their former partners were remarried or had made plans to remarry by the time we first interviewed them. This distribution attenuates the following associations. Men and women with a new partner wanted less contact with their former partner ($r = -.22$ for total sample). Remarriage was related to less contact ($r = -.28$) and less personal conversation ($r = -.23$) with the former wife among men, but was unrelated to contact and conversation among women. There was a greater chance that men and women still felt some form of love for the former partner (love or love and hate) if they had no new serious involvement than if they had a new partner. This pattern was the same for men and women but was only statistically significant among women ($X^2 = 14.2$, 4 df, $p < .01$). There were no women who were remarried or planned to remarry who still expressed love for their former husbands, although two men said they still loved their wives of old even if they had a new partner. Remarriage was not connected with thinking and wondering about or longing for the former partner. Remarriage was related only marginally to attachment in Kitson's (1982) study.

The former spouse's remarriage was not related to attachment to or feelings for the erstwhile husband or wife. The spouse's remarriage also was not connected with the desire for contact, but did reduce actual contact ($r = -.21$ for total sample) and rapport in conversation ($r = -.22$ for total sample). Weiss (1975), as well as Hetherington and her associates (1978), report that the former partner's new involvement may arouse hostility and regret among separated or divorced people. When the partner has found someone new, he or she is no longer seen as suffering from the breakup; and the observing husband or wife may feel a sense of loss similar to that experienced with the initial breakup. One young woman expressed it this way:

> Now he's living with this 18-year-old girl. I'm sure he loves that. Now I think he never did care. Well, he couldn't have cared if he's living with someone else already. And I'm the one who wanted the divorce. In a couple of months he's living with someone else. He's divorced but he can get another woman just like that. He probably loves that.

Others are pleased for their former partners. A woman told us about her relations with her former husband:

> We talk on the phone two or three times a week. Sometimes we mention the people we're seeing. He's got a new lady, and he told me when she moved in. . . . I felt really good because I wasn't upset, because I was just glad he was happy.

To tap the respondents' current social opportunities, we tried to order their involvement from remarriage, through steady dating (daily to a few times a week) and sporadic dating (once a week to a few times a month), to slight social involvement (dating once a month or never). Using the four categories, current social opportunities were not connected with the continuing tie with the former marital partner. We got more information by comparing simply those who planned to remarry or were already remarried with those who had no plans for remarriage.

Among those who had not already remarried (n = 74 men and 95 women), we considered frequency of dating, satisfaction with dating, and frequency of sexual activity. These measures of new social opportunities had very little to do with the relationship with the marital partner after separation. The only exception was the connection between frequencies of dating and sexual activity and attachment. Those who longed for the former partner were less sexually active than those who did not long for the partner of old ($r = -.24$ for women and $-.17$ for men). Although frequency of dating was not related to attachment to the former wife among men, it was related to thinking and wondering about husband ($r = -.28$) and longing for the husband ($r = -.19$) among women who had not remarried.

A subjective evaluation of current social opportunity is loneliness. Overall loneliness and loneliness experienced as boredom, longing for a new involvement, or a dearth of social activity were not linked to contact and conversations with the former marital partner, feelings for, or attachment to the partner.

Goode (1956) suggests that there are different causes of antagonism toward the former partner for those with and without a new involvement. Those with a new involvement (either remarried or going steady) temper their feelings for the former partner by comparing him or her to the new love. Those without a new involvement base their antagonism toward the former partner on an antipathy toward love and marriage in general. We could not test the first conjecture with our data, but we could attend to the second. Among those who had not already married or planned to remarry (n = 69 men and 84 women), their attitude toward remarriage was unrelated to their continuing tie with the former partner. Attitude toward remarriage ranged from eager to remarry to would never remarry. Attitude toward remarriage was not connected with feelings toward the partner (affection, apathy, or antagonism) or with anger.

Other researchers have found that a new intimate is the most powerful factor easing the intensity and distress of separating from the partner of old (Hetherington et al., 1978; Weiss, 1975). They also remark on the persistence of attachment and the ability to sustain strong feelings over time and circumstance. Lamentably, in our study we did not measure the level of intimacy in new involvements. And so few of our respondents were remarried by the time of our first interview that we could not attend thoroughly to the connection between old and new ties.

## Profiles of Partnership

Partnership after marriage is something each couple has to arrange for themselves. There are no objective standards by which couples can judge their continued connection. There is ambivalence among the divorced, and among those who study divorce, about what is the appropriate tie between marital partners after separation. On the one hand, resolution of the breakup is conceived as leaving the partner and marriage of old behind. On the other hand is the contemporary idea that part of the creative experience of ending a marriage is friendship between former partners. Separation and divorce have no rituals to ease the transition for couples. Most people have never learned to temper close relations, to cut an intimate out of their life, or to transform love (or hate) into liking or indifference. Relations between partners after separation are confounded by old wounds and pleasures, the perplexity of breaking up, the emotional tangle of separation distress. Old and new ties must be comprehended; children must be considered. Out of this muddle, husbands and wives try to find a place for each other in memory, hope, and actuality.

Partners who have separated most likely believe that they should not feel much for each other anymore. Their reports to us, therefore, are probably biased toward indifference. Even so, there is diversity among couples in their contact, conversation, feelings, and attachment. There appear to be three general profiles of the partnership after marriage. There are partners who remain close, partners who desire or tolerate some exchange, and partners who prefer to have nothing to do with each other. We only talked with one member of the partnership, so we cannot say that the profiles represent couples. The scenarios are one partner's view of the couple after separation. Each partnership is novel. Still, the typical patterns we offer below give order to boundless variety.

About a quarter of the separated men and women maintain a closeness to the partner of old after separation. Although the closeness is not a strong emotional dependency, it is a complex of wanting close contact, love (or at least liking) for the partner, and attachment (thinking and wondering about and longing for). Men are somewhat more likely to love and long for their partners after separation than women, but there are no gender differences in preoccupation and desire for contact with the erstwhile spouse.

Continuing sympathy and rapport sustains affection and attachment in close couples. Partners who discuss personal rather than mundane matters and who do not avoid sensitive topics in conversation tend to care about each other. Affection, then, is connected with disclosure about personal problems and relations between partners both past and current. Former partners that care about each other even talk about new intimate ties in their lives. This level of sympathy in separated couples also leaves each partner aware that the breakup may have hurt the other badly.

Contact among close couples is linked with the complex of feelings, but contact is not as important to persistent affection and attachment as is depth of conversation. Among women, contact with the former husband helps to sustain love, while contact is not related to affection among men. On the other hand, there is evidence that men tend to act on their attachment more readily than women. That is, if men think and wonder about or long for their former wives, they also want to maintain close contact. If they long for their wives, men tend to initiate contact themselves rather than depend on the partner or mutual arrangement. Not surprisingly, then, men who are more attached to their partners also are more apt to have spoken with their former wives in the past few weeks. Women are much less prone to desire, initiate, or have contact because of preoccupation or pining for the partner.

The following is an example of partners who have maintained close ties after separation. A woman in her late fifties was content with her marriage except that her husband had "affairs" for sexual variety throughout their time together. When asked who had been her major source of emotional support since separation, she named her former husband:

> He helped me whenever I needed it. Even loaned me money when I was strapped. . . . I spend a lot of time with my husband. In fact, we talk more since we separated. I'm much happier now that we separated. I call him when I need help with the car or

something. He would do anything to help. I still think about him, but I can't say it's love. More like concern.

Even after the divorce was final, she and her husband would go on vacation together, sometimes with their grown children.

At the other extreme are partners who prefer to have nothing to do with the former spouse. About a quarter of the men and women appear to fit this type of partnership after separation. These people make an effort to avoid seeing the partner, stick to mundane topics of conversation, and avoid sensitive and personal issues when they do come in contact. They either hate or have no feeling for the partner of old, and they are angry at each other. One woman put it this way:

> I hate his guts. I'm resentful and have no good feelings toward him at all. He's really done me wrong after 28 years of marriage. There's no way I'd take him back. I'm making a life for myself now. . . . I only call him when I'm desperate, only when I have to settle some business.

Most common, however, is the middling partnership after separation. At least half of the men and women report this type of relation. They prefer some contact, but only when necessary. They may have spoken to their former partners in the past few weeks but had no more intimate contact. Conversation is neither wholly mundane nor personal. Feelings tend to be absent or perhaps there is mild affection. Preoccupation and pining are rare. Most of the separated men and women in our sample, then, are no longer emotionally touched or in close contact with the person to whom they used to be married. A man who struggled with his wife about housework and who was going to get his or her own way throughout marriage described their current relations:

> We are very friendly with each other. You might say it is the ideal divorce. Her boyfriend and her came over to see me the other day about keeping the boys this weekend, so they could go out of town. Most of our relationship concerns the boys.

Many participants report that even at separation, their feelings were tempered and so-so feelings have persisted. Others have achieved friendliess or apathy only since separation, leaving love and hate behind. Still others, at least one-quarter of the men and women, have managed to sustain feelings of love and/or hate over months and years.

The three profiles do not reflect the complicated arrangements couples develop after separation. There are those, particularly women, whose desire for close contact is connected to their guilt about the breakup. There are others who love their partners, but will make every effort to avoid seeing him or her. The profiles, nevertheless, give a sense of how most partners settle themselves after separation.

We thought the following circumstances might be connected with partnership after separation: children, memories of the final months and breakup, and social opportunities outside of the partnership. Couples with children are more likely to see and speak with one another than couples without children. Couples who do not share children discuss more intimate matters, however, than couples with children. All in all, there are few differences in the postseparation relations of partners who do and do not have children. Children are not necessary to bind former partners together. Partners' desire to maintain contact with, and their affection and attachment for one another, are not contingent upon the presence of children.

## Summary

Understandably, current relations between partners of old are connected with recollections of the final months of marriage and circumstances of the breakup. Overall, the desire for contact, personal conversation, affection, and attachment after separation are related positively to memories of marital quality. Among women, there is a consistent link between the quality of marriage in its final months and couple dimensions after separation, contact and conversation. Women have a greater continuity than men in their view of relations from marriage and after marriage. With more intimate contact and conversation after the breakup, women recall greater compatibility, companionship, and calm in their erstwhile marriages.

Men have discontinuous views of what went on then and what goes on now. Among men, however, there is a stronger link than among women in the quality of marriage in its final months and personal desires, feelings, and thoughts for the partner after separation. Although men may not tie what went on during marriage with what actually goes on now, they do weave together what went on then with what they feel and want now. Women express this continuity as well, but not as strongly as men. Men who still love and pine for their wives after separation remember a marriage characterized by relative compatibility, harmony, and commitment in the final months.

We can only speculate about what cognitive or interpersonal processes might account for these different continuities between former husbands and wives. Women may make an effort to maintain the once-affable partnership after separation. We have already offered some evidence, however, that this is probably not the case. Women are no more likely than men to preserve postseparation arrangements actively. It is more likely that women have an account of the end of the marriage that is consistent with current relations. Women may be more likely than men to alter their account of the breakup based on current contact with their husband. Recall that current affection for the husband was connected to contact among women but not among men. Men seem to preserve their view of the marriage regardless of how the partnership progresses after separation. Husbands base their desires, feelings, and thoughts on how they remember the marriage. Women, on the other hand, seem to be able to mold their account to fit current circumstances of the partnership. Men appear yet again as the more romantic, holding fast to their memories.

Men and women who are left by their marital partners are more apt than leavers to maintain strong feelings of either love or hate and pine for their partner after separation. Along with position in the breakup, allocation of blame emerges as an important part of the account for women. Among former wives, there is a twist in the previously offered profiles: There are women who blame their husbands or an outsider for the breakup, continue to love or hate them, long for them; but they want no contact with their husbands, avoid seeing them, and avoid sensitive topics when they do see them.

Blame is related to the partner's sexual relations outside of marriage (see Chapter 3). We found that the partner's extramarital social opportunities put a damper on the partnership after separation. However, at least among women an alternative partner for oneself is related to a more affable relationship after separation. Perhaps a woman with an alternative can afford to be magnanimous. Yet, among both husbands and wives the other's alternative is an affront.

Current social opportunities (dating, sexual activity, and remarriage) do not have the dramatic effect on postseparation relations that we anticipated. This may be because few of our participants have remarried or made plans to remarry. Among those who are not remarried, frequency of dating and sexual activity tempers attachment, especially among women, but is not related to the partnership in other ways. Again, women's feelings are tied more closely to current conditions than are men's feelings.

The partnership between husband and wife does not end with separation. The partnership continues in memory or hope, if not in actuality. What happens between partners after separation, however, depends as much on memory as on current circumstance.

## Notes

1. Given our sample size, there are too many combinations of shifting feelings to allow analysis of change. We tried to use three categories of change (maintain strong feelings, maintain moderate feelings, and change from strong to moderate feelings), but the attempt told us no more than when we looked at current feelings.

2. Other researchers have found time since separation unrelated to attachment (Brown et al., 1980; Kitson and Sussman, 1976). In each case, we thought that their time since separation (median time around 4 to 6 months) was too brief to reflect the slow wane of attachment. The median time since separation in our study was 16 months.

3. Length of marriage was not related to contact, conversation, feelings, or attachment after separation (Brown et al., 1980; Kitson, 1982). In Weiss's (1979) experience, it does not matter how long the marriage endured, only whether or not it was integrated into the life pattern of the individual, which takes about two years. Very few of the men and women in our study had been married less than two years.

CHAPTER 6
# Friends and Relatives

Almost by definition, friends and family are those people who are around when you need them. Kith and kin are supposed to rally and uphold in times of trouble. The plight of marital breakup, however, confuses tradition. The couple have gotten themselves into this predicament. Others may disapprove. Loyalties are split. Obligations are unclear. In this chapter we look at how relations with friends and family have changed since marriage and its demise. We also describe help from friends and relatives, what induces others to help, and how help is connected to the emotional aftermath of separation.

## Changes in Social Relations After Separation

Part of the upheaval after marital breakup is changes in the alignment of old friends and kin and the securing of new social ties. We asked our participants several questions about their social relations during marriage and since separation. Participants listed the three persons they felt closest to during the last year or two of marriage. For each person, we asked the nature of the tie (family, in-law, or friend), marital status, and frequency of contact. Using the same format, we asked participants about the three closest persons at the time of the interview. Men were more likely than women not to have three people close to them. At the time of the interview, 11 men (12 percent) could not come up with three names; only 4 women (4 percent) had such a dearth of intimate ties. This pattern was more pronounced during marriage where 6 men (as compared to 1 woman) could not think of a single person they felt close to aside from their marital partner. Most participants combined family and friends in their circles of intimates, although 30 percent of the men and women named only friends as close at the time of the interview. Only 7 percent of the women and 10 percent of the men named all family members. One woman said, "It bothers me not having friends, because I need something more than my family." Even at the time of the interview, two men chose all three of their closest people from the former spouse's family; no women did so. Understandably, the biggest shift since marriage was dropping in-laws as intimates. While one-fifth of the men and women named at least one in-law as close during the last year or two of marriage, only about 11 percent did so at the time of the interview. Surprisingly, 2 women and 4 men actually had acquired an in-law as an intimate since separation.

There have been previous attempts to describe affinal kinship patterns after divorce. Divorced persons have a difficult time maintaining ongoing relations with their former spouse's kindred, and contact with in-laws declines dramatically with the end of marriage (Anspach, 1976; Spicer and Hampe, 1975; Weiss, 1975). Weiss (1975) reports that most men drop relationships with their in-laws, probably because men only infrequently establish bonds with in-laws strong enough to survive the marital breakup. Women often maintain relationships with in-laws (Anspach, 1976; Spicer and Hampe, 1975; Weiss, 1975), many of whom they have learned to think of as family or friends. Weiss concluded that more women than men regret the loss of affinal relationships after divorce, but few consider it a "tragedy." Our data show, however, that women are no more likely than men to consider an in-law an intimate, either during marriage or after separation.

A small minority of men, as well as women, were able to build close ties with at least one member of their partner's family and sustain the tie beyond the end of marriage. A middle-aged man told us the following:

> I see her parents quite a bit even now. I occasionally have dinner with them. Before I left I went to them and told them what I was doing and why because they had been close to me. They agreed that it was the best thing to do so we still have a good relationship.

Another man sometimes plays golf with his father-in-law but they "never talk about the divorce or anything like that." Affinal relationships after separation may be troubled by divided loyalties and a sense of awkwardness in trying to redefine the connection. A young woman described her troubled ties with former in-laws:

> I'm not welcome there any more because of his mother, because I hurt her little Joey. It makes me feel a little bad because I liked Joe's father and my brother- and sister-in-law.

Another woman, married over 20 years, spoke more sadly and sympathetically about her husband's parents:

> I loved them dearly, and they were good to me. We have no relationship now, no contact whatsoever. It hurts, but I guess they figure it was their son.

Often, members of the partner's family were involved in the breakup. One woman whose marriage was racked with drinking and violence stayed with her former sister-in-law "because it was the only place I could think of that he wouldn't think to look for me." Coming out of a marriage of almost 30 years in which the husband was seeing another woman, one wife said her husband's family "all turned against me. I don't know what my husband told them, but the whole family . . . for some reason, they were blaming me."

A man whose wife had a lover outside of marriage had strained street meetings with his former mother-in-law:

> I'm still upset about the fact that she knew what was going on and also knew when I talked with her how upset I was in not knowing what was wrong, but she never told me or tried to get my wife to tell me.

Hostility toward former in-laws is not common among divorced men and women (Spicer and Hampe, 1975), but for some the feelings run dark and deep. A man in his thirties whose mother-in-law had lived with him and his wife for much of their marriage railed as follows:

> I think her and her daughter planned to get as much out of me as they could. I don't see her or talk to her at all. I guess I'm really the most bitter towards her. I sometimes think I'd like her to go senile and stay that way for a long time and not get better or worse, so my ex-wife would be stuck with her. I know I shouldn't think things like that but I think she deliberately wrecked our marriage, and I'm still really bitter towards her.

Although they are not as obliged to maintain contact with in-laws now that the marriage is over, some divorced men and women keep up with in-laws because of affection, common interests, or interests in the children (Spicer and Hampe, 1975). One woman was very friendly with her former sister-in-law, another named her husband's brother and his wife as her greatest source of emotional support; former parents were invited up for birthdays or over for Thanksgiving; and a man referred affectionately to his former mother-in-law as "a gem."

We thought the separated men and women in our study might surround themselves with other single people. Although we found a slight shift toward intimates who were single (either never married or divorced) with separation, we did not find that participants were keeping company only with other singles. Dating and seeking out others with similar experiences accounts for the shift to single people. A middle-aged woman explained her need for other singles: "You can't talk to married people; they just don't understand. You need to talk to divorced people." A middle-aged man concurred: "Married people just don't understand if they haven't been through it." Both felt emotionally stranded because they had no one who could empathize with their circumstances. Several people mentioned the comfort of talking with someone else who had been through the end of a marriage:

> I met this girl who also was just divorced and going through some of the same problems. . . . She's been the biggest help to me.
>
> My boss is a woman and she's great. She's younger but we're very close. She was divorced once and now remarried, but they've separated, too. So we can talk very intimately. I need that.

The majority of people named as intimates by our participants were married, however, even at the time of the interview. Only 10 percent of the men and women said that all or most of their friends were separated or divorced, while about 15 percent said that none of their friends had experienced the end of a marriage. The remaining 75 percent, then, reported that some or a few of their friends were separated or divorced. Similar to Goode's (1956) results, we did not find that men and women were living in a social ghetto of the divorced after separation. Several women, in fact, complained about Parents Without Partners because it was a coterie of divorced women. It can be oppressive being around too many others struggling with a breakup. As one man said,

> It seems like I've run into a lot of people lately who are going through the same thing. . . . A lot of those people who also have problems are friendlier. I've about decided that there are not many happy people around any more.

Next, we looked at changes in social participation with separation. During marriage, husbands and wives were in contact with the three people closest to them on the average about once a week. About 30 percent of the men and women were in touch daily with the person they felt closest to. After separation, at the time of the interview, about 50 percent of the men and women were in touch with the closest person daily. On the average, frequency of contact with intimates did not change much with separation. At the time of the interview, average contact with the three closest people was between once and a few times a week. We explored individual changes in social contact with intimates since separation, as well as group differences over time. The sample split evenly: About a third of the participants were in touch with the three closest people more often now than during marriage; about a third showed no change in frequency of contact; and a third were in contact with intimates less often now than during marriage. Later, we examine what factors are related to change in contact since separation.

Marital breakup can cause intimate relations outside of the pair to change (Goode, 1956; Weiss, 1975). A woman who was having a difficult time of it said,

> I didn't really know what I was doing. I'd lost so many supports, like the church. Our friends were divided. I had never even known a divorced person before. . . . I felt so strange that I resisted meeting anyone.

Being single is different from being a couple. Experiencing a stressful event also alters the amount and nature of support from others. From everyone's point of view, social conditions have changed drastically. Social and emotional ambiguity abounds (Goode, 1956; Miller, 1970). There are few norms to guide the actions of family and friends, and the newly single person has needs and preferences that are much different than when he or she was part of a couple. A young woman talked about her family after she broke up with her husband:

> I felt like I was going out into this big world of strangers. . . . I felt like a threat to them. It was so strange. I was single again, and nobody wanted to spend time with me.

She kept her distance for awhile, then visited but stayed in the background. Eventually, her family became less uncomfortable, and relations are fine now. A woman married almost thirty years told us this:

> I feel awkward. I have an odd feeling even among friends that they'll think, "Oh, that divorcee is flirting" when I joke with someone. Now people will think I'm hunting a man, and that I won't do.

Some participants felt awkward because they knew others were discussing their personal lives behind their backs or taking sides. Others felt like a third wheel or that their couple friends might consider them a "threat" now that they were single. Still others had given up their friends or family as part of settling down in marriage and found their "old friends started coming around again" after the breakup. Many simply recognized that their needs and preferences had changed with separation and began to build up new social ties.

We asked participants how the people they felt closest to during marriage treated them now that they were separated. A man in his late thirties whose two children were living with him described the attentiveness of others:

> At first the women . . . were concerned about how I would cope. They would want to bring food over or take care of the children or help clean the house; but I kept telling them that I appreciated their wanting to help, but that I could manage. As they saw that I could cope, they became less concerned but still supportive. The males assured me that they were around if I needed anything even if it was only someone to talk to.

Another man resented and refused the concern of others:

> Right after I moved out of the house they all began to invite me to dinner, as if they were feeling sorry for me. I just refused to get involved in any of that.

We get an inkling that others gauge their attentiveness to the apparent need of the separated person, and that the separated person may turn down succor or resist the implication that he or she is in distress.

Table 6.1 shows how select behaviors changed since separation; the results were the same for men and women. A little over half saw no change in offers of help, discussion of personal problems, and visiting patterns. About one-quarter of the men and women perceived that the people they were closest to during marriage were more attentive now that they were separated. Somewhat less than a quarter saw intimates as less attentive since separation. The behaviors were highly interrelated, and we created an attentiveness index by summing the five items (Cronbach's alpha = .88).

Friends, at first, rally around; then they become aware that circumstances have changed; and finally, the friendship is either reinterpreted or it fades (Weiss, 1975). This can be a very painful process on top of all the other changes that are occurring. Friendships are particularly vulnerable if they were shared with the marital partner (Goode, 1956; Weiss, 1975). One woman whose friends during marriage centered around her husband's work place felt very hurt:

> I've been isolated and ostracized by my former friends. Around here if your husband doesn't work at the university you're nowhere—nobody knows you. . . . I don't get invited anywhere anymore. It's like I was just cut off. . . . My emotional feeling is like being an Eskimo stranded on an ice floe. I'd always felt like I belonged somewhere, but not now. I've got nothing, no place.

In our sample, about 70 percent of the men and women reported that they saw less of the friends shared with the former partner now that the marriage was over. More contact with mutual friends was rare. The more friends women shared with their husbands during marriage, the more likely they were to wish they had more friends after separation (r = .22). Almost half the men and women (43 percent) expressed a desire for more friends. Of the participants 14 percent had made no good

**TABLE 6.1**
**Behavioral Change Since Separation in People Closest to While Married (in percentages)**

| Behavior | Change Since Separation | | |
| --- | --- | --- | --- |
| | More Often | Same Amount | Less Often |
| Offer to help | 24.9 | 60.0 | 15.1 |
| Talk over their personal problems | 24.4 | 57.1 | 18.5 |
| Listen to personal problems | 27.8 | 58.5 | 13.7 |
| Drop by | 21.0 | 45.4 | 33.7 |
| Invite over to see them | 30.2 | 45.4 | 24.4 |

friends since separation, while the median number of new friendships was four among both men and women.

Making new friends can take more energy and confidence than the separated person has left in reserve after ending a marriage. We asked one woman if it wouldn't help if she saw more people, and she said, "No. I want to be left alone. It's a real chore to have people here, to be smiling." Another young woman—pregnant and married at 16—told us the hardest part about her separation:

> My husband had always said I was stupid and unattractive, and that no one could like me. I got so I couldn't believe anyone liked me, and I didn't have any real friends. I had a horrible inferiority complex. So I was always suspicious when someone was friendly.

New friends can help. A woman in her late fifties with three adult children said,

> I've found that once you're divorced, you get different friends. They're better friends, though. They helped me cope. In fact, I have more friends now than when I was married.

Based on his sample of divorced women, Goode (1956) thought that friendships are made and maintained primarily if they help the woman to find a new mate. We have no way of addressing this single-mindedness with our data. We can report, however, that friends were offered as the best source of meeting dates, especially among women. Since separation 60 percent of the participants had met at least one date through friends. As we might imagine, no one mentioned family intervention as the best way to meet new partners. Among women, increasing social contact with closest people from marriage to the time of the interview was connected with a positive approach to remarriage. Women whose social participation had picked up since separation were more likely to consider remarriage ($r = .26$) and agree that remarriage to the right person would make them happier than they are right now ($r = .21$). There is some evidence, therefore, that rather than seeking out friends and relatives as replacement for a marital partner, women may use social contact as a way to find a new partner.

## Help from Family, Former In-Laws, and Friends

Besides providing new partners and being more attentive, there are other forms of help that family and friends supply. Table 6.2 summarizes receipt of support from family members (both own family and in-laws), friends, and coworkers. Three types of support are included: moral, financial, and service. Services refer to babysitting, errands, housework, home repairs, and so on. The separated men and women relied on parents and siblings for moral support as well as on friends and work associates. Even in-laws provided moral support in a sizable minority of cases. With regard to financial help, women relied primarily on parents, but also on friends. Men also looked to their parents for financial aid, but were less likely to receive money than women were. Services also were provided by parents and siblings, as well as friends and coworkers. In all but two instances, women received more support than men.

A picture of fairly extensive friend and kin support emerges from the data. In the sections that follow, we examine some of the circumstances that may account for the provision of support: geographic proximity of kin, inclusion of family and friends among intimates, disapproval of the breakup, presence of children, financial instability and strain, and well-being at the time of separation. In each case, inclusion of intimates is coded as a dichotomous variable. For example, 1 is assigned if a member of one's own extended family is one of the three closest people at the time of the interview; 0 if no kin are included. The same coding is assigned for in-laws and friends. Financial instability and strain are addressed by three variables: (1) instability of income since separation, (2) an index of two items measuring current financial strain and decline in financial status since separation, and (3) whether or not the person is currently employed. Well-being at the time of separation is assessed by an item asking the participant how things were just after separation, taking all things together (work, home, way of life, things done for enjoyment, and health). The variable was coded to express emotional distress; that is, a high score indicated things were "not good at all." We look at these predictors of help separately for family, former in-laws, and friends.

## TABLE 6.2
### Percentage Reporting Receipt of Support from Family Members, Friends, and Coworkers

| | Type of Support | | | | | |
|---|---|---|---|---|---|---|
| | Moral | | Financial | | Service | |
| Source of Support | Women | Men | Women | Men | Women | Men |
| Mother | 90.3 | 86.1 | 52.4 | 18.8 | 48.1 | 35.4 |
| Father | 83.9 | 70.8 | 49.4 | 27.0 | 50.6 | 35.2 |
| Brothers or sisters | 83.0 | 73.3 | 18.9 | 11.4 | 50.9 | 29.9 |
| Mother-in-law | 30.0 | 20.7 | 9.0 | 2.4 | 14.4 | 9.6 |
| Father-in-law | 19.3 | 23.0 | 5.8 | 2.6 | 12.4 | 8.1 |
| Brothers-in-law, sisters-in-law | 34.6 | 30.9 | 1.9 | 0.0 | 20.2 | 6.1 |
| Friends | 95.6 | 84.6 | 32.5 | 6.6 | 76.3 | 54.9 |
| Coworkers | 80.8 | 71.1 | 1.9 | 4.4 | 41.9 | 30.0 |

## FAMILY

The vast majority of separated men and women received moral support from their parents, brothers, and sisters since separation. The receipt of services is also common, with half of the women reporting help from parents and siblings. Services from family members are not quite as commonly rendered for separated men. Financial aid is common from parents to their daughters, with about half of the women receiving money. Financial aid to men from parents and to both men and women from brothers and sisters is more unusual. A man in his late thirties who has custody of his two children recounted the comfort provided by his family:

> I come from a very beautiful family. . . . Everyone is very close. The one word I heard most from my family all my life was "love." I have always known that they are always there if I need them and that they will always stand by me whatever I want to do. I guess they have helped most just by letting me know that they're there.

In our assessments of support from family, the correlations between help from mother and help from father ranged from .5 to .7 across types of support. We created, therefore, a parental score for each type of support. The types of support were interrelated. If parents provided one kind of help, they were likely to provide other kinds as well. The same was true of help from brothers and sisters. Support from brothers and sisters was connected with help from parents. In the case of services, the correlation was as high as .6. If help is received from parents, therefore, help is likely to be received from brothers and sisters as well. The family of origin appears to rally together and supply a breadth of assistance.

Kitson and her colleagues (1982) report that help received from kin is related marginally ($r = .12$) to approval of the separation and divorce. We found no evidence of a connection between support from parents or siblings and approval of the breakup. A severe case of parental conflict came, surprisingly, from a mother who was in favor of the divorce:

> She always hated Larry, so it was kind of like, "I told you so." . . . She just knows I'm not going to succeed at living alone. I'll show her. I have to. . . . She thinks I have very weird ideas. Her idea of weird is anything she doesn't like. . . . When she's here she tries to tell the kids how bad their father was. I've tried to

explain to her that that just makes it worse, but she doesn't stop. . . . [now] she's telling the kids how bad they are. Finally she told them they were so rotten I should send them to their rotten father. I got really angry and she hasn't written to me since.

Goode (1956) concluded that it is not whether parents approve or disapprove of the divorce but whether they are involved in the decision at all that matters. We created a dichotomous variable of parental involvement: Parents encouraged the person to go through with it or not to go through with it (coded 1) or they stayed out of it (coded 0). Among men, encouragement one way or the other was related to parental provision of moral support ($r = .20$) and services ($r = .24$). There was no connection between parental intrusion in the divorce decision and aid among women. Overall, then, it seems that family members help out after separation regardless of their feelings about the divorce or their attempts to sway the decision. A man who had persistent and cordial relations with his family before the breakup told us,

> They are opposed to divorce in general but since there wasn't anything they could do about it, they've accepted it. I don't have the kind of relationship with them where I seek advice or support from them, so they don't give any. We're just friendly and they still accept me, and we still get along the same since the divorce.

Choosing a member of one's own family as an intimate (68 percent of the women and 55 percent of the men) was related to parental services ($r = .28$ for total sample) and sibling services ($r = .26$ for total sample). There was no other evidence among men of a connection between emotional closeness and succor from family members. Among women, naming a family member as an intimate also was related to financial help ($r = .34$) and moral support ($r = .24$) from siblings. We would guess that women often had close bonds with sisters. We asked about geographical closeness of kin as well. As we might suspect, the more relatives that lived within an hour's drive, the more likely it was that parents provided services ($r = .33$ for total sample) and brothers and sisters provided services ($r = .33$ for total sample). Other forms of help—financial and emotional support—were not dependent upon living close by. In general, family members give moral and financial aid regardless of whether or not they are emotionally and geographically close to the separated person. Services, however, are another matter.

Physical and emotional closeness accounts at least in part for why family members babysit, run errands, do chores, and so on.

An important service provided by many parents was taking the child back into their home. A young woman escaping an abusive husband lived with her parents and said, "They were wonderful to me." Another young man lived with his parents until he could get on his feet again and appreciatively told us his mother and father helped him "in any way they could." Many parents, then, see that their help is needed and make provisions. A woman with four children who was having a hard time of it reported,

> I asked my parents if I could live with them until I got something together, but they said no. . . . My family didn't really know what was going on. They apologized later and said they didn't realize it was so bad. . . . They gave me a car and offered to pay the lawyer's fees.

We thought that help might depend on whether or not the separated man or woman had children. We also wondered if financial aid from family members was tied to the financial instability or strain of the separated person. Finally, we wondered if support—particularly moral—was connected with a low evaluation of life at separation. All of these circumstances indicate need in one form or another. Researchers are often confused by the finding that support from others after marital breakup is positively related to current distress (Chiriboga et al., 1979; Kitson et al., 1982). The common explanation is that distressed people seek out or elicit help from others, not that help is itself distressing. We cannot untangle these causal connections with our data, but we can address the issue. Those indicators of a need for support (children, financial upheaval, unemployment, poor view of life at separation) are unlikely to be results of the intervention of others.

Among both men and women, having children increased the likelihood of receiving services from parents ($r = .34$ for men and $.21$ for women). Money and moral support from parents were not related to the presence of children. Among women, but not among men, having children was connected with financial help ($r = .23$) and moral support ($r = .19$) from brothers and sisters. Financial instability since separation was related to financial help from parents ($r = .29$) and from siblings ($r = .26$) among men but not among women. Financial strain and decline also was connected with money from parents among men ($r = .24$) but not among women. Women are more likely than men to receive financial help from their families, but their receipt of money is not as closely tied to their perceived financial need as it was for men. Unemployment was not linked with financial support from family members among men, but unemployed women were more likely to receive money from brothers and sisters than were employed women ($r = .21$).

Among women, a bleak view of life right after separation was associated with moral support from parents ($r = .18$), services from parents ($r = .29$), money from siblings ($r = .33$), and services from siblings ($r = .19$). Among men, only moral support from brothers and sisters was related to low morale at separation ($r = .19$). It appears, then, that family members help out because they are needed. The emotional distress of women and their burden of children are somewhat more likely to evoke help from family members than similar circumstances among men. Among men, financial need calls forth appropriate relief from family members. This does not rule out the possibility, however, that the receipt of help is distressing. Our culture encourages parents to keep their distance from adult children, especially if they are married. Moving back into the parents' home and accepting money or advice can be comforting, but also a strain on relations.

## FORMER IN-LAWS

In-laws are, of course, not as prone to provide support as one's own family. As Table 6.2 indicates, moral support is the most common mode of assistance from in-laws. About a third of the women received emotional support from in-laws, usually from mothers-in-law or the former partner's brothers and sisters. Men did not find quite as much support, but about a quarter of them received moral support from in-laws. Services and money were rendered less frequently by in-laws, especially to former sons-in-law.

Similar to own kin, we created parental scores for each type of support for in-laws. Correlations between help from mother-in-law and help from father-in-law ranged from .7 to 1.0 across types of support. Modes of support were interrelated within source. In-laws, whether parents or siblings, who provide one type of assistance were likely to provide other types as well. Help from brothers-in-law and sisters-in-law was connected with help from parents-in-law, except for financial aid. Money from former in-laws was so rare that correlations between this mode of support and other variables are unreliable.

Among men, disapproval of the separation and divorce by in-laws was related positively to some forms of assistance. The more mothers- and fathers-in-law disapproved of the breakup, the more likely they were to give their services to their daughter's former husband after separation ($r = .26$). The receipt of money from parents-in-law was also related to parental disapproval of the divorce among men ($r = .20$) as well as women ($r = .21$). The former wife's siblings were also somewhat more likely to provide moral support if they disapproved of the breakup ($r = .18$). It seems confused that disapproval would be connected with the provision of aid. Recall, however, that disapproval is from the perspective of participants, not the in-laws themselves. Participants who are close to in-laws may be aware of their disapproval, whereas others may have to guess how their in-laws evaluate the situation. It may well be that, if in-laws like the former husband and thus disapprove of the breakup, they would be more likely to provide help after separation.

Among both men and women, naming a member of the former spouse's family as an intimate at the time of the interview was related to provision of services from parents-in-law ($r = .17$ for men and .25 for women), services from brothers- and sisters-in-law ($r = .41$ for men and .42 for women), and moral support from the former partner's sibling ($r = .21$ for men and .24 for women). In addition, women who chose an in-law as an intimate were more likely to receive moral support from parents-in-law ($r = .43$). This is further evidence that provision of support from in-laws is based on affection. Geographical closeness of in-laws (number of affines within an hour's drive) was not important to the provision of services from members of the former marital partner's family.

As with the participant's own family, having children meant greater receipt of services from parents-in-law ($r = .26$ for men and women) and from brothers- and sisters-in-law ($r = .17$ for men and .22 for women). Financial need and low morale after separation was not connected with the provision of support from in-laws. All in all, it appears that in-laws help out because they like the former family member and because of the children they share as relatives.

## FRIENDS

Friends were the most likely source of moral support and services among the participants in our study. Almost all of the separated men and women had received emotional succor from friends after separation. Some friends gave sympathy by revealing their surprise that "the marriage lasted as long as it did." A few friends offered a haven to the homeless. Others looked to the future and tried to help the separated person start a new life. Some of the friends were unlikely. A young man, when asked if there was any one person who had been especially helpful, described his friend to us:

> There's this older lady. . . . I guess she's about 60 now. I've always been close to her. I sort of call her my adopted mother. She's very easy for me to talk to and helps a lot. She doesn't offer a lot of advice or anything, she's just there when I need to talk.

Half of the men and three-quarters of the women had friends who babysat, ran errands, helped with chores, or rendered other services. A third of the women received financial aid from friends, while only a small minority of the men did so. Coworkers did not give or lend money. They did, however, provide services and moral support.

There is little variance in our assessment of moral support from friends, especially among women; so the relationships of moral support with other variables will be attenuated severely. Among men, disapproval of the separation and divorce by friends was related negatively to the receipt of services from friends ($r = -.24$). Otherwise, there were no connections between friends' evaluations of the breakup and their provision of support. We asked participants if they felt they acted differently with friends now that they were separated or divorced. About 60 percent of the men and women said no, while about 40 percent reported that the nature of their behavior with friends had changed since separation. Among men, the perceived disapproval of friends was tied to changes in their behavior ($r = .25$). We do not know the proportion of current friends that came before and after the marital breakup. Both old and new friends probably make up the current social circle. Among both men and women, those who shared friends with the marital partner were less likely to receive services from friends after divorce than those who had separate friends during marriage ($r = -.23$ for men and $-.17$ for women). Among men, but not among women, the number of new friends made since separation was connected positively to all forms of support from friends—moral ($r = .25$), financial ($r = .22$), and services ($r = .32$). Men may be more likely to receive comfort from new friends than women.

Women with children were more likely to receive service support ($r = .32$) and money ($r = .32$) from friends than were women without children. There was no difference in the receipt of assistance from friends among men with and without children. Financial instability among men was connected to financial aid from friends ($r = .17$) and coworkers ($r = .26$). Work associates also were more likely to give or loan money if the separated man was experiencing financial strain and decline ($r = .20$). Women received money ($r = .22$) as well as moral support ($r = .19$) from friends under these financial conditions. Low morale at separation elicited service support from friends among women ($r = .26$) and financial backing among men ($r = .24$).

## SUMMARY

Moral support from one's own family and friends appears unvarying from our global assessment. Regardless of circumstances, kith and kin bolster the separated man and woman. We do not know, however, the nature and depth of the emotional succor. We do not know, for instance, about attempts by others to sabotage the rising spirit or denials of support. The receipt of services from family is connected with emotional and geographic closeness and the presence of children. Among men, financial need brings forth money from parents and siblings. Women seem more likely than men to receive financial aid from family members regardless of their perception of need. Among women, a dim view of life at separation brings forth all modes of support from kin. Services from friends are connected with low morale and children among women. Money from friends also is linked with children among women as well as with financial need. Men receive money from friends because of emotional or financial straits.

Family and friends, therefore, give moral support because it is their place to do so. Parents also may give or loan money to daughters because of this feeling of responsibility. It appears that sons' receipt of money depends more on particular need. Services from kin are not as constant as moral support and depend on a variety of conditions—affection, living close by, presence of children. Money and services from friends are not as unconditional as moral support; their receipt depends on need and circumstance. There is also some indication that men are more likely than women to receive comfort from friends that they have made since the breakup. Finally, in-laws help out because they are fond of the former family member and because of children. They help because they want to rather than out of obligation or responsibility.

Children are not included as a source of support in Table 6.2. Among those with children, over 80 percent of the women and 60 percent of the men reported emotional succor from their children. Financial aid was extremely rare. Three-quarters of the separated women and one-quarter of the men received service support from sons or daughters. The age of the child dictates his or her ability to provide support. Among parents with younger children, a child may serve simply as a constant reminder that life must and should go on. As one mother said about her five children, "I can't afford to fall apart. I keep picking up the pieces. I have to be responsible for them." Among middle-aged parents with adult children, a son or daughter may be a confidant and supply a great deal of comfort. Another woman, close to 60 years old and living with her daughter on savings, spoke of her sons and daughters fondly: "My children are wonderful. The oldest . . . kept things together for me." Dependence is frightening, however. The woman, with tears, went on to say,

> The kids fill my life. I don't know what I'll do now that they're all going away. I'm afraid I'll be lonesome. . . . I want to get settled. I have to. I can't depend on my kids to support me. I don't want them to keep me.

Children may not be comforting. A woman who was having a desperately difficult separation told us the following:

> My kids don't understand why I don't just straighten up and do everything, why I'm so messed up. . . . They're always asking why I'm such a mess, "Why aren't you back on your feet?" . . . My 17-year-old daughter treats me like we had no prior relationship. She's openly resentful and rebellious. She has more sympathy for the woman my husband married.

Unfortunately, children can be confused confederates in battles of loyalty. Relations with a child can be painfully treacherous:

> I can't even trust my oldest son. He tells his father things I've said.
>
> The kids stuck by me. They really resent their father. He said [we heard] that I turned them against him. But my kids say, "No sir, he did it himself."

## Social Support and Participation

In this section, we take a broader view of social support and participation. We look at the number of sources of support within each mode of assistance. We examine how the breadth of support and attentiveness are connected to our indicators of need for help. Finally, we consider how support, attentiveness, social participation, and changes in social relations are tied to separated men's and women's reactions to the marital breakup. Reactions, in this case, include thoughts and attempts of suicide, loneliness, and acceptance of the end of marriage.

Within each mode of support (moral, financial, services), we added up the six potential sources of support (parents, brothers and sisters, parents-in-law, siblings-in-law, friends, and coworkers). Only 2 percent of the women and 8 percent of the men received no moral support from anyone since separation. The average number of sources of emotional support was about four for women and men. No financial aid had been received from families or friends after the breakup by 35 percent of the women and twice as many men (70 percent). On the average, women received money from only a single source. Men, of course, typically received no financial help. Of the women 15 percent and 35 percent of the men did without service support from anyone. On the average, men and women seemed set on facing the separation alone:

> I'm pretty much of a loner. I have friends, but not very close ones that I would discuss this with very much. . . . I really don't need any friends.

> I didn't expect support. I'd gotten myself into it; I was going to get myself out.

> I'm pretty self-sufficient, so I won't be looking for someone to help me through this divorce. I don't have to ask for help.

Among men, the increased attentiveness since the breakup of people they were closest to during marriage was connected with the breadth of support in all areas: moral support ($r = .35$), financial aid ($r = .32$), and services ($r = .26$). There was no connection between attentiveness and the three modes of support among women. When we looked more closely at which sources of support men tied to perceptions of attentiveness, it was clear that they were thinking about family. All three types of help from parents, brothers and sisters, and parents-in-law were linked with attentiveness. Friends were not taken into account. This is another indication that the closest relationships that persisted after separation for men were family, while friends who helped out were often new.

Table 6.3 summarizes the relationships between indicators of need for support and assistance from others since separation. Women with children have a broader base of moral, financial, and service support than women without children. Men in financial need are more likely to receive money from a range of sources than men who are not in such straits. The lower a man's morale at separation, the more likely he is to receive moral support, money, and the attention of others after the breakup. Women get money and services from a broader base of support if their view of life was bleak at separation. It appears likely that friends and family rally around because the separated need their help. This conclusion is supported further when we look at the connection between assistance from others since separation and reactions to the marital breakup. Overall, there was not much tie between the three modes of support from specific sources or the range of sources and reactions to the breakup. Men who received money were more likely to think about or attempt suicide than those who did not get financial aid ($r = .22$). Women who had difficulty accepting the end of marriage received moral support from a broader range of people than women who were more accepting ($r = -.20$). Among men, attentiveness was related to thoughts of suicide ($r = .17$), loneliness ($r = .18$), and difficulty accepting the separation and divorce ($r = -.23$). Attentiveness of others was not related to reactions to the breakup among women.

A striking exception to the overall lack of connection between support and reactions to the breakup was the instance of in-laws. Table 6.4 presents the linkage between dimensions of in-law relations since separation and acceptance of the end of marriage. Either in-laws are more prone to approach and intervene when the separated person is having trouble accepting the breakup, or continuing ties with former in-

## TABLE 6.3
### Indicators of Need for Support and Assistance from Others

| | Assistance from Others | | | | | | | |
|---|---|---|---|---|---|---|---|---|
| | Moral Support | | Financial Aid | | Services | | Attentiveness | |
| Indicators of Need | Women | Men | Women | Men | Women | Men | Women | Men |
| Presence of children | .16 | ns | .29 | ns | .34 | .23 | ns | ns |
| Financial instability | ns | ns | ns | .36 | .17 | ns | ns | ns |
| Financial strain and decline | ns | ns | .16 | .24 | ns | ns | ns | ns |
| No employment | ns | ns | ns | .32 | ns | ns | ns | ns |
| Low morale at separation | ns | .20 | .25 | .20 | .27 | ns | ns | .21 |

NOTE: Only correlations significant at $p < .05$ are reported; others are nonsignificant (ns).

laws after the end of marriage hinders the process of acceptance. Another explanation that emerged from the qualitative reports is that men and women who are having trouble understanding their separation turn to in-laws for insight into their former partner's motives and actions. The pattern was particularly evident among women: Involvement with and assistance from members of the former partner's family were related negatively to acceptance of the end of marriage. Family researchers may have underestimated the importance of former affines in the process of adjusting to separation and divorce (Anspach, 1976).

Turning to social participation, we consider average frequency of contact with intimates, change in contact since marriage, number of good friends made since separation, and desire for more friends. Social participation following divorce has been found to be critical in reducing distress (Goode, 1956; Raschke, 1977). Current frequency of contact with intimates and change in frequency since marriage were not related to thoughts of suicide, loneliness, or acceptance of the breakup in our study. Among men, the number of friends made since separation is related positively to distress. The more new friends a man made, the more likely he was to have had thoughts about suicide ($r = .28$), felt lonely ($r = .20$), and have had a hard time accepting that the marriage was over ($r -.17$). There was no such connection among women. Hetherington and her colleagues (1978) report that men, particularly, are prone to a frenzy of social activity after separation. Again, the

**TABLE 6.4**
**In-Law Relations and Acceptance**
**of the End of Marriage**

| | Acceptance | |
|---|---|---|
| Dimensions of In-Law Relations | Women | Men |
| In-law one of closest people | −.31 | ns |
| Parents-in-law involved in divorce decision | ns | −.21 |
| Moral support from parents-in-law | −.36 | ns |
| Moral support from brothers-in-law, sisters-in-law | ns | ns |
| Financial aid from parents-in-law | −.24 | ns |
| Financial aid from brothers-in-law, sisters-in-law | ns | * |
| Services from parents-in-law | −.20 | −.24 |
| Services from brothers-in-law, sisters-in-law | −.19 | ns |

* In no case did a man receive money from brothers-in-law, sisters-in-law.
NOTE: Only correlations significant at $p < .05$ are reported; others are nonsignificant (ns).

causal connections are unclear, but it is clear that the process of acquiring a number of new friends is related to distress among men. We do not know the nature and depth of these new social ties. Among women, wanting more friends is tied to distress. The desire for more friends among women is related to thoughts of suicide ($r = .16$), loneliness ($r = .25$), and difficulty accepting the breakup ($r = -.18$). The link between social participation and distress, like that between support and distress, turns out to be more complicated than we had anticipated.

## The Limits of Support

We cannot report simply that friends and relatives gather around after separation, offer aid and comfort, and relieve the pain of ending a marriage and starting a new life. Friends and relatives also can forsake, sabotage, and interfere. We cannot say that separated men and women accept whole-heartedly the solicitous attentions of others. The need for autonomy may be as strong as the need for the comfort of others. The need for support is a burden itself. One woman said, "Other people will listen, but they're just being polite. . . . A close friend tells me how well I'm doing. Sometimes it helps, but sometimes I just don't believe her." Another woman, in tears, told us, "Inside I wish I had someone to share all this with. . . . Talking to my sister or neighbor doesn't really do any good. It's not their problem." Yet another woman expressed the ambivalence of needing and shunning others:

> Those that are happy, I don't want to go near. They make me feel terrible. I don't really have any close friends any more. I've lost contact with them over the years. The one couple I'm friends with, they've helped. I didn't know whether to feel good that they were concerned or mad at them for interfering. In some ways I just want my own life. I want to be left alone. It's hard dealing with other people.

The love, esteem, and succor of others can do much to buffer the distress of marital breakup. Most people report that they would not have made it without the support of family or friends. Yet, we have to acknowledge the complexity of offering and providing help, on the one side, and needing, seeking, and accepting help on the other side.

CHAPTER 7

# Dating and Sex

Men and women who have been separated and divorced have in common one noteworthy characteristic—namely, they have not dated in any traditional way for years. This fact is often the focus of discussion in groups such as Parents Without Partners, and is thought about often by men and women who have separated. There are some individuals who are eager to begin dating again and others who avoid it. Many wish to date but do not feel confident about it. Others begin dating even before the separation or divorce has occurred. Still others launch into active dating relationships with several individuals. We have demonstrated earlier the important role that friends and relatives play in the adjustment to marital separation, and we have discussed how extramarital sexual relationships figure in the termination of some marriages. In this chapter we look at dating and sex and the role they play in marital separation and its aftermath.

Our qualitative interviews gave some hints as to the diversity of dating experience for persons who have divorced. The case studies also revealed that one's social life after marriage was an important contributor to one's self-concept. Three of our respondents reveal the continuum of experience. A 37-year-old woman with two children who worked part-time was asked if she dated at all. She replied,

> The only place I go to is work. And it's all women there. I'm tired of women. I went to a Parents Without Partners meeting once, but they're mostly women, too. I met this one 56-year-old man there, though, and he's been calling me and driving me crazy. I just don't like him, so I was leaving the phone off the hook.

A 31-year-old man with no children resembled many of our respondents who had been dating a little, but was not yet fully comfortable with his role as a dating partner:

> Well, I was doing a little casual dating but not a lot and I haven't gotten serious with anyone yet. It's kind of hard when you've been

out of circulation for eight or ten years, counting the time I was married and the time before when we were going steady.

A 46-year-old man was similar to many respondents who had a rather optimistic evaluation of their dating experiences:

> I've dated several different girls. Two or three have been sort of close but nothing really serious. I have really enjoyed getting back into dating and, after the first time, I have found it pretty easy. I know people who say they feel rather weird dating again, but I never had any problems after the first time.

## Dating and Separation

Do men and women approaching separation or divorce begin plans for future relationships? How do such relationships figure into the termination of the marriage? And what role do dating relationships play after the separation has taken place? Our data show that some separated persons are reluctant to begin dating, often for reasons perceived to be very pragmatic. Note the interviewer's question and the respondent's answer below:

> I: Have you had any romantic involvements or started dating or anything like that since the separation?
> R: Not really, I didn't do any dating or anything for quite a while but in the last couple of months I've had a few very casual dates, but not many. For one thing I don't want to give my wife any ammunition if she should want to try to get the children and besides I haven't really wanted to get involved yet. I don't want to just jump into anything to get a mother for the kids or something like that. I've proved that I can cope very well on my own. Also I don't think the kids are ready to handle anything like that yet.

Another man began dating before the final separation. Following a brief period of hesitation, he began to date, reporting that it probably helped his transition.

> I: You said that you started dating some during the first separation. Did that help you in adjusting to the situation then or did it make it more difficult?
> R: Well in some ways it did both. It probably helped more than it hurt. At first I wanted to date since she was seeing someone and I

didn't like being on my own; but I had mixed emotions about it. I had been brought up in an old fashioned way and I knew that you didn't do that kind of thing when you were married. However, at the time of our first separation I was living in a building with a nice bar downstairs and I used to go down there a lot, and there were usually some girls there. Finally, I picked one up. We had a very good time, and after that first time it was easy for me to get back into dating.

One in nine of our respondents reported that they were already dating someone or planning on dating someone in particular before the separation. Another 35 percent of the respondents reported that their spouses were dating or planned to, and an additional 12 percent reported that *both* they and their spouses were in this situation. It is noteworthy that two-fifths of the sample reported that this actual or planned dating activity was not a factor in the separation process.

By the time of the interview, however, approximately two-fifths of the reported relationships had terminated. Reported one respondent, "I just don't want to get serious right now with anybody. My life is too unsettled." Yet, one in six had already ended in marriage, and another one in six was forecasted to end in marriage. It is important to note, however, that these responses may contain one important bias; specifically, respondents are far more likely to report that their *spouses* began dating before separation and that subsequent remarriages were based on relationships that began before the separation than they are to recall such scenarios for themselves. Nevertheless, we find that most dating relationships that begin before divorce do not end in marriage although a minority do.

Reactions to a spouse's preseparation relationship can be varied:

> I knew they didn't get along very well. . . . She was a bitch. I could have shot them both and not cared—if I could get away with it.
>
> [I felt] self-pity, because he found somebody and I didn't.

Further evidence for the characterization that dating before divorce is primarily a way of coping with the failing marriage is available in the data about the length of the dating relationships that had begun shortly after the separation. Respondents report that one-third of their relationships had ended within three months and one-third of their spouses' relationships had ended within six months of the time they began. Only a minority of such relationships—*including* those that resulted in remarriage—persisted for longer than one year.

A divorce can be dragged out by one or both parties for months or years beyond the separation for any number of reasons. When interest develops on the part of one of the spouses to remarry, however, the legal action to divorce becomes necessary. A 25-year-old man married since high school reported that his wife had moved to a different state. He went for a time and returned to Central Pennsylvania.

> About the time I first started coming up here regularly I met this girl who also was just divorced and going through some of the same problems. . . . Anyway, we met and started dating, and now we are engaged. We plan to be married as soon as my decree becomes final. That's the main reason why I'm getting the divorce now even though it's costing so much.

Turning now to the postseparation period, we explored in some detail the nature and extent of dating relationships. Excluding the 21 respondents who had already remarried by the time of the interview, 44 percent of the sample were dating daily or a few times a week. This projects a picture of very socially active men and women following their divorce. Another 28 percent dated about once a week or a few times a month. About one in nine respondents dated only occasionally, and one in six respondents never dated. A majority of the respondents—including those who report not dating at all at the time of the interview—had begun dating within a month of their separation, and nearly all had begun dating within six months of the separation. These data suggest that both men and women discover the importance of establishing new dating relationships following separation and lose very little time in beginning a social life.

By the time of the interview, only three respondents had never dated since their separation. Most respondents had dated a few partners; more than half had four or more different dating partners. Of the sample, 10 percent had already dated at least ten different individuals since separation. The majority of those who are dating report that they have only one partner at the moment. This is the typical pattern, with men and women alike reporting that they tend to date a succession of individuals, going "steady" with each one until the relationship tapers off. Fewer than 10 percent of the respondents were attempting to date more than two individuals at the same time. Although there is no factual basis for the comparison, it is likely that the extent of dating activity, including number of partners and frequency, would rival any age-equivalent group of never-married persons, and perhaps would rival individuals in the typical mate selection years for first marriages.

When asked whether they felt that dates treated them differently upon learning that they were separated or divorced, 31 percent of the sample responded affirmatively. This awareness of the very special status they occupy may account for some feelings of awkwardness felt by recently separated or divorced individuals. In fact, nearly half of the sample reported feeling at least a little awkward when dating. Many separated people consider dating a contrived, embarrassing, and perilous social activity (Weiss, 1975).

Where do separated individuals look for dating partners, and which of the many methods of establishing a social life seem to work the best? In our qualitative interviews, reentry into dating was a common topic of discussion. We found almost every conceivable way of meeting someone mentioned. We also found a great reluctance on the part of many respondents to meet people in some particular settings. For example, a 37-year-old woman said,

> I know it sounds bad, but I can't help feeling why should I join another bunch of losers [at Parents Without Partners]. Some of the people were really nice, but there are mostly women. . . . Where do you go to meet people? I can't bring myself to go to a singles club. There should be a happy medium, somewhere between Parents Without Partners and a singles club. I just don't have the nerve to go to a singles club.

**TABLE 7.1**
**Ways in which Dating Acquaintances Have Been Met**

|  | Yes | No |
|---|---|---|
| Through your family | 10.6 | 89.4 |
| Through a friend | 61.1 | 38.9 |
| At a party or social gathering | 42.4 | 45.4 |
| In a singles bar | 9.4 | 90.6 |
| At a bar | 42.8 | 57.2 |
| At work | 46.1 | 53.9 |
| Through a church | 5.7 | 94.3 |
| Because you knew them before | 65.6 | 34.4 |
| Other | 20.7 | 79.3 |

A 25-year-old man, when asked about his dating, indicated the following:

> Just pickups. When I'm out drinking with the guys sometimes I get hooked up with a particular female. There is something in my head that tells me to avoid getting tied up with another woman now, I guess I'm afraid that I might get into a marriage that would fail like the last.

Finally, a 57-year-old woman was having trouble finding places to meet men.

> I meet a lot of people at work but they're married usually. Mostly through friends, I'd say. I haven't dated that much. In fact, I spend a lot of time with my husband.

Data from the structured interviews are reported in Table 7.1. It appears that dating most often emerges from acquaintances made through friends, at parties or social gatherings, at bars, or at work. Many dating opportunities develop because individuals were acquainted before the separation, although this is not listed as the best source of meeting dating partners. Friends are cited as being the best sources; dating opportunities provided through families, singles groups, or church apparently are not very promising.

There are many reasons why new social involvements are beneficial to separated men and women (Weiss, 1975). Dating is a distracting and engaging social activity. It helps to keep one busy so that there is some relief from thinking about the breakup. It provides something to anticipate. Dating can be a remedy for loneliness and offer someone new with whom to chat about mundane matters or confide. For separated men and women, someone new also can reaffirm one's worth. As one woman said, "My sense of self-worth has been restored by my relationship with Peter. I know I'm desirable as a woman, for me." In contrast, she felt that her husband had neither known nor appreciated the woman she really was during her 22-year marriage. A number of respondents discussed how important romantic relationships were for their adjustment to separation. A statement by a recently divorced man was typical:

> Getting involved with a woman has helped me to realize I can now communicate intimately and establish a relationship with

someone. This has been very helpful. It's made the adjustment much easier.

Another man talked about the effects of his ex-wife's new relationship:

> I also think that forming another relationship helped my ex-wife. Shortly after the separation she got involved in another relationship, and I noticed a real change after that. . . . The separation bothered her at first because of her insecurities, but after she formed a new relationship, then she adjusted rapidly and we became friends again. I think more than anything, that helped to ease things between us, so we stopped fighting.

Despite the rather high level of social activity reported by our respondents, more than one-fourth of the sample would like to date more often. Many of those not dating discussed how much they wanted to form new relationships. A common set of problems was where to meet others and how to start dating again after not dating for so long. Several women also said that it was difficult to establish new relationships because "the only thing men want from a divorcee is sex."

Many people leaving marriage are fearful of being hurt again. The ordeal of ending a marriage has left them unsure of themselves and their desirability, cautious about risking new problems, and concerned about rejection (Weiss, 1975). They are sensitive particularly to the perils of involvement. As one woman explained,

> I'm dating a man now who has a gentleness I never knew. He's older too. In the past couple of weeks I've had to cool it. I'm very much afraid to get too involved. I want a relationship, but I fear too much intimacy. I don't want to hurt him either. . . . I have sexual desires, but I have to have some feeling for someone before going to bed with them. . . . I want opportunities to meet the opposite sex without pressure for sex. But where and how? I have a great fear of loneliness. . . . I would like to remarry someday, but it scares me.

A man said very much the same thing:

> This woman I've been dating has helped to soothe things over lately. Since I met her, I don't miss my wife so much. It's a budding relationship. I wouldn't say it was just a casual relationship. It's beginning to present some problems, because it's

getting deeper faster than I want it to be. We have decided to keep it nonsexual for the moment. . . . I doubt that the relationship will ever go anywhere much. I'm not sure that I want it to. I realize I'm in a bad position to get in another relationship. It's helping a lot now, but I don't want to go out of the frying pan into the fire.

A good indicator of the value of dating experience following separation are the respondent's self-reports of the relationship between dating and postseparation adjustment. Again excluding those who are already married, half of the respondents report that dating has helped a great deal in adjusting to separation. Another fourth of the sample indicated that it helped a little, and one in five suggests that it has had no effect one way or another. According to 6 percent, it has made the adjustment harder. Children are reported to decrease chances for dating by about one-third of those with custody of children. The majority of respondents, however, report that children are not a factor in dating opportunities; a few respondents with children, particularly those *with* custody, report that it enhances their dating prospects.

Sexual activity after divorce, of course, is closely related to dating activity. We asked our respondents about the extent of sexual relations since separation and their degree of satisfaction with them. We found some significant differences between men and women on these items. Men were more likely to be having sexual relations frequently, with 47 percent of the men and 33 percent of the women reporting frequent sexual intercourse. Occasional sexual relations are reported by 22 percent of the men and 38 percent of the women. Fifteen percent of both men and women reported sexual relations rarely, and only 15 percent of the men and 14 percent of the women reported sexual relations not at all. A picture emerges of rather active sexual involvement within the framework of dating relationships.

Although men were having sex more frequently than women, they were less pleased with the frequency and reported lower degrees of satisfaction than the women. Half of the men desired sexual intercourse more often, whereas less than one-third of the women desired sex more often. In our sample 48 percent of the men and 62 percent of the women were "satisfied as is" with the frequency, and only 1 percent of the men and 6 percent of the women wanted to have sexual relations less often.

Nearly half (48 percent) of the men indicated their sexual relations were very satisfactory since separation, compared to 63 percent of the women; 38 percent of the men and 24 percent of the women said their sexual relations were somewhat satisfactory. One in ten men and 4 percent of the women reported their sexual relations as a little unsatisfactory. Finally, women were more likely to say their relations were very unsatisfactory (9 percent); men indicated this level of evaluation 4 percent of the time.

Weiss (1975) points out behavioral and motivational differences in the sexual activity of men and women after separation. Neither men nor women have many clues about what is appropriate behavior; and casual sex can be very distressing, especially among women. Weiss suggests that separated men can gain reassurance of their worth from the sexual consent of their partners; men can interpret consent as acceptance. Separated men may indulge in a frenzy of sexual encounters to bolster their confidence and then settle down once they get back their self-assurance. Women cannot interpret readily the sexual consent of their partners as reassurance of their own worth and are more likely than men to feel undermined personally by their own sexual accessibility. Women, says Weiss, more likely use sex to enhance a new attachment rather than to shore up depleted self-assurance. We will comment further on these gender differences in subsequent sections of this chapter.

We wanted to know what dating and sexual circumstances were connected with participants thinking that dating eased the aftermath of separation. The results in Table 7.2 show that the number of people dated (either since separation or currently) and awkwardness about dating are not tied to the perception that dating is helping one get through the separation and start a new life. What matters is the frequency of and satisfaction with dating and sexual relations. Among women, a short lag between separation and starting to date is also important.

Dating and sexual activity after separation may be influenced by the relationship with the marital partner during or after marriage. Although the themes of complaints women level against their husbands and marriages were not related to dating after divorce in Goode's (1956) study, the person who suggested the divorce was. Goode reports that women who first suggested the divorce dated more frequently afterward than women whose husbands suggested the divorce or arrived at divorce by mutual conclusion. Being left by the partner and leaving an unpleasant marriage may dampen the appeal of dating. In our sample, marital quality in the final months, who suggested the

**TABLE 7.2**
**Correlations Between Circumstances of Dating
and Reports that Dating Helped in Adjustment to Separation**

| Dating Circumstance | Dating Helped Adjustment | |
|---|---|---|
| | Men | Women |
| Frequency of dating | .44 | .48 |
| How soon started dating | ns | .23 |
| Number of people dated since separation | ns | ns |
| Number of people currently dating | ns | ns |
| Feel awkward about dating | ns | ns |
| Frequency of sexual relations | .45 | .42 |
| Want sex more often | −.34 | −.27 |
| Satisfaction with sexual relations | .27 | .27 |

NOTE: ns = correlation nonsignificant at $p < .05$

separation, and who is blamed for the breakup are not connected to dating and sexual experience after separation.

Goode also reports that feelings for the partner after separation are connected with dating. Women who still loved or felt friendly toward their husbands dated more after divorce than women who hated or were indifferent to their husbands. Goode speculates that the latter group is resentful toward men in general. His results are somewhat surprising. It would seem likely that separated men and women who persist in their attachment to and affection for the former partner would be less likely to date after the breakup. We already considered this issue in Chapter 5. To summarize our results from Chapter 5, dating and sexual experience are not related to contact and rapport with the former partner or feelings for the partner after separation. Attachment, however, is related to dating and sexual experience. Particularly among women, current attachment to the former partner (thinking and wondering about, longing for the partner) is characteristic of separated people who are less socially and sexually active.

## Age, Sex, and Dating

Dating involves men and women, and it is reasonable to hypothesize that the experiences are different for men and women, particularly after marital separation. We have already pointed out that men have somewhat more frequent sexual relations than women and are less satisfied with their frequency of relations. Recall that women also expressed more satisfaction than men with extramarital sexual relations although their evaluation of marital sex was bleaker. There were no differences between men and women in their awkwardness in dating or in their perception of the healing qualities of new social ties after separation. Overall, there are few differences in the dating and sexual experiences of men and women after separation.

Age is another critical variable that should be considered. Demographic research (Spanier and Glick, 1980) indicates that remarriage rates are much higher for men than women, and that women have a rapidly declining chance of remarriage as they get older. Although there are many reasons for this phenomenon—including higher mortality rates for males (and a consequently smaller field of eligibles for females) and the tendency of men to marry younger women—it is nevertheless likely that age is a relevant factor in the dating experience of men and women in the postseparation period. Inasmuch as dating is a precursor to remarriage, the data on remarriage trends are likely to reflect the dating situation for men and women of different ages.

Among men, we found two instances where age is related to extent of dating activity. The older a man is, the fewer people he is likely to have dated since separation ($r = .21$). Older men are more satisfied with frequency of sex ($r = .17$) and the quality of sexual relations ($r = .22$). Otherwise, age is unrelated to dating and sexual behavior after separation for men.

Among women, however, there are many more instances where age appears to play a role in dating and sexual experience. Older women date less frequently ($r = .37$) than younger women, feel more awkward about dating ($r = .21$), would like to go out more often then they do ($r = .21$), and feel that dating has not helped them to grow accustomed to separation ($r = .22$). Older women have sexual relations less frequently after separation ($r = .27$), are less satisfied with sexual relations ($r = .19$), but would prefer sex more often ($r = .21$) than younger women.

To see what age groups are affected, we did cross-tabulations of dating and sex variables with age categories of women in their 20s, 30s, and 40 and over. The relationships are linear: The older a woman gets, the less she dates, the less she has sex, and the more dissatisfied she is with the experience. For example, 55 percent of the women in their 20s go out daily or a few times a week; 35 percent of the women in their 30s go out that frequently; only 17 percent of the women in their 40s are frequent daters. Dating after separation for women who are no longer young can be a particularly baffling and discouraging experience.

Goode (1956) also found that older women had fewer opportunities to date and dated less frequently than younger women. As Goode bluntly states, women over 30 have "lost much of their appeal." He thought that perhaps older women had unfavorable attitudes toward love and marriage, and that their lack of desire to remarry explained their limited social activity. This did not turn out to be the case in either Goode's study or our own. Controlling for the effects of attitude toward remarriage, the connection of age with dating and sexual experience remains.

## Attitudes Toward Remarriage

To many men and women who have separated, dating and sexual activity after separation is prominently thought of as a road to remarriage. To many others, however, remarriage is a rather distant vision that has nothing to do with their current social relationships. Some individuals have been so soured on members of the opposite sex, generally as a result of their divorce, that they have vowed never to remarry. We investigate remarriage more fully in the companion volume by Furstenberg and Spanier *(Recycling the Family)*. Here we focus on attitudes toward remarriage at the time of the initial interview with our respondents following separation.

In our case-study interviews we found examples of the diversity of thinking about remarriage mentioned above. One woman in her 50s who had little interest in dating would have welcomed an opportunity to remarry. She reported a particular dilemma she was facing, however:

> The one man I'm involved with is married, and I don't want to do to someone else's marriage what someone did to mine. I censor myself. I don't see him for weeks at a time, and I don't even answer my phone. But I can only do that for so long. I haven't met anyone else that I like as much as I like him. I don't know what to do.

Several women noted that their opportunities seemed to be limited to men who were already married to someone. A man, 46 years old and with four children living with their mother, expressed little interest in remarriage:

> I don't have any desire now to remarry. As I said, I like my life the way it is now. I think I'm well adjusted and I don't have any major problems. I'm not saying I won't marry again; it could happen but I don't have any desire to right now.

A 31-year-old man who had been married for six years began his interview by asking the interviewer if he had any suggestions on how to meet "nice" girls who were interested in settling down and not playing around. Later in the interview he said,

> I think I would like to get married again. I'm not sure that I really had a chance to find out what marriage was all about. I think I would like to find a girl who had been married before, maybe one who had been ripped off like I was. I've not been too successful in finding the kind of girl I'm looking for. Most of the ones I've met are just out for a good time and don't seem to have any values or principles anymore. And I'm just not interested in going to bars or partying all the time. I like it better just being settled down.

We asked our respondents how they felt about remarriage. Table 7.3 shows that only a small minority of respondents (13 percent of the men and 8 percent of the women) felt that they will probably never remarry. About half the sample reported being reluctant to remarry, but may nevertheless do so. About one in six respondents said he or she may remarry, and reported being eager. Of our sample, 9 percent were

**TABLE 7.3**
**How Respondents Feel About Remarriage**
**(in percentages)**

|  | Men | Women |
|---|---|---|
| Will probably never remarry | 13 | 8 |
| May remarry, but reluctant | 47 | 55 |
| May remarry, and eager | 19 | 15 |
| Definite plans to remarry | 6 | 9 |
| Already remarried | 10 | 8 |
| Have never thought about it | 6 | 5 |
| Total percentage | 100 | 100 |

already remarried by the time of the interview, and at the time we talked to them, another 8 percent had definite plans to remarry.

We also asked about feelings toward the statement, "I would never consider remarriage." Only 7 percent of the men and 5 percent of the women indicated that this was very much their feeling. Two-thirds of the men and three-fourths of the women reported that it was "not at all" their feeling. One in four men and one in five women said it was somewhat their feeling. A woman who would not consider remarriage told us, "I think men are all alike. I know they're not, but I guess I made one mistake and that's one too many. I'd hate it if I made the same mistake."

Do separated men and women perceive that remarriage to the right person would make them happier than they are right now? More than half of both men (54 percent) and women (58 percent) indicated that they very much believed it would. Thirty percent of both men and women said "somewhat"; and 16 percent of the men and 12 percent of the women indicated that it was not at all their feelings that remarriage to the right person would make them happier than they were right now. A man approaching 40 expressed his situation in this way:

> I think it has made me less trusting and more hesitant to start new relationships. At first, I thought that I would never want to get married again, but now I guess I'm changing some. I'm not actively looking for anything, and I think I've shown I can get along fine without a wife, so I'm not in a panic to get married like some people I've known. But if the right person came along, I'd get married again.

Earlier we considered shifts in financial security in the aftermath of separation. We also asked our respondents to give us their feeling about the statement "I am basically happy now and would remarry mostly for financial reasons." Only 5 percent of both men and women reported that this statement very much described how they felt, 7 percent of the men and 13 percent of the women said that it somewhat described their feelings. The large majority of the sample (89 percent of the men and 81 percent of the women) said it did not at all describe them. Despite the skewedness of the responses, it is interesting to note that 15 percent of the respondents (combining the first two response choices) did indicate that they might consider remarriage for financial reasons. As one woman said, "I want somebody better than I had. If I do remarry, the man will provide for me. Money isn't everything, but it sure helps." Another woman, in her middle 40s, said,

> I won't get involved in a relationship unless it's emotionally and financially beneficial to me. I want to be on my own and not need men, because I think basically you can't trust them. I really believe that.

Would respondents who are basically happy now remarry mostly for companionship reasons? Here we see a different response pattern. Nearly one in three respondents reported that this was very much how they felt. Four in ten men and one in three women said it was somewhat how they felt, and 28 percent of the men and 34 percent of the women indicated it was not at all how they felt. One woman put it this way when we asked her what had changed most since her separation.

> The only thing that's really changed is that I don't have a man. I'd welcome and accept that any time. I'm used to having a man, going out to dinner or dancing. I miss that. I miss married life, but I'm sure I'll be married some time in the future. I like the responsibility of running a home. One of these days there will be a man in my life.

We sought to discover whether there was a link between circumstances in the previous marriage and attitudes toward remarriage. We found that attitudes toward remarriage are not related to the conditions of the old marriage. Disappointment in the erstwhile partner's role performance, marital quality in the final months, and who suggested the breakup are not connected with the person's propensity to desire remarriage.

What about current dating circumstances? How are they related to the desire for or the dread of remarriage? Among men, only the wish to date more often than they do is linked with a positive attitude toward remarriage. They are more likely to report that they would be happier married to the right person ($r = .19$), would marry for companionship ($r = .24$), and deny that they would never consider remarriage ($r = .20$) than men who are content with how often they date.

Among women, a positive attitude toward remarriage is tied to dating more often ($r = .26$ with never consider remarriage) and more frequent sexual encounters ($r = .24$ with never consider remarriage). Admitting that they would marry mostly for financial reasons is connected with having dated a greater number of men since separation ($r = .34$). Women who are currently dating only one man are more likely than women dating more than one man to say that marriage to the right person would make them happier than they are right now ($r = .24$).

Attitudes toward remarriage are undoubtedly developed in greatly varying contexts. For some, religious influences may be quite important. For others, the desire to demonstrate that one is attractive and desirable to another partner may heavily influence one's attitude about remarriage. Rejection of marriage as an institution is not common, but some individuals become soured on members of the opposite sex for a period of time following separation. In this sample, we find that our respondents are not heavily influenced by the circumstances they just left, although many in our case study interviews talked about being shy or leery of marriage. As one man said,

> I'll be wary, though, and extremely careful if I [remarry]. It certainly won't be for love alone. I'll make sure I can have some freedom that I need, and whoever I marry will have to be responsible—responsible with money—and of course faithful to me.

Attitudes about remarriage may also be influenced by one's self-concept as a parent. A 28-year-old man whose first marriage ended when his wife became involved with another man told the interviewer the following: "I think that I would like to [remarry] eventually. I enjoy being a father and a husband and I think I am good at it." The desire for or dread of remarriage is connected tenuously with current dating circumstances, indicating either that dating is used for mate selection purposes or else dating reassures men and women about the promise of a favorable remarriage in the future.

For those separated men and women who are wary of remarriage, cohabitation may be considered as an alternative or prelude to another marriage. Unmarried cohabitation has increased dramatically in the United States over the last two decades, but the extent to which this phenomenon has been influenced by separated and divorced individuals has not received as much attention as cohabitation by never-married young men and women. A recent demographic analysis of unmarried and married cohabitation (Spanier, 1983) found that a substantial proportion of unmarried couples involved men and women who have been previously married. It is clear from these data that cohabitation is becoming increasingly normative as a part of the process leading to remarriage. We asked our respondents how they would feel about living together before a remarriage. Half of the sample (55 percent of the men and 43 percent of the women) said they would prefer to live together; a third of the sample reported they would consider it (31 percent of the men and 36 percent of the women); only one in six of the respondents (14 percent of the men and 21 percent of the women) said they would be against it.

## Dating and Response to Breakup

Dating and sexual relations typically are begun during a period when the separated man or woman is both getting used to the breakup and starting anew. The process of leaving the old life behind is tied to the process of putting together a new life. Trouble accepting the breakup may undermine new dating relationships and contribute to negative attitudes toward remarriage. Conversely, new dating relationships may foster acceptance of the end of marriage and favorable attitudes toward remarriage, as well as dispel loneliness after separation. Although we cannot address these causal subtleties with out data, we can consider the link between emotional response to the breakup (acceptance and loneliness) and attitudes toward remarriage and dating after separation.

Loneliness since separation is marginally related to a desire to remarry. The more loneliness men have experienced, the more likely they are to say that they would remarry for reasons of companionship (r = .19); lonely women are more likely to report that marriage to the right person would make them happier than they are now (r = .27). Many of the men and women we interviewed told us that they simply do not want to be alone. The need for intimacy and companionship may squelch the reluctance to consider remarriage. Trouble accepting the end of marriage is characterized by an abiding attachment to the former spouse, obsessive review and preoccupation with the event, and a sense of regret about having done the wrong thing (see Chapter 4). Somewhat surprisingly, acceptance of the end of the old marriage is not related to desires for a new marriage among men and women.

Acceptance of the breakup, however, is connected consistently with the circumstances of dating after separation. Table 7.4 presents the associations of acceptance and loneliness with dating and sexual experience. The correlations presented demonstrate the importance of

**TABLE 7.4**
Correlations Between Circumstances of Dating
and Acceptance and Loneliness After Separation

|  | Acceptance | | Loneliness | |
| --- | --- | --- | --- | --- |
|  | Men | Women | Men | Women |
| Frequency of dating | .23 | .34 | ns | ns |
| How soon started dating | .27 | ns | ns | −.29 |
| Number of people dated since separation | ns | ns | −.18 | ns |
| Feel awkward about dating | −.26 | −.31 | .34 | .21 |
| Frequency of sexual relations | .17 | .16 | ns | ns |
| Want sex more often | −.26 | ns | ns | ns |
| Satisfaction with sexual relations | .26 | .43 | ns | −.17 |

NOTE: ns = correlation not significant at $p < .05$

dating circumstances in accepting the loss of the former partner and marriage and, subsequently, reducing loneliness after separation. Acceptance was greater for both men and women who were dating more frequently. Men who began dating more quickly after the separation were more accepting of the breakup than were those who waited to begin dating, but no similar significant relationship was found for women. As might be expected, those who were most accepting of the divorce felt the least awkward about dating, had a greater frequency of sexual relations, and were most satisfied with sexual relations. Wanting to date more often was not related to acceptance of the breakup. This is an indication that dating experiences help separated people get over the loss of the former partner and marriage rather than the converse—that nonaccepting people have less desire to date.

The pattern was somewhat less clear with regard to how loneliness is related to dating circumstances. Among women, those who were least lonely were more likely to have started dating soon after the separation. Women were also more likely to report a lower degree of loneliness if they had more current dating partners. Those who felt most awkward about dating were most likely to be lonely. Satisfaction with sexual relations among women were greater when loneliness was less prevalent. Among men, only the number of people dated since separation and awkward feelings about dating were related to loneliness. Men who were least lonely had the most partners since separation, and those who felt more awkward about dating were more likely to be lonely.

The data reported in this chapter give no indication that sexual activity is connected differentially to the emotional aftermath of separation among men and women. In both the connections of sexual experience to the perceived benefits of dating (Table 7.2) and to acceptance of the breakup and loneliness (Table 7.4), the results are very similar for men and women. We will see in the next chapter, however, that sexual experience is linked more closely to the emotional well-being of men after separation than women. Even in the case of women, however, the data reveal that frequency of sexual activity enhances rather than undermines emotional organization after separation. Unfortunately, we have no way of knowing the intimacy involved in the sexual encounters of the separated men and women in our study. Hetherington and associates (1978: 160) measured intimacy as "love in the sense of valuing the welfare of the other as much as one's own, a deep concern and willingness to make sacrifices for the other, and a strong attachment and desire to be near the other person." They found that under conditions of high intimacy, frequency of sex was positively related to happiness; while under conditions of low intimacy, frequency of sex was negatively related to happiness after separation. This negative consequence of casual sex was found in men as well as women.

The interrelationship between loneliness, sex, and dating is also found in selective accounts from our case studies. On the positive side, we interviewed a man who had been married for more than 20 years and consequently had been out of the social arena associated with dating. He had, nevertheless, established several dating relationships. We asked him whether he thought that being able to get back into the dating circle successfully and easily made it easier to adjust to being separated and single again. He replied,

> Oh definitely! I think it would be a lot harder to adjust if I wasn't dating. I think that's one of the main reasons that I really like the way my life is right now.

On the other side of the spectrum is a man in his thirties who described painfully for us the loneliness he feels:

> I just usually stay home here but like I said that gets lonely after a while, and I guess that's what bothers me the most. Being alone. Of course that wasn't as sudden as it might have been because my wife wasn't around much during the last months. . . . Life's been

pretty dull since we separated. I've been kind of scared to really start circulating.

Finally, we can highlight one case where a 44-year-old woman with five children complained about her loneliness and what she considered to be a rather awkward, even hostile, environment for doing something about it:

> I don't even have sexual freedom. Technically, I do, but just try to find it. You don't just go out to the street corner and say, "Why don't you come over and look at my etchings?" You can go to the Holiday Inn and pick someone up, but everybody knows it if you do. And there's still a double standard. A male can still get away with more than a female in that area. It's all this role playing, and it's all so phony.

## Summary

In this chapter we have found that dating plays an important role in postseparation adjustment, with virtually all men and women seeking dating opportunities. Those who have become involved in a particular dating relationship prior to separation, however, do not usually continue that relationship to remarriage. Rather, relationships established in the course of a waning marriage primarily serve the purpose of providing emotional support and intimacy as the termination of the marriage is logistically and psychologically negotiated. We also found that there are links between the propensity to consider remarriage and dating experience. In addition, some aspects of dating and sexual experiences are tied to acceptance and loneliness.

What have we learned about the dynamics of dating and sexual relations for separated men and women? First of all, our study illustrates a tremendous amount of diversity in experiences. Generalizations are difficult as circumstances vary so greatly. Some men and women seek out dating opportunities, and the social interactions that follow become important in facilitating adjustment to separation. Establishing new dating relations can greatly enhance one's self-esteem, particularly in showing the individual that he or she is still desirable to members of the opposite sex. Some men and women are eager to experience the freedom they have fantasized about during the marriage.

Still others have begun dating before the separation, but now the dating can be more open and "legitimate."

Some individuals, we pointed out, have difficulty establishing new relationships or are reluctant to do so. One may be soured on members of the opposite sex in general. Some persons still are emotionally attached to their spouse and find it difficult to date until they can reconcile the fact that the marriage is over. There are also those who are simply uncomfortable dating. They have been away from it for many years; they may not know how to go about it. Their field of eligibles may be small—or perhaps perceived as small. There is also some concern about how to meet people. Bars, parties, and singles clubs are often avoided. Among those who frequent such places or activities, many of our respondents report being pessimistic about finding suitable dating partners in these ways.

The connection between sex and dating is obviously different for previously married persons than it is for never-married persons. Thus, there is little that can be learned about this connection for separated men and women from the general courtship literature, which almost exclusively focuses on never-married individuals. As all separated or divorced persons are sexually experienced, we suspect that there is less focus on the novelty of sex than on the novelty of a new partner. Sex, we can speculate, is more likely to be considered earlier in dating relationships for our respondents; and there are some hints in our data that this is true.

Our respondents generally are positive about their sexual relationships after separation. There is an interesting contrast between reports of sexual dissatisfaction in marriage and sexual satisfaction after the breakup of the marriage. This confirms the suggestion that much sexual conflict and dissatisfaction in marriage is circumstantial—related to the interaction with the partner rather than to sexual dysfunctions that are attributable to physical or organic dysfunction.

Although some separated individuals are rather casual in their approach to sex following the dissolution of their marriage, there are others who are critical of this casual attitude in those they encounter and avoid such relationships. Some men and women have had sexual intercourse with only one person in their lifetime or at least with only one person in the last several years. To consider new sexual involvements now is scary and is approached gingerly. The role that dating relationships play in well-being and overall adjustment to separation is considered briefly in Chapter 8.

In the final chapter of the book we consider well-being. The physical and psychological consequences of separation are of keen interest to those experiencing the dissolution of a marriage as well as those who study families or practice family therapy. We now embark on the task of describing the current physical and emotional well-being of the men and women in our study and seeking predictors of well-being.

CHAPTER 8
# Well-Being

In Chapter 4 we characterized adjustment to the end of marriage as a stable and resilient pattern of life, separate from the previous marriage and partner and based on anticipation rather than memory (Goode, 1956; Hetherington et al., 1978; Hunt, 1966; Spanier and Casto, 1979; Weiss, 1975). In subsequent chapters, we described the disorganizing and integrating consequences of separation and divorce. We considered what changes and what stays the same in life when a marital breakup occurs. We examined social, psychological, and economic upheaval and found that such changes are not always traumatic nor do they always have the lasting effect that many would presume. In this chapter, we consider current physical and mental well-being. By well-being, we mean how people feel about themselves and their new lives. We begin the chapter with an overview of the physical and psychological well-being of the separated men and women in our study. Then, we examine how these subjective judgments of self and life are connected with the circumstances of ending a marriage and putting together a new life. We gather circumstances from each of the previous chapters (end of marriage, outsiders, emotional response to separation, continuing relations with partner, social support and participation, and dating) to discover what factors contribute to current well-being.

## Physical and Emotional Well-Being

The concept of well-being has come to serve as a general term in the literature on separation and divorce, encompassing such concepts as happiness (Glenn, 1981), trauma (Goode, 1956), adjustment (Kitson and Raschke, 1981), impact (Thompson, 1981), health status (Renne, 1971), and stress (Chiriboga et al., 1978). Several studies have assessed various aspects of well-being by considering a range of indicators (Bachrach, 1975; Bloom et al., 1978; Campbell et al., 1976; Weingarten, 1980). Dozens of studies conducted over the past decade have confirmed Goode's (1956) earlier finding that the majority of persons whose marriages are disrupted struggle and find their well-being tested, if not threatened.

In this study, we use a general concept of well-being as meaning contentment with oneself and life. We highlight from our data some of the physical health concerns that often follow separation. We also consider positive and negative affect, self-esteem, and life satisfaction as aspects of psychological well-being that may yield to the ordeal of marital breakup.

## PHYSICAL HEALTH

One's physical health can become a dramatic indicator of well-being, and our respondents often told us of the physical manifestations of their separation difficulties. One woman noted,

> I get terrible headaches, nausea, and blurred vision. I'm on welfare now since I can't work an eight-hour day. If it weren't for my health, I'd work. . . . I have to get a lot of rest or I get nervous. Then I'm a mess. . . . I get so restless.

Another woman, married five years and separated for only a few weeks, appeared distracted throughout the interview in her living room. Her television was on, but she wasn't watching it. She smoked continuously, was overweight, nervous, and repetitious. She acted confused, almost in a state of shock. During the interview, she revealed numerous instances of health-related problems including one particularly unusual incident.

> My blood pressure was up to 190/160 from worrying. I ended up in the emergency room. I was very upset. I would call my sister and cry. One day, while I was talking to her—I was really upset—I passed out. I stayed out for one-half to three-fourths of an hour. My sister got really upset and sent her husband over and called an ambulance. I didn't want to go to the hospital at first but they convinced me.

We read our respondents a list of common psychosomatic symptoms that people experience. For each condition mentioned, we asked them to tell the interviewer whether the condition had increased, remained the same, or decreased since the separation, or whether they never had

## TABLE 8.1
### Changes in Psychosomatic Symptoms

| | Percentage Reporting Condition | | | |
|---|---|---|---|---|
| | Increased | Remained the Same | Decreased | Never Had Condition |
| Sleeplessness | 25.4 | 27.3 | 22.9 | 24.4 |
| Nervousness | 27.3 | 26.8 | 33.2 | 12.7 |
| Being tired | 28.8 | 41.5 | 24.4 | 5.4 |
| Headaches | 13.7 | 30.7 | 27.3 | 28.3 |
| Indigestion | 13.2 | 31.2 | 18.5 | 37.1 |
| Allergies | 6.8 | 24.4 | 5.9 | 62.9 |
| Colds, flu, or fever | 7.8 | 61.0 | 16.6 | 14.6 |
| Irregularity | 7.4 | 41.2 | 13.2 | 38.2 |
| Moody spells | 29.4 | 32.3 | 28.4 | 8.8 |
| Trouble with periods (women only) | 15.7 | 40.0 | 12.2 | 32.2 |

the condition at all in the last couple of years. These responses are summarized in Table 8.1.

Among those who had ever experienced the various conditions mentioned, the plurality reported that the condition remained the same for all symptoms except nervousness. And for several symptoms (allergies; colds, flu, or fever; irregularity), only small portions of the sample reported increases. For most of the symptoms listed, however, there are significant numbers of individuals who reported changes in conditions, either increases or decreases. It is important to point out that changes occur in both directions—increasing for some individuals and decreasing for others. This finding is consistent with the conclusion stated in our discussion of relief and distress where we pointed out that for many individuals the end of marriage comes as a great relief and is the beginning of an improvement in mental and physical health.

The other side of the picture, however, is that many persons experienced increases in the conditions listed. More than one-fourth of the respondents reported increases in sleeplessness, being tired, and moody spells. More than one in eight respondents experienced increases in headaches and indigestion; 16 percent of the women reported increases in trouble with periods. The data demonstrate the close relationship between emotional and physical conditions and suggest that the transition from marriage to divorce has an important physical component for many men and women. Over all, women experienced greater fluctuation in symptoms since separation than men. Men were more likely to maintain an even keel while women were more prone to swings in symptoms, both up and down. Differences between men and women were evident particularly in nervousness, tiredness, headaches, and colds or flu.

We compiled an index of health for further analysis using the responses to the following three items: (1) Since your separation, would you say your health has been excellent, good, fair, or poor? (2) How many times have you seen a doctor within the past year? (3) Do you have any health or physical problems that bother you now? A high score indicates poor health. About one-third of the sample reported their health was excellent (33 percent). Health was reported as good by 43 percent, and 20 percent stated fair health. Only 4 percent considered their health poor since their separation; 14 percent reported poor health before the separation. Thus, there was improvement in reported health from before to after separation. Nevertheless, 44 percent of the respondents reported that they had health or physical problems that bothered them at the time of the interview. A doctor had not been seen at all within the last year by 11 percent; 45 percent had seen a doctor only once or twice; 27 percent had three to seven visits to a doctor; and 17 percent of the respondents had sought medical help at least eight times. In a national sample, adults under 65 averaged 2.4 visits to a physician each year (National Center for Health Statistics, 1983). In our recently separated sample, the mean is approximately one visit higher.

## PSYCHOLOGICAL WELL-BEING

Psychological responses to marital separation can be particularly debilitating since the symptoms that emerge can be difficult to interpret. Our respondents reported a variety of psychological distresses that adversely affected their well-being. A 22-year-old woman who married at age 16 because of pregnancy reported the following:

> My husband had always said I was stupid and unattractive, and that no one could like me. I got so I couldn't believe any one liked me, and I didn't have any real friends. I had a horrible inferiority complex. So I was always suspicious when someone was friendly.

Another woman, a 27-year-old mother of two, found little positive to report about her well-being after the divorce:

> I was in a hurt state of shock for three or four months. I didn't want to do anything. It hurt to even see the house. I was numb. I felt so alone even with my Mom. Detached. I'd go through periods of ignoring [her son]. Real extremes, like then I'd spank him and holler. I couldn't get interested in anything, even my old favorites like horses. I had no friends. I felt like people blamed me.

Others, however, reported that their well-being was enhanced by the breakup. A 46-year-old woman who had been married for 26 years and had three children reported positive well-being and displayed much confidence in her psychological state following the separation:

> I feel stronger. It's been a lot of work. I haven't done any wavering since my decision. I feel I did all I could. I know it's better for all concerned.

We offer, as a final example of the range of diversity in reaction, the comments of a 45-year-old man with two grown children. We asked him how he thought things would be for him in one year. His comments reflect a mixture of positive and negative well-being:

> I might be dead. That's always an option if other things don't work out. I really think that I will be happier, but you never know what will happen. . . . I know now that one minute I will feel good and free, and the next I will be alone and depressed.

We included several measures of psychological well-being in our study. The Bradburn scales (Bradburn and Caplovitz, 1965) are concerned with the affective experience of life rather than specific events or circumstances. A positive affect dimension taps pleasurable, favorable feelings about current existence. Respondents are asked how often in the past week they have experienced the following feelings: particularly excited or interested in something; that things were going your way; on top of the world; pleased about having accomplished something; and proud because someone had complimented you on something you had done. A negative affect dimension taps unpleasant, unfavorable feelings about current existence. Negative feelings include the following: so restless you couldn't sit long in a chair; upset because someone criticized you; very lonely and not close to other people; bored; and down or discouraged because nothing seemed to be going right for you. In general, the items tap feelings of pleasantness and activation and have a "generalized nowadays" time perspective. The two affect dimensions were found to be independent, and Bradburn used their balance as a measure of general happiness. Subsequent researchers recommend that the positive and negative affect scales be used separately, however, since they are related to different factors (Cherlin and Reeder, 1975; Robinson and Shaver, 1973).

About 10 percent of the men and women in our sample reported that they had not experienced the positive feelings listed above in the past week. About 20 percent of the sample reported that they had experienced the positive feelings once in the past week. The large majority of men and women (about 70 percent across items) had experienced the pleasurable feelings several times or often in the last week. The experience of negative feelings showed a reversed distribution, with the large majority of separated men and women reporting that they had unfavorable feelings only once or not at all in the past week.

We also assessed attitudes toward the self with the self-esteem scale (Rosenberg, 1965). A high score on the scale means that the person respects himself or herself and considers the self worthy.

Finally, we included two measures of life satisfaction. Some scholars differentiate between affective and cognitive evaluations of personal circumstance. Life satisfaction is a person's cognitive judgment of the current situation laid against a private standard of aspiration and needs. Affective and cognitive evaluations, however, are highly related and are both aspects of psychological well-being. One measure is the Cantril (1965) self-anchoring scale on which the respondent places his or her current situation on a ladder, the ends of which represent the best and the worst possible life. The other measure is a single item asking the respondent how, taking all things together, things are going for him or her these days. We also asked how things were just after the separation. Table 8.2 presents the results of both life evaluations. The vast majority of separated men and women (almost 80 percent) felt that life is at least pretty good these days. Only 11 percent of the men and 28 percent of the women recalled that life felt this good right after the separation.

We did a cross-tabulation between the two life evaluations to see how people had changed. Among men, only one saw his life as getting worse since just after the separation. Eleven percent of the men stayed the

## TABLE 8.2
### Life Evaluation Now and Just After the Separation (in percentages)

|                | Now | | After Separation | |
|---|---|---|---|---|
|                | Men | Women | Men | Women |
| Very good      | 32 | 30 | 3 | 7 |
| Pretty good    | 45 | 48 | 8 | 21 |
| So-so          | 19 | 15 | 30 | 20 |
| Not so good    | 3 | 4 | 32 | 24 |
| Not at all good | 1 | 3 | 27 | 28 |
| Total          | 100 | 100 | 100 | 100 |

same, most in the pretty good to very good categories even right after the separation. The remaining 88 percent of the men felt that life was brighter for them now. Among women, 7 percent felt that life had gotten bleaker, with half of them plunging from pretty or very good to not at all good. Among women 14 percent stayed the same, while 79 percent felt life had improved since just after the separation.

Looking over all the measures of well-being, roughly 20 percent of the separated men and women in our sample did not have a sense of well-being at the time of the interview. These people had a dim view of their current life, their health, and themselves. We found no differences between men and women on the measures of well-being. A history of research has shown that married persons generally report greater happiness and satisfaction with life than separated or divorced persons (Bradburn and Caplovitz, 1965; Robinson and Shaver, 1973; Wilson, 1967) although the results are sometimes reversed among women (Campbell et al., 1976). We compared our sample with a probability sample of 1000 persons from Central Pennsylvania interviewed in 1975. Both studies included the Bradburn and Cantril measures. Differences between the two samples were small, but consistent: Our separated sample reported lower well-being than the sample of the general population. Our purpose is not so much to compare our separated sample with a married sample or national norms, but rather to discover what factors in the process of ending a marriage and building a new life are connected with well-being after separation. That is, what accounts for diversity in well-being after marital breakup?

## TABLE 8.3
### Correlations Among Measures of Well-Being

|  |  | $Y_1$ | $Y_2$ | $Y_3$ | $Y_4$ | $Y_5$ |
|---|---|---|---|---|---|---|
| Poor health | $Y_1$ | | | | | |
| Self-esteem | $Y_2$ | −.29 | | | | |
| Positive affect | $Y_3$ | −.20 | .51 | | | |
| Negative affect | $Y_4$ | .29 | −.51 | −.36 | | |
| Life evaluation | $Y_5$ | −.33 | .42 | .42 | −.47 | |
| Life ladder | $Y_6$ | −.24 | .34 | .45 | −.45 | .64 |

As Table 8.3 indicates, our measures of well-being are interrelated. We view the measures as multiple indicators of the global construct of well-being. In the sections that follow, we gather significant variables from each of the previous chapters and explore their relationships to well-being. We consider circumstances from the end of marriage, outsiders, emotional response to the breakup, continuing relations with the partner, social support and participation, and dating. We will look for patterns across the measures of well-being, not isolated relationships. It is very unusual to find strong relationships between measures of perceived well-being and reports of most life conditions and behaviors (Andrews and Withey, 1976). Even though relationships are small, however, we can be confident in their existence if they occur across several measures of well-being.

## The End of Marriage

What is left behind in marriage and how the separation comes about may influence well-being after separation. Life may not seem whole without a fondly remembered partner or marriage. Ending a marriage may chip away at a person's self-esteem and sap energy. Marriage, as well, can undermine well-being and escape may lead to an expansion of self and life.

A 40-year-old woman recited the traditional complaints of temper, drunkenness, and running around against her husband. She told us about her marriage:

> Even from the beginning I feared his temper. I always had to
> analyze everything I said first to be sure it wouldn't make him

angry. I was in a trap, subconsciously, and wasn't really happy. . . . When we did fight, he never let the past drop. Always bringing things up in anger. He'd belittle me and make me feel small in front of my family. He'd say things that I could tell he loved me and, in the next breath, he'd be yelling. . . . I became more and more aware of what I was doing to myself over the years. I was making myself ill because I was so unhappy, but I didn't know how to handle it. I had been divorcing myself from him for years, to preserve myself. The hurt came years before, and it killed anything I felt. If it hadn't gone in stages, it would have broke me . . . [Now] I have to rid myself of all that resentment. I have to or I'll make myself ill.

Reflecting many of the circumstances described in this chronicle, we entered marital quality and commitment to marriage in the final months, length of time anticipating the separation, who suggested the divorce, and assignment of blame for the breakup into a series of multiple regressions with each measure of well-being as the criterion variable. We thought that higher marital quality and commitment, a short anticipation period, being on the receiving end of the suggestion to divorce, and externalizing the blame for the breakup would be related to lower levels of well-being after separation. A 29-year-old man who had been married eight years explained how anticipation of the end and withdrawal from the marriage before separation affected his well-being after the breakup:

> I was kind of surprised that I didn't feel depressed about it all. I have really felt great since then. I was down to about 150 pounds [before the separation] and now I'm back up to about 185. I had been thinking about divorce so long before it happened that it wasn't a really big adjustment for me. I'm pretty much of a loner anyway. I always have been, so I kind of enjoy being by myself a lot. I feel a lot better physically now.

The circumstances at the end of marriage accounted for only 1 percent to 10 percent of the variance in well-being. Among both men and women, all of the multiple correlations were statistically nonsignificant. Escaping a dismal marriage may be a relief, but the marriage may leave the separated person depleted in confidence and morale. Circumstances can pull well-being in both directions. It is also the case that measures of well-being may be appropriate to concurrent predictors but not more distal predictors (Bradburn, 1969).

Although the multiple correlations were not statistically significant, there were a couple of noteworthy patterns among the simple correlations. Among men, higher marital quality in the final months was related to better health ($r = -.24$) and higher positive affect ($r = .19$) after separation. These results are contrary to our prediction that leaving a relatively content and calm marriage would reduce well-being after separation. Perhaps it's more likely that the disconnection and squabbles of the final months take their toll. Among women, however, commitment to the marriage in its final months was linked with negative affect ($r = .21$) and lower life satisfaction ($r = -.21$ with ladder) after separation. Although marital quality and commitment to marriage are connected, they have different consequences for well-being after separation.

Finally, the assignment of blame was related to well-being among women. Placing the blame for the breakup outside of herself, either solely on the spouse or another person, was related negatively to self-esteem ($r = -.19$) and life satisfaction ($r = -.18$) after separation. Blame has been particularly important for women throughout our analysis. Women who blamed someone other than themselves for the breakup were less accepting of the end of marriage, more likely to still love and/or hate the partner, wanted less contact with the partner, would make an effort to avoid seeing him, avoid sensitive conversational topics, but would long for the former husband nevertheless. Although the connection ultimately of blame with well-being is tenuous, it is consistent with our other results.

## Outsiders

The difficulty of breaking out of a marriage and the costs incurred in the process may have consequences for well-being after separation. The disapproval of family and friends, financial upheaval, and legal barriers drain emotional and monetary reserves. Children also may be a resource to help sustain the separated mother or father through difficult times. There are other sources of well-being outside of the former partner and marital relationship besides children that can bolster the flagging spirit: The recollection of alternative sexual partners during marriage or a stable job and income. In this section we consider the connections of extramarital sexual partners, disapproval of others, legal barriers, children, and economics with well-being after marital breakup.

## EXTRAMARITAL SEXUAL PARTNERS

We predicted that the experience of extramarital coitus (EMC), the number of extramarital partners, higher reported quality of extramarital sexual relations, and lower feeling of guilt after engaging in EMC would characterize separated men and women with greater well-being after separation. No significant relationships were found, however, between extramarital sexual experience and well-being.

There are several reasons why EMC may have no effect on postmarital adjustment. Other variables such as disapproval by one's spouse and duration of the extramarital relationship may mediate the effects of EMC on postmarital well-being. EMC may have increased self-efficacy with respect to establishing new relationships, but other events may be more important during postmarital adjustment. Thus, the *total* experience of the extramarital relationship is likely to vary from respondent to respondent. Some respondents may have been affected positively, others negatively, and some not at all. In this event, the positive and negative effects across respondents would "cancel" each other out.

It is quite possible, however, that participation in EMC has *no* effect on postmarital well-being. First, it is possible that extramarital sexual relationships affect respondents only during the course of the extramarital relationship. Once the relationship has ended, respondents no longer may think about their extramarital involvement. It may be simply a passing experience. Given that respondents who engaged in EMC did not have different perceptions about their marital quality (during the months preceding marital separation) compared with respondents who did not engage in EMC, the preceding suggestion may have some validity. Second, EMC may have an effect on respondents only while their marriage is intact. They may experience increased emotional satisfaction, self-worth, guilt, or self-depreciation due to maintaining two concomitant relationships. Once their marriage has ended, many of these emotions may be dulled. Even if extramarital sexual experience is not related directly to global well-being after separation, it is related to the emotional response to the breakup—particularly among men. As we reported earlier, for men the presence, pleasure, and persistence of extramarital sexual relations are linked with greater acceptance of the breakup, less loneliness, and fewer thoughts of suicide after separation. As we shall discover, these feelings are in turn connected with well-being.

There is a significant relationship, however, between respondents' attitudes toward spouses' extramarital sexual relationships and two of the measures of postmarital well-being—satisfaction with life ($X^2 = 7.9$, 3 df, $p < .05$) —and self-esteem ($X^2 = 10.6$, 3 df, $p < .02$). Of the respondents reporting low satisfaction with life, 78 percent had strongly disapproved of their spouses' extramarital relationships. Similarly, a higher percentage of those in the low self-esteem category (73 percent) had strongly disapproved of their spouses' extramarital relationships than did those in the high self-esteem group (56 percent).

Respondents who strongly disapproved of their spouses' extramarital relationships probably were more deeply affected than respondents who did not disapprove as strongly. They may have felt hurt, angry, or deceived. Thus, this strong attitude of disapproval may have affected other aspects of the respondents' lives and influenced satisfaction with life and self-esteem. Furthermore, it is worth noting that no significant relationship was found between whether one's spouse engaged in EMC and respondent's postmarital well-being. Thus, it is not the mere occurrence of an extramarital relationship by one's spouse that affects postmarital adjustment but one's reaction to this occurrence.

## DISAPPROVAL AND INTRUSION OF OTHERS

Goode (1956) reports that disapproval of the divorce by family and friends is characteristic of women who experience high trauma after the breakup. He further suggests that it is not so much whether others approve or disapprove but whether or not they intrude on the decision to end the marriage. If others remain detached and neutral, the reaction to divorce will be less severe than if others try to advise or judge one way or the other.

We entered disapproval from parents, parents-in-law, and friends into a series of multiple regressions along with parental intrusion in the divorce decision and intrusion of parents-in-law. Intrusion was defined as encouraging the child or child-in-law to go through with it rather than just staying out of the decision. The five variables were regressed on each measure of well-being. None of the multiple correlations of disapproval and intrusion with well-being were worthy of remark. Even though disapproval was connected with the emotional response to breakup (trouble accepting the breakup, loneliness, and symptomatic distress), the judgments of others did not relate directly to general well-being after separation.

## LEGAL BARRIERS

In an earlier analysis (Spanier and Anderson, 1979), we used both cross-tabular and multivariate analyses to assess the impact of the legal system on the adjustment to marital separation. The analyses indicated that the problems encountered in the legal arena, as identified in the present study, do not significantly influence postseparation well-being. In other words, being encouraged by the lawyer to make a bigger issue of the separation or divorce than the respondent wanted to, having the lawyer advise the respondent to do things that might aggravate his or her spouse, lying or trumping up statements in the hearing to make sure the divorce was decreed, and the level of satisfaction with the legal process were not significantly associated with well-being after separation. Thus, although individuals who have gone through a divorce report numerous problems with the legal system, there is no evidence to suggest that such problems later influence their social-psychological adjustment.

## CHILDREN

Wrangles over custody and changes in accessibility to and closeness with children are part of marital breakup for many mothers and fathers. A woman whose 14-year-old son chose to live with his father tearfully described what the separation has meant to her:

> I fought a long, hard battle for the children's sake. I feel I've lost a child, my son, who lives with his father. . . . I want what's best for him, but he's torn between us. . . . I worry he's not getting the attention he needs. They go out a lot, and I think the children are neglected. I don't know what to do about it. I feel so powerless.

We considered whether the presence of children in the marriage, custody responsibilities, time spent with children, and changes in closeness with children since separation were related to well-being. We did not think the simple presence or absence of children in marriage would be connected with well-being after separation. Our results have shown repeatedly that children per se do not account for differences in the aftermath of separation among either men or women. The only exception was in the receipt of help from friends and relatives. Among former marital partners with children, however, the conditions of parenthood are likely to affect well-being after separation. We predicted that satisfaction with the custody arrangement and confidence that one can handle the responsibilities of custody would be tied to greater well-being. We also predicted that infrequent contact with children, dwindled contact since separation, and the desire for more time with children would be tied to lower well-being among fathers. Circumstances of reduced accessibility to children do not occur typically for mothers after separation. Finally, we predicted that the sense that one had drifted away from one's children would undermine well-being after separation among both mothers and fathers.

Among men, *none* of the child-related variables was a factor in well-being after separation. Neither the presence of children in the marriage nor the conditions of parenthood after separation was connected to well-being. Even longing for the children—a common form of loneliness among fathers—was unrelated to well-being.

The account among women was much different. Although there was no difference in the well-being of women with and without children, the experience of parenthood among mothers was tied strikingly to their well-being after separation. Among women with children (n = 66), satisfaction with the custody arrangement was unrelated to well-being; however, feeling that custody was a burdensome responsibility was connected consistently with well-being among mothers with custody (n = 63). Mothers who have problems with custody have lower self-esteem ($r = -.37$), lower positive affect ($r = -.40$), higher negative affect ($r = .28$), and lower life satisfaction ($r = -.28$ with global item and $-.32$ with ladder) than do mothers who do not feel custody is a burden. Mothers who spend more time with their children now than before separation report poorer health ($r = -.26$) than mothers who have not noticed much change in the amount of time they spend with their children. One woman put it this way:

> If I could get some relief from the kids, I think I could cope better. Mornings around here are the worst. The two girls are fighting and screaming from the minute they get out of bed. I just don't want to face it. I want to bury myself in bed and pretend it's not there.

Hetherington and her associates (1978) document the special circumstances of a woman alone with children. Mothers often feel trapped in a world of children and tormented by their own sons and daughters. Mothers in our study who reported an increase in closeness to their children since separation also reported higher self-esteem ($r = .36$), lower negative affect ($r = -.41$), and higher life satisfaction ($r = .22$) than mothers who reported that their relations with children have not changed or deteriorated since separation.

Women, then, typically must bear the consequences of sole responsibility for ever-present children after separation. Men with custody expressed similar distress in the qualitative interviews although their numbers were too few for quantitative analysis. We were surprised, however, that the changes in father-child relations with separation did not emerge as predictors of well-being.

## ECONOMICS

In Chapter 3 we considered the role of economics in the adjustment to marital separation. Given the importance of economics in parting, we were not surprised to find disturbances in well-being associated with economic hardship. A young unemployed mother of two children who had complained in the interview about her "spendthrift" husband started crying when she told the interviewer the following:

> He [ex-husband] sold his car, he's in debt again, so he comes over to use mine. I let him, but I resent it. It's hard on us, but we're trying to make ends meet; he's not even trying. . . . I guess I do resent being left so insecure financially when I've worked so hard to be careful. Here he is using my car, and not contributing anything. I guess I'm afraid he'll end up marrying someone else and we'll be left with nothing.

We wanted to know the relative contribution of socioeconomic factors to well-being after separation. There is evidence that the important dimensions are economic stability (Cherlin, 1979) and control over funds (Kohen et al., 1979) rather than actual income. An economic instability index was constructed from responses to the following three items: (1) How stable has your income been since your separation: very stable, somewhat stable, somewhat unstable, or very unstable? (2) Since your separation, would you say your financial status is better off than before, about the same as before, or worse off than before? (3) How about now? Do you feel a lot of financial strain, some financial strain, very little financial strain, or no financial strain at all? A high score reflected financial instability and strain. We also included employment status, occupation, education, and income as predictors of well-being.

Table 8.4 presents the results for all multiple regressions except those with poor health as the criterion variable. The health regressions are deleted because the multiple correlations were not statistically significant for either men or women. Among men, financial security and occupation were consistent contributors to well-being after separation. Actual income, education, and employment (although 88 percent of men were employed) were not as important. Among women, financial security and education were consistent contributors to well-being after separation. Income, occupation, and employment (with 73 percent of the women employed) did not contribute at all to well-being among women.

Women were somewhat more likely than men to decline in financial terms and to experience financial strain after separation, although financial security was important to the well-being of both men and women. Actual income was not the critical economic circumstance.

We thought perhaps occupation emerged as important for men while education emerged for women because discrimination in the labor market may make education a better indicator of socioeconomic class than occupation among women. In our sample, however, the correlation between education and occupation was about .65 for both men and women. As we reported earlier, education also was connected with greater acceptance of the breakup and less loneliness after separation among women but not among men. For many women, education and training ease the upheaval and distress of ending a marriage. The independence education provides may have allowed women to leave the marriage in the first place (Cherlin, 1979; Nye, 1979).

Actual employment did not make much of a difference in well-being, although the sample was heavily biased toward the employed—especially among men. The majority of women who were not working were home taking care of the children or not working by choice, rather than unable to get a job. These women, then, apparently did not sense a deprivation from paid work; and their well-being was comparable to those women who were employed after separation.

## TABLE 8.4
## Multiple Regressions of Economic Variables on Well-Being Measures for Males (Females)

| Predictor Variables | Self-Esteem | | Positive Affect | | Negative Affect | | Life Satisfaction | | Life Ladder | |
|---|---|---|---|---|---|---|---|---|---|---|
| | Simple r | Beta | Simple r | Beta | Simple r | Beta | Simple r | Beta | Simple r | Beta |
| Financial instability | −.13 (−.10) | −.19 (−.11) | .01 (−.33**) | −.05 (−.32**) | .14 (.16) | .15 (.16) | −.36** (−.33**) | −.27* (−.32**) | −.36** (−.44**) | −.35** (−.42**) |
| Employment | .03 (.09) | −.08 (.01) | .01 (−.15) | .03 (−.18) | −.03 (.01) | .05 (.09) | .29** (−.06) | .16 (−.13) | .24** (−.09) | .09 (−.17) |
| Occupation | .37** (.20) | .31 (−.01) | .25** (.11) | .34 (−.09) | −.34** (−.14) | −.46** (.11) | .30** (.10) | .44** (−.16) | .34** (.09) | .44** (−.24) |
| Education | .26* (.31**) | .09 (.32*) | .19* (.14) | .01 (.24) | −.13 (−.26**) | .15 (−.35**) | .05 (.20**) | .18 (.33**) | .13 (.21**) | −.07 (.39**) |
| Income | .22** (.04) | .01 (−.03) | −.02 (.06) | −.21 (.01) | −.19* (−.06) | .02 (−.02) | .27** (.13) | −.04 (.07) | .23** (.19*) | −.10 (.12) |
| n | 91 (114) | | | | | | | | | |
| Multiple R | .41 (.33) | | .30 (.40) | | .39 (.32) | | .51 (.42) | | .51 (.53) | |
| R² | .17 (.11) | | .09 (.16) | | .15 (.10) | | .25 (.18) | | .26 (.28) | |
| F | 2.7* (1.6) | | 1.3 (2.5*) | | 2.5* (1.5) | | 4.6** (2.8*) | | 4.8** (5.2**) | |

\* p < .05
\*\* p < .01

## Response to the Breakup

We have defined acceptance as the extent to which a person accepts separation and divorce as an inevitable decision that is correct rather than a regretful mistake.

Examples of several different responses to the breakup highlight how parting and well-being are interrelated. A 36-year-old, career-oriented man illustrates a rather positive response.

> After the divorce from my wife I felt freedom, a sense of starting over emotionally, of having a less complicated life. So it has been pretty easy, but it could have been harder if she had objected to the divorce.

Mixed feelings were reported by a 26-year-old woman who was married only two years before the divorce:

> I had really mixed feelings. You know, you're only supposed to get married once. I was supposed to make it work. But I wasn't getting any help working it out, can't do it by yourself. And I worried about how the families would feel. But I knew I had to do something. I was a wreck, down to 86 pounds . . . I was nervous, always shaking inside, very unsure.

Finally, there are those—like the 37-year-old man quoted below—whose responses reflect the trauma of separation which often adversely affects well-being for some time after the breakup.

> At first I was pissed off, hurt, mad. I felt like I wanted to kill someone. I was really in bad shape. I really got depressed, to the point of having suicidal thoughts. I just couldn't function. I'm just now getting to where I don't mind getting up in the morning to face a new day.

The scale we used to measure acceptance includes a range of feelings about the end of marriage—disbelief, regret, preoccupation with the former partner, relief, sense of tragedy. Throughout our study, acceptance has been connected with both the circumstances of ending a marriage and the circumstances of organizing a new life.

Acceptance of the breakup was related to well-being after separation among both men and women. Those persons who were more accepting of the end of marriage had higher self-esteem (r = .34 for men and .24 for women), lower negative affect (r = −.22 for men and −.32 for women), and higher life satisfaction (r = .18 for men and .26 for women with global item) than did men and women who were having trouble accepting the breakup. Women with higher acceptance also had higher positive affect (r = .20) and higher ratings on the life ladder (r = .39). There is little doubt that feelings about the breakup enhance or undermine psychological well-being after separation.

Bouts of loneliness since separation were related to well-being, particularly among women. Lonely women had lower self-esteem (r = −.32), positive affect (r = −.28), and life satisfaction (r = −.33 with global item and −.38 with ladder); they also had higher negative affect (r = .39). Lonely men also had lower life satisfaction (r = −.24) and higher negative affect (r = .19), although the negative affect scale includes an item on loneliness which exaggerates the connection.

The specific forms of loneliness (boredom, longing for the husband or someone else, and social isolation) were not linked consistently with well-being among women. Among men, boredom and a sense of social isolation undermined well-being. Bored men had poorer health (r = .20), lower self-esteem (r = −.26) and higher negative affect (r = .34) although, again, the negative affect scale includes an assessment of current boredom. Men who felt socially isolated had lower self-esteem (r = −.36), positive affect (r = −.25), and life satisfaction (r = −.21); they also had higher negative affect (r = .18).

Weiss (1975) says that the pain and distress of separation are due to persistent attachment to the partner and loneliness. Our data clearly show that difficulty giving up the erstwhile partner and marriage and bouts of loneliness tear away at well-being after separation.

Many of the separated men and women we talked with described the almost overwhelming confusion and distress of the first few weeks after separation. A 28-year-old man who had been married for seven years before the separation experienced a dramatic plunge in his overall well-being, but then seemed to recover after the initial shock.

> At first I wasn't able to concentrate at all and felt sort of disoriented. I essentially did nothing for awhile. It's getting better now, but I'm still not back to capacity. At least, I'm back moving and active. I've had a change in attitude toward work lately. When we were living together, I was blaming my work all the time for

the problems. I felt like I was working on a time bomb. I really like the slower pace that I have now.

This change in well-being as life progressed was characteristic of many of our respondents. We found no connection, however, between time since separation and well-being in our quantitative data. There were very few in our sample, however, who were newly separated. Many people found their well-being took a turn upward only to fall again. A young women separated several months described it this way:

> I was feeling pretty good till about a month ago. Then it seemed to hit me like a sledge hammer. I've felt so depressed, so alienated, so lonely.

## The Partners After Marriage

If difficulty in giving up the former partner and marriage weakens well-being, then continuing ties with the partner after separation may also work against physical and psychological health. We considered the desire for contact with the former partner, actual contact, rapport between partners, and feelings toward the partner. With a series of multiple regressions, we regressed desire for contact (ranged from not even speaking to the partner to having sex), topics discussed in conversation (ranged from the mundane to the personal), and topics avoided in conversation (ranged from widely acceptable to the more sensitive) on each measure of well-being. We addressed feelings toward the partner separately.

All of the multiple correlations of relationship with partner variables and well-being were negligible. Continuing ties with the former partner contributed little to well-being after separation. There were some noteworthy patterns, however, among the simple correlations even if the multiple correlations were not statistically significant. Among men, the desire to maintain close contact with the former wife was related to negative affect ($r = -.21$) after separation and lower satisfaction with life ($r = -.21$) after separation. Similarly, among both men and women, actual contact with the former partner was connected with negative affect ($r = .17$ for men and .16 for women) and with lower life satisfaction ($r = -.20$ for men and $-.24$ for women with global item; and $-.23$ for men and $-.19$ for women with ladder). The desire for contact and actual contact can be interpreted as an abiding attachment to the former partner.

Among women, rapport with the former husband also was connected with well-being after separation. Avoiding personal and sensitive topics in conversation was related to poor health ($r = .18$), lower self-esteem ($r = -.26$) and negative affect ($r = .24$). If partners are going to maintain a partnership after marriage, it is healthier—at least from the woman's perspective—if former marital partners are able to discuss joys and woes freely rather than skirt sensitive issues. The most sensitive issue is new romantic relationships.

Feelings toward the old partner were entered as dummy variables into a series of multiple regression analyses. Current feelings toward the old partner (love, like, no feeling, and love/hate) were unrelated to well-being among men. Among women, multiple correlations with self-esteem (.34), positive affect (.29), negative affect (.33), life satisfaction (.35), life ladder (.43) were noteworthy and significant at $p < .05$ level. In every case, it was the women who had strong ambivalent feelings about their husbands (both love and hate) who had a lower sense of well-being. This only represents 14 percent of the women, so the distribution is very skewed and should be considered cautiously. In looking at the simple correlations of ambivalence versus other feeings with well-being, we find the mixture of love and hate connected with lower self-esteem ($r = -.32$), lower positive affect ($r = -.24$), and lower life ladder ($r = -.31$). Women were more prone than men to combine love and hate; in fact, strong ambivalence was the most common feeling expressed about husbands at the time of separation. This ambivalence does not have a dramatic effect on well-being if it persists into the aftermath of separation, but it does take its toll.

## Social Support and Participation

To what degree does social support and participation enhance or detract from well-being? We found examples in our case study interviews of support that seemed to promote well-being, support that seemed to hurt well-being, and support that was forthcoming but unimportant for well-being. A young woman who had been married five years and couldn't understand why her husband wanted a divorce is an example of the latter situation:

> No. My family's been really good, and his too. They don't understand what the problem is, either. And I have a divorced friend at work who has really been helpful. But it doesn't seem to make a big difference. I still get so depressed.

Previous research has found the support of others to be crucial during life transitions. In this section, we consider several dimensions of social support: service support from friends and relatives, financial support from friends and relatives, moral support from friends and relatives, and attentiveness. Attentiveness means that the people closest to the respondent during marriage have increased their offers of help, discussion of personal problems, and visiting behavior since separation. Social participation includes average contact with the three people closest to the respondent at the time of the interview, number of close friends made since separation, and the desire for more friends.

Among men, there was no case in which one aspect of social support and participation was connected with well-being in any consistent way. The only remarkable pattern was the connection of positive affect with several aspects of social support and participation. Positive affect was linked with average contact ($r = .21$), attentiveness ($r = .22$), number of friends made since separation ($r = .24$), financial support ($r = .35$), and emotional support ($r = .32$). Previous research has also found positive affect to be related positively to social participation (Bradburn and Caplovitz, 1965). On the other hand, service support was related to negative affect ($r = .24$), especially if the support came from one's parents ($r = .25$) or siblings ($r = .23$).

There were few connections, either, of social support and participation with well-being among women. Average contact, attentiveness, service support, and emotional support were unrelated to well-being after separation. The more sources of friends and relatives from whom women received financial aid, however, the lower the self-esteem ($r = -.24$) and the higher their negative affect ($r = .20$). We know from a previous chapter that financial aid is tied to financial instability and strain. This is further confirmation of the importance of financial security and control.

The number of close friends made since separation and the desire for more friends were related to well-being among women. Women who made more friends had higher positive affect ($r = .26$) and life satisfaction ($r = .25$ with global item and .21 with ladder) than women who had not made as many close friends since separation. Wanting more friends meant lower self-esteem (r = −.19), positive affect (r = −.21), and life satisfaction (r = −.26 with global item and −.25 with ladder); negative affect was also higher (r = .25) among women who would like more friends. This confirms the threat of loneliness to well-being, particularly among women.

Over all, social support has little connection with well-being. We have to remember, however, that while support can ease distress, it is also offered because the separated person is in need of help. Receiving help and attention can be humbling and add to the distress of separation. The results on social participation are somewhat more conclusive, but hardly striking. At best, they serve to validate our other evidence that loneliness gnaws at well-being. The relationships of social support and participation with well-being might be stronger if we knew the content of support and the intimacy involved in ties to others.

## Dating, Sex, and Remarriage

Among men and women who are not yet remarried, dating experience was not related to well-being in any consistent way. Frequency of dating, timing of dating after separation, number of people dated since separation, and number currently seeing were not connected with well-being. There were some stray and small associations between a circumstance of dating and a single measure of well-being, but no consistent pattern of relationship of any magnitude. The only exception was awkwardness about dating. Among both men and women, feeling awkward was tied with lower self-esteem (r = −.18 for men and −.38 for women), high negative affect (r = .30 for men and .22 for women), and lower life satisfaction (r = −.18 for men and −.21 for women). It is impossible to say what the causal connections are between being socially awkward and having negative evaluations of oneself and one's life. The dearth of relationships between dating experience and well-being is unexpected. We would have predicted that dating contributes to a sense of well-being. Yet, as with social participation in the previous section, we do not know the emotional content of the dating encounters. If dating does not introduce intimacy or ease loneliness, then it probably does not enhance well-being either.

Table 8.5 demonstrates that sexual experience after separation did have a consistent link with well-being, particularly among men. As Weiss (1975) suggests, sex reassures men and bolsters their confidence

**TABLE 8.5**
Correlations Between Sexual Experience After Separation and Well-Being

|  | Frequency of Sex | | Want More Sex | | Satisfaction with Sex Relations | |
|---|---|---|---|---|---|---|
|  | Men | Women | Men | Women | Men | Women |
| Poor health | ns | ns | ns | ns | ns | ns |
| Self-esteem | .25 | ns | −.24 | ns | .38 | ns |
| Positive affect | .37 | ns | −.20 | ns | .20 | .17 |
| Negative affect | −.19 | ns | .18 | ns | −.37 | −.18 |
| Life evaluation | ns | .21 | .28 | ns | .28 | ns |
| Life ladder | ns | .17 | .17 | ns | ns | .25 |

NOTE: ns = not significant at $p < .05$

and contentment. Current sexual experience does not detract from well-being among women, but sex is not the boon to them that it is to men. Recall that sexual activity was also related to acceptance of the breakup.

Remarriage signifies that intimacy has, indeed, entered life again. Remarriage—either being already remarried or having definite plans to remarry—was connected with greater well-being among the men and women in our sample. Divorced people who are committed to a new marriage had a higher positive affect ($r = .21$ for men and .31 for women) and higher life satisfaction ($r = .30$ for men and .28 for women with global item and .23 for men and .38 for women with life ladder) than those who had no plans for remarriage. Men who were involved in a new marriage also were less apt to report poor health ($r = −.17$) and negative affect ($r = −.18$) than men without plans for remarriage.

Among those who had not already remarried, the attitude toward marriage was not tied to well-being. The only exception was among women. Women who said that they would be willing to marry for financial reasons had lower self-esteem ($r = −.16$), lower positive affect ($r = −.23$), higher negative affect ($r = .26$), and lower life satisfaction ($r = −.26$ with global item and $−.23$ with ladder) than women who did not feel this way. Once again, monetary worries undermine the well-being of women.

## Summary

There is no doubt that marital separation and its aftermath can affect a man or woman in most any way. We have learned that it is not really possible to predict what the sequel to separation will be like from one individual to the next. Many respondents are surprised themselves how easy the adjustment is, and others are dismayed, upset, depressed, or discouraged by what they are confronted with. We found that, overall, about 20 percent of the separated men and women in our study are discontented with themselves and life and/or suffer troublesome health problems. The vast majority appear to have gone on with their new life after separation with some degree of pleasure and enthusiasm.

Our search for factors that would help us predict well-being after separation has been extensive. Although experience is diverse, we can draw some conclusions. We found no connection between current well-being and circumstances of the impending separation or actual breakup. For most, whatever happened then—the months of bickering, being left by the partner, the intrusion of others, extramarital sexual partners, legal barriers—seems not to affect well-being seriously. It is the current circumstances of picking up the pieces and moving on that threaten or assure well-being.

We do not mean that the marriage did not bequeath something to the separated man or woman. Their ability to accept the end of the marriage contributes largely to well-being after separation. Among both men and women, persistent attachment to and contact with the former marital partner shadows well-being. Women have complicated connections between their continuing ties with the erstwhile husband and well-being. Well-being is enhanced if women can broach sensitive topics with the husband of old, but is undermined if they still harbor strong feelings of love and hate or blame their husband for the breakup.

Loneliness chips away at well-being, especially among women. Women who have not made many close friends since separation want more friends, report bouts of loneliness, and are more dissatisfied with themselves and their lives. We did not find any evidence that dating is connected with well-being although feeling awkward about dating is related negatively to positive evaluations of self and life among both men and women. Particularly among men, sexual activity bolsters confidence, morale, and contentment. Finally, commitment to a new marriage is tied to well-being among men and women.

Economic security is linked closely with well-being after separation. This is true among both men and women, although the consequences of economic instability are more insidious among women. For example, receiving financial aid from family and friends undermines well-being, as does the attitude that they would marry again mainly for financial reasons. A higher level of education is related to well-being among women, while occupation is an important socioeconomic factor among men.

Women also suffer the consequences of single-parenthood. For many mothers, the burden of custody and the growing amount of time they must spend with their often recalcitrant children wear away at well-being.

Just because we found no connection between many of the factors considered throughout the book and well-being does not mean that these circumstances have no ultimate consequences for separated men and women. Our measures of well-being are subjective judgments and, therefore, are more likely to be related to other emotional or cognitive appraisals than to behavioral or objective reports. That is, such objective reports as average contact with intimates or dating frequency are not as likely to be tied to subjective well-being. Circumstances that occurred in the past are not as likely as concurrent conditions to influence well-being directly. Well-being is also a global concept, and we would not expect it to be as closely related to separation circumstances as measures that are more specific to the divorce experience—for instance, acceptance of the breakup is more closely related to separation circumstances. Many circumstances probably influence well-being indirectly through factors such as acceptance. Other circumstances are simply too complex and diverse for us to capture them quantitatively. In fact, when we are faced with the richness and variety of experience shared with us by the separated men and women in our study, we feel somewhat presumptuous making any general statements.

We have tried throughout the book to portray the process of bringing a marriage to an end and starting anew. Experience accrues as people marry, falter, cherish and tolerate outsiders, separate, respond to a breakup, and go on in a new life. We hope we have conveyed this sense of time and transition.

# References

ABEL, R. L. (1973) "Lawbooks and books about law." Stanford Law Review 26: 175–227.
ACKERMAN, C. (1963) "Affiliations: structural determinants of differential divorce rates." American Journal of Sociology 69: 12–20.
ALBRECHT, S. L. (1980) "Reactions and adjustments to divorce: differences in the experiences of males and females." Family Relations 29: 59–68.
ANDREWS, F. M. and S. B. WITHEY (1976) Social Indicators of Well-Being. New York: Plenum Press.
ANSPACH, K. F. (1976) "Kinship and divorce." Journal of Marriage and the Family. 38: 323–330.
ATHANASIOU, R., and R. SARKIN (1974) "Premarital sexual behavior and postmarital adjustment." Archives of Sexual Behavior 3: 207-255.
BACHRACH, L. L. (1975) "Marital status and mental disorder: an analytical review." DHEW Publication (ADM) 75–217. Washington, DC: U.S. Government Printing Office.
BANDURA, A. (1977) Social Learning Theory. Englewood Cliffs, NJ: Prentice-Hall,
BEAL, E. W. (1979) "Children of divorce: a family systems perspective." Journal of Social Issues 35: 140–154.
BELL, R. R., S. TURNER, and L. ROSEN (1975) "A multivariate analysis of female extramarital coitus." Journal of Marriage and the Family 37: 375–384.
BERNARD , J. (1972) The Future of Marriage. New York: World.
——— (1956) Remarriage: A Study of Marriage. New York: Dryden Press.
BERSCHEID, E., J. DION, E. WALSTER, and G. W. WALSTER (1971) "Physical attractiveness, and dating choice: a test of the matching hypothesis." Journal of Experimental Social Psychology 7: 173–189.
BLAKE, N. M. (1962) The Road to Reno: A History of Divorce in the United States. New York: Macmillan.
BLOOM, B. L., S. J. ASHER, and S. W. WHITE (1978) "Marital disruption as a stressor: a review and analysis." Psychological Bulletin 85: 867–894.
BLOOM, B. L., S. W. WHITE and S. J. ASHER (1979) "Marital disruption as a stressful life event," in G. Levinger and O.C. Moles (eds.) Divorce and Separation: Contexts, Causes, and Consequences. New York: Basic Books.
BOWLBY, J. (1969) Attachment and Loss, Vol. I: Attachment. New York: Basic Books.
BRADBURN, N. (1969) The Structure of Psychological Well Being. Chicago: Aldine Publishing.
——— and CAPLOVITZ, D. (1965) Reports on Happiness. Chicago: University of Chicago Press.

BROWN, P. (1974)"A study of women coping with divorce," in D.G. McGuigan (Ed.) New Research on Women and Sex Roles. University of Michigan: Center for Continuing Education.

―――― B. J. FELTON, V. WHITEMAN and R. MANELA (1980) "Attachment and distress following marital separation." Journal of Divorce 3: 303–317.

BUKSTEL, L. H., G. D. ROEDER, P. R. KILMAN, J. LAUGHLIN, and W. M. SOTILE (1978) "Projected extramarital sexual involvement in unmarried college students." Journal of Marriage and Family 40: 337–340.

CAMPBELL, A., P. E. CONVERSE, and W. L. RODGERS (1976) The Quality of American Life. New York: Russell Sage Foundation.

CANTRIL, H. (1965) The Patterns of Human Concerns. New Brunswick: Rutgers University Press.

CHERLIN, A. (1979) "Work life and marital dissolution," in G. Levinger and D.C. Moles (eds.) Divorce and Separation: Contexts, Causes, and Consequences. New York: Basic Books.

―――― and L. G. REEDER (1975) "The dimensions of psychological well-being." Sociological Methods and Research 4: 189–214.

CHIRIBOGA, D. A. (1977) Marital Separation: A Study of Stress. Symposium presented at the Annual Meeting of the Western Psychological Association, Seattle.

―――― and L. CUTLER (1979) "Stress responses among divorcing men and women." Journal of Divorce 1: 95–106.

CHIRIBOGA, D. A. and M. THURNHER (1980) "Marital lifestyles and adjustment to separation" Journal of Divorce 3: 379–390.

CHIRIBOGA, D. A., J. ROBERTS, and J. A. STEIN (1978) "Psychological well-being during marital separation.' Journal of Divorce 2: 21–36.

CHIRIBOGA, D. A., A. COHO, J. A. STEIN, and J. ROBERTS (1979) "Divorce, stress and social support: a study of helpseeking behavior." Journal of Divorce 3: 121–135.

CHRISTENSEN, H. T. (1958) Marriage Analysis. New York: The Ronald Press.

CRONBACH, L. J. (1951) "Coefficient alpha and the internal structure of tests." Psychometrika 16: 297–334.

CUBER, J. F. (1969) "Adultery: reality versus stereotype," in G. Neubeck (ed.) Extramarital Relations. New Jersey: Prentice-Hall.

―――― and P. B. HARROFF (1965) Sex and the Significant Americans. New York: Pelican Books.

DEAN, D. G. and G. B. SPANIER (1974) "Commitment: an overlooked variable in marital adjustment?" Sociological Focus 7: 113–118.

――――and B. S. BRESNAHAN (1969) "Ecology, friendship patterns, and divorce: a research note." Journal of Marriage and the Family 31: 462–463.

DION, K., E. BERSCHEID and E. WALSTER (1972) "What is beautiful is good." Journal of Personality and Social Psychology 24: 285–290.

DUNCAN, O. D. (1975) Introduction to Structural Equation Models. New York: Academic Press.

EDWARDS, J. (1973) "Extramarital involvement: fact and theory." Journal of Sex Research 9: 210–224.

FREDERICO, J. (1979) "The marital termination period of the divorce adjustment period." Journal of Divorce 3: 93–106.

FREUND, J. (1974) "Divorce and grief." Journal of Family Counseling 2: 40–46.

FURSTENBERG, F. F., Jr. (1982) "Conjugal succession; reentering marriage after divorce," in P.B. Baltes and O.G. Brim (eds.) Life Span Development and Behavior, Vol. 4 New York: Academic Press.
—— and G. B. SPANIER, (1980) "Marital dissolution and generational ties." Presented at the annual meeting of the Gerontological Society, San Diego, CA.
FURSTENBERG, F. F. Jr., C. W. NORD, J. L. PETERSON, and N. ZILL (1983) "The life course of children of divorce: marital disruption and parental contact." American Sociological Review 48: 656–668.
GLASS, S. P. and T. L. Wright (1977) "The relationship of extramarital sex, length of marriage, and sex differences on marital satisfaction and romanticism: Athanasiou's data reanalyzed." Journal of Marriage and the Family 39: 691–703.
GLENN, N. D. (1981) "The well-being of persons remarried after divorce." Journal of Family Issues 2: 61–75.
—— and C. N. WEAVER (1979) "Attitudes toward premarital, extramarital, and homosexual relations in the U.S. and the 1970's." Journal of Sex Research 15: 108–119.
—— (1978) "A multivariate multisurvey study of marital happiness." Journal of Marriage and the Family 40: 269–282.
GLICK, P. C. and A. J. NORTON (1976) "Number, timing and duration of marriages and divorces in the U.S.: June 1975." Current Population Reports, Series P-20, No. 297. Washington, DC: U.S. Government Printing Office.
GLICK, P. C. and G. B. SPANIER (1980) "Married and unmarried cohabitation in the U.S." Journal of Marriage and the Family 42: 19–30.
GOETTING, A. (1979) "The normative integration of the former spouse relationship" Journal of Divorce 2: 395–414.
GOODE, W. J. (1956) After Divorce (Women in Divorce) New York: The Free Press.
—— (1949) "Some problems in post divorce adjustment." American Sociological Review 14: 394–401.
GOTTMAN, J. M. (1979) Marital Interaction. New York: Academic Press.
HARMSWORTH, H. and M. MINNIS (1955) "Non-statutory causes of divorce: the lawyer's point of view." Marriage and Family Living 17: 316–321.
HARVEY, J. H., G. L. WELLS, and M. D. ALVAREZ (1978) "Attribution in the context of conflict and separation in close relationships," in J.H. Harvey et al. (eds.) New Direction in Attribution Research, Vol. 2. Hillsdale, NJ: Lawrence Erlbaum.
HETHERINGTON, E. M., M. COX and R. COX (1978) "The aftermath of divorce," in J.H. Stevens, Jr. and M. Mathews (eds.) Mother-Child, Father-Child Relations. Washington, DC: National Association for the Education of Young Children.
—— (1976) "The aftermath of divorce." Presented at the Annual Meeting of the American Psychological Association, Washington, DC.
HILL, C. T., Z. RUBIN, and L. A. PEPLAU (1979) "Breakups before marriage: the end of 103 affairs," in G. Levinger & O. C. Moles (eds.) Divorce and Separation: Contexts, Causes, and Consequences. New York: Basic Books.
HOLMES, T. S. and R. H. RAHE (1967) "The social readjustment rating scale." Psychosomatic Research 11: 213–218.
HULTSCH, D. and J. PLEMONS (1979) "Life events and life span development," in P.B. Baltes and O. Brim (eds.) Life Span Development and Behavior, Vol. 2. New York: Academic Press.
HUNT, M. (1974) Sexual Behavior in the 1970's. Illinois: Playboy Press.

—— (1966) The World of the Formerly Married. New York: McGraw-Hill.
JOHNSON, R. E. (1970) "Some correlates of extramarital coitus." Journal of Marriage and the Family 32: 449-456.
KELLEY, H. H. (1979) Personal Relationships: Their Structure and Processes. Hillsdale, NJ: Lawrence Erlbaum.
KINSEY, A. C., W. B. POMEROY, and C. E. MARTIN (1948) Sexual Behavior in the Human Male. Philadelphia: Saunders Co.
—— and P. H. GEBHARD (1953) Sexual Behavior in the Human Female. Philadelphia: Saunders Co.
KITSON, G. C. (1982) "Attachment to the spouse in divorce: a scale and its application." Journal of Marriage and the Family 44: 379-393.
—— and H. J. RASCHKE (1981) "Divorce research: what we know, what we need to know." Journal of Divorce 4: 1-37.
KITSON, G. C. and M. B. SUSSMAN "Marital complaints, demographic characteristics, and symptoms of mental distress in divorce." Journal of Marriage and the Family, 1982, 44: 87-101.
—— (1976) "The process of marital separation and divorce: male and female similarities and differences." Case Western Reserve University. (unpublished)
—— (1974) "Unpublished interview schedule," Case Western Reserve University.
KITSON, G. C., R. N. MOIR, and P. R. MASON (1982) "Family social support in crisis; the special case of divorce." American Journal of Orthopsychiatry 52: 161-165.
KOHEN, J. A., C. A. BROWN, and R. FELDBERG (1979) "Divorced mothers: the costs and benefits of female control," in G. Leginger and O.C. Moles (eds.) Divorce and Separation: Contexts, Causes, and Consequences. New York: Basic Books.
KOO, H. P. and C. M. SUCHINDRAN (1980) "Effects of children on women's remarriage prospects." Journal of Family Issues 1: 497-515.
KRAUS, S. (1979) "The crisis of divorce: growth promoting or pathogenic." Journal of Divorce 3: 107-119.
LACHMAN, M. (1977) "Dating: a coping strategy during marital separation." Presented at the annual meeting of the Western Psychological Association, Seattle.
LEICHTER, J. J. and W. E. MITCHELL (1967) Kinship and Case Work. Hartford: Communication Printers.
LERNER, R. M. and C. D. RYFF (1978) "Implementation of the lifespan view of human development: the sample case of attachment," in P. B. Baltes (ed.) Life Span Development and Behavior, Vol. 1. New York: Academic Press.
LEVIN, R. J. (1975) "Premarital and extramarital sex." Redbook 145: 38-44, 190-192.
—— and LEVIN, A. (1975) "Sexual pleasure; the surprising preferences of 100,000 women." Redbook 145: 51-58.
LEVINGER, G. (1979) "A social psychological perspective on marital dissolution," in G. Levinger and O.C. Moles (eds.) Divorce and Separation: Context, Causes, and Consequences. New York: Basic Books.
—— (1966) "Sources of marital dissatisfaction among applicants for divorce." American Journal of Orthopsychiatry 36: 803-807.
—— (1965) "Marital cohesiveness and dissolution: an integrative review." Journal of Marriage and the Family 27: 19-28.
LEWIS, R. A. and G. B. SPANIER (1979) "Theorizing about the quality and stability of marriage," in W. Burr et al. (eds.) Contemporary Theories About the Family. New York: The Free Press.

LOPATA, H. Z. (1972) "Social relations of widows in urbanizing societies." Sociological Quarterly 13: 259–271.

LOWENTHAL, M. F. and C. HAVEN (1968) "Interaction and adaptation: intimacy as a critical variable," in B.L. Neugarten (ed.) Middle Age and Aging. Chicago: University of Chicago Press.

LOWENTHAL, M. F., M. THURHNER and D. CHIRIBOGA (1976) Four Stages of Life. San Francisco: Jossey-Bass.

MILLER, A. A. (1970) "Reactions of friends to divorce," in P. Bohannon (ed.) Divorce and After. Garden City, NY: Doubleday.

MOWRER, E. R. (1924) "The variance between the legal and natural causes of divorce." Journal of Social Forces 3: 388–392.

NAGER, L., D. CHIRIBOGA, and L. CUTLER (1977) "Stress and relief during the process of divorce: a psychosocial study." Presented at Western Psychological Association, Seattle.

NASS, G. D., R. W. LIBBY, and M. P. FISHER (1981) Sexual Choices: An Introduction to Human Sexuality, Belmont, CA: Wadsworth.

National Center for Health Statistics (1983) 1981 Summary: National Ambulatory Medical Care Survey 88, March 16, Vital and Health Statistics. Washington, DC: U.S. Department of Health and Human Services.

NYE, F. I. (1979) "Choice, exchange, and the family," in W.R. Burr et al. (eds.) Contemporary Theories About the Family, Vol. 2. New York: The Free Press.

RANDS, M., G. LEVINGER and G. D. MELLINGER (1981) "Patterns of conflict resolution and marital satisfaction." Journal of Family Issues 2: 297–321.

RASCHKE, H. J. (1977) "The role of social participation in postseparation and post divorce adjustment." Journal of Divorce 1: 129–140.

RAUSH, H. L., W. A. BARRY, R. K. HETEL, and M. SWAIN (1974) Communication, Conflict and Marriage. San Francisco: Jossey-Bass.

REISS, I. L. (1980) Family Systems in America. New York: Holt, Rinehart and Winston.

——— and B. C. MILLER (1974) A Theoretical Analysis of Heterosexual Permissiveness. University of Minnesota Family Studies Center, Technical Bulletin 2, August.

RENNE, K. (1971) "Health and marital experience in an urban population." Journal of Marriage and the Family 33: 338–350.

RHEINSTEIN, M. (1971) Marriage, Divorce, Stability, and the Law. Chicago: University of Chicago Press.

ROBINSON, J. P. and P. R. SHAVER (1973) Measures of Social Psychological Attitudes. Ann Arbor, MI: Survey Research Center, Institute for Social Research.

ROSENBERG, N. (1965) Society and the Adolescent Self-Image. Princeton, NJ: Princeton University Press.

RUBIN, L. B. (1979) Women of a Certain Age. New York: Harper & Row.

SINGH, B. K., B. L. WALTON, and J. S. WILLIAMS (1976) "Extramarital sexual permissiveness: conditions and contingencies." Journal of Marriage and the Family 38: 701–712.

SPANIER, G. B. (1983) "Married and unmarried cohabitation in the United States: 1980." Journal of Marriage and the Family 45: 277–288.

——— (1979) "Measuring dyadic adjustment: new scales for assessing the quality of marriage and similar dyads." Journal of Marriage and the Family 41: 605–613.

────── and E. A. ANDERSON (1979) "The impact of the legal system on adjustment to marital separation." Journal of Marriage and the Family 41: 605–613.

SPANIER, G. B. and R. F. CASTO (1979a) "Adjustment to separation and divorce: a qualitative analysis," in G. Levinger and O.C. Moles (eds.) Divorce and Separation: Context, Causes, and Consequences. New York: Basic Books.

────── (1979b) "Adjustment to separation and divorce: an analysis of 50 case studies." Journal of Divorce 2: 241–253.

SPANIER, G. B. and F. F. FURSTENBERG Jr. (1982) "Remarriage after divorce: a longitudinal analysis of well-being." Journal of Marriage and the Family 44: 709–720.

SPANIER, G. B. and P. C. GLICK (1981) "Marital instability in the United States: some correlates and recent changes." Family Relations 30: 329–338.

────── (1980) "Paths to remarriage." Journal of Divorce 3: 283–298.

SPANIER, G. B. and S. HANSON (1981) "The role of extended kin in the adjustment to marital separation." Journal of Divorce 5: 33–48.

SPANIER, G. B. and M. E. LACHMAN (1980) "Factors associated with adjustment to marital separation." Sociological Focus 13: 369–381.

────── (1979) "Indicators of adjustment to marital separation and social policy issues." Presented at the meeting of the Eastern Sociological Society, New York.

SPANIER, G. B. and R. L. MARGOLIS (1983) "Marital separation and extramarital sexual behavior." The Journal of Sex Research 19: 23–48.

SPANIER, G. B. and L. THOMPSON (1983) "Relief and distress after marital separation." Journal of Divorce 7: 31–49.

SPANIER, G. B., R. A. LEWIS, and C. L. COLE (1975) "Marital adjustment over the family life cycle: the issue of curvilinearity." Journal of Marriage and the Family 37: 263–275.

SPICER, J. W. and G. D. HAMPE (1975) "Kinship interaction after divorce." Journal of Marriage and the Family 37: 113–119.

STETSON, D. M. and G. C. WRIGHT Jr. (1975) "The effect of laws on divorce in American states." Journal of Marriage and the Family 37: 537–547.

STRAUS, M. A. (1979) "Measuring intrafamily conflict and violence." Journal of Marriage and the Family 41: 75–88.

TESSLER, R. and D. MECHANIC (1978) "Psychological distress and perceived health status." Journal of Health and Social Behavior 19: 254–262.

THOMPSON, L. (1981) "The aftermath of separation and divorce." Ph.D. dissertation, Pennsylvania State University.

────── and G. B. SPANIER (1983) "The end of marriage and acceptance of marital termination." Journal of Marriage and the Family 45: 103–113.

U.S. Bureau of Census (1979) Divorce, Child Custody, and Child Support. Series P-23, No. 84, Current Population Reports, June. Washington, DC: U.S. Government Printing Office.

WALLERSTEIN, J. S. and J. B. KELLY (1980) Surviving the Breakup. New York: Basic Books.

WALSTER, E., J. TRAUPMAN, and G. W. WALSTER (1978) "Equity and extramarital sexuality." Archives of Sexual Behavior 7: 127–142.

WEINGARTEN, H. (1980) "Remarriage and well-being: national survey evidence of social and psychological effects." Journal of Family Issues 1: 533–559.

WEISS, R. S. (1975) Marital Separation. New York: Basic Books.

WHITEHURST, R. M. (1969) "Extramarital sex: alienation or extension of normal behavior," in G. Neubeck (ed.) Extramarital Relations. Englewood Cliffs, NJ: Prentice-Hall.
WILSON, W. (1967) "Correlates of avowed happiness." Psychological Bulletin 67: 294–306.
WRIGHT, G. C. and D. M. STETSON (1978) "The impact of no-fault divorce law reform on divorce in American states." Journal of Marriage and the Family 40: 575–580.

# Index

Abel, R. L., 91
Ackerman, C., 116
Adjustments to divorce, 103–129
    acceptance, 104–106, 113, 114, 116, 117, 118, 119, 122, 123
    alternative gratification, 123–129
    and extramarital sex, 125, 127–128
    anger, 106, 113, 114, 116, 119, 121
    blaming, 122, 128, 129
    distress, 111, 112, 113, 115, 116, 120, 121
    educational alternatives, 126, 128, 129
    external pressures, 115, 120
    family and friends, 125–126
    gender differences, 106, 107, 108, 110, 112, 113, 114, 118, 120, 122, 127, 128, 129
    guilt, 106–107, 110, 113, 114, 116, 121, 122
    loneliness, 107–109, 110, 112, 113, 114, 116–119, 120, 121, 123
    relief, 111, 112, 113, 114, 115, 116, 118, 120, 122
    stability, 113
    suicide, 109–110, 113, 114, 116, 125, 127
    tables, 108, 109, 117, 124
Abuse
    and divorce, 15
    and women, 15
    before separation, 50
Albrecht, S. L., 45
Anderson, E. A., 95, 221
Andrews, F. M., 216
Anspach, K. F., 84, 126, 164, 184
Bachrach, L. L., 209
Beal, E. W., 145
Becker, H., 18

Bell, R. R., 61
Bernard, J., 45
Blake, W. M., 90
Bloom, B. L. 209
Bowlby, J., 140
Bradburn, N., 213, 215, 217, 230
Bresnahan, B. S., 22
Brown, P., 111, 140, 142, 145, 147, 150
Burgess, E., 15
Campbell, A., 45, 209, 215
Cantril, H., 214, 215
Caplovitz, D., 213, 215, 230
Casto, R. F., 73, 97, 103, 209
Cherlin, A., 84, 87, 214, 223, 224
Children
    and consequences of breakup, 75
    and contact, 76, 77
    and divorce, 15-16, 24, 57, 72–80, 100
    and postponement of divorce, 73
    and threats, 74
    and well-being, 221–223
    as barrier to breakup, 72–80
    child rearing, 77
    custody, 21, 24, 72, 73, 75, 76, 77, 78, 79, 80, 100
    family planning, 12
    of working women, 86
    quality of parent-child relationship, 75–76, 77
    source of support, 79, 80
    table, 75
    uses (against spouse), 74
    visitation, 75, 76–77
Chiriboga, D. A., 24, 30, 106, 111, 115, 118, 175, 209
Christensen, H. T., 61
Cohabitation

alternative to marriage, 13, 202, 203
Communication
  expectations, 30
Companionship
  and separation, 51
  expectations, 30
Complaints
  and divorce, 27, 30–34
  disagreement, 27, 29, 30
  involvement, 27, 29–30
Conflict
  attack tactics, 42
  avoidance of conflict, 41–42, 56
  before separation, 41-44, 52, 56
Contraception
  unwanted pregnancy, 12–13
Counseling
  clergy, 97–98
  gender differences, 97
  professional, 97–99, 101
  satisfaction, 98
  table, 97
Cuber, J. F., 27, 28, 53, 61, 111, 115, 116
Cutler, L., 111, 115
Custody, 21, 24, 72, 73, 75, 77, 78, 79, 80, 100, 146
  adjustments, 78–79
  and discipline, 79
  and guilt, 78, 80
  and satisfaction, 77–78
  and well-being, 221, 223
  joint, 77, 78
  shared, 73
  split, 77, 78, 80
  visitation, 75, 76–77
Dating
  and age, 197–198
  and ex-spouse, 196
  and loneliness, 205–206
  and sex, 194–198, 205
  and well-being, 231–232
  attitudes toward remarriage, 198
  awkwardness, 195
  benefits, 192–193
  differential treatment, 191
  fears, 193–194
  gender differences, 194–195, 199–200, 201–202
  hesitation, 188-189

opportunities, 192
  pre-separation, 189
  tables, 191, 196, 199, 204
  timing, 190
Dean, D. G., 22, 115
Death of spouse
  United States rates, 7
Deliberation
  and children, 47
  and divorce, 46–53
  and length of marriage, 47
  and mutual conclusion, 54
  and role performance, 51
  certainty, 46–53, 54, 57–58
  events, 46
  foreboding, 46–51, 54
  gender differences, 46–47
  table, 46
Disagreement
  and involvement, 43–44
  attack tactics, 42
  avoidance of conflict, 41–42, 56
  before separation, 41–44, 56
  issues, 43
Divorce
  and abuse, 15
  and children, 24, 72–80
  and dating, 187–208
  and discrimination, 86–87
  and economics, 84–90, 101
  and extramarital sex, 19–20, 59–72, 99–100
  and gender roles, 27, 28
  and race, 13
  and religion, 15, 23
  and sex, 187–208
  and significant others, 163–185
  and suicide, 109–110
  and teenage marriage, 12
  and the family, 14, 15–16, 17, 163–185
  and the legal system, 90–97, 101
  and well-being, 209–234
  arguments, 28
  causes, 27, 30
  complaints, 27
  deliberation, 46–53
  diversity of experience, 9
  help for marital problems, 97–99, 101

increased rate, 13, 18
lack of communication, 28–29
likelihood, 13
mixed fault grounds, 24
no-fault divorce, 15, 24, 91
outside influences, 59-101
paucity of research, 9, 18
reaction and adjustments, 103–129
reactions of others, 80–84
rejection of spouse, 14
relationships after separation, 131–161
responsibility, 23, 53–56
similarities, 9
social stigma, 15
timing, 13, 23–24, 46–53
unexpected, 27–28, 29
United States, 7, 11
Economics
  and marriage, 12
  and suicide, 88, 104
  and well-being, 223, 225
  as barrier to divorce, 87
  causes of unemployment, 88, 89
  changes after separation, 88–90
  economic independence, 13
  economic stability, 84–86
  economics and divorce, 84–90
  gender differences 86–90, 126, 224
  points of conflict, 87
  tables, 86, 87, 89, 90
Education
  and divorce rates, 13
  and marriage, 13
Eligibles, field of, 12
Emotional support
  family function, 17
Expectations
  and communication, 30
  and companionship, 30, 56
  and income, 31, 33
  and role performance, 30–34, 56
  gender differences, 30–34, 56
  housework, 31–33, 56
  parental, 30
  sexual, 30–31, 56
  table, 31
Extramarital sex, 59–72, 123, 125, 127–128
  and guilt, 67, 70, 71–72
  and love, 66, 68
  and marital problems, 67, 68–69
  and marital quality, 62
  and marital sex, 67
  and religiosity, 61
  and satisfaction, 66–67, 71–72, 125
  and separate vacations, 62
  and separation, 66, 68, 99–100, 151–153, 157, 160
  and suicide, 69
  and well-being, 219–220
  blame, 69, 70–71
  disapproval, 68
  explanations, 61
  frequency, 62
  gender differences, 59, 62–73, 123, 125
  group marriage, 60
  kissing and petting, 65, 67
  number of partners, 65–66
  of spouse, 67–68
  tables, 63–65, 71
  women, 59
Family
  and divorce, 14, 15–16, 17, 163–185
  and marriage, 12
  change, 10
  family planning, 12
  functions, 17
  future, 14
  ill health, 11
  interest, 12
  problems, 11, 14
  stability, 14, 15–16
Feelings
  gender differences, 44–45
  table, 44
  toward partner, 44–45
Frederico, J., 52, 71, 115, 122
Furstenberg, F. F., 7, 10, 76, 198
Gender Roles
  and divorce, 27
  gender role performance, 30–34
Glenn, N. D., 45, 59, 209
Glick, P. C., 77, 197
Goetting, A., 133, 145, 147
Goode, W. J., 9, 18, 27, 39, 43, 45, 46, 53, 54, 81, 82, 83, 103, 106, 111, 115, 116, 119, 120, 121, 122, 123, 129, 132, 133, 138, 144, 145,

146, 155, 166, 167, 169, 170, 174, 184, 195, 196, 198, 209, 210, 220
Gottman, J. M., 43
Hampe, G. D., 164, 165
Happiness
  and marriage, 14, 15, 41, 44–45
  gender differences, 44–45
Harnsworth, H., 91
Harroff, P. B., 27, 28, 53, 111, 115, 116
Harvey, J. H., 148, 151
Hetherington, E. M., 30, 75, 103, 115, 129, 136, 137, 144, 145, 147, 154, 155, 184, 205, 209, 222
Hill, C. T., 45, 106, 121
Holmes, T. S., 111
Household composition, 11
  at final separation, 49
  one-parent households, 16
Housework
  expectations, 31–33, 56
  table, 31
Hunt, M., 30, 59, 66, 68, 103, 115, 209
Income
  expectations, 31
Kelley, H. H., 69
Kelly, J. B., 75
Kinsey, A. C., 59, 66
Kitson, G. C., 24, 27, 29, 111, 115, 118, 140, 141, 144, 150, 154, 173, 175, 209
Kohen, J. A., 85, 203
*Kramer vs. Kramer*, 16
Kraus, S., 111
Legal system
  adversary divorce arrangement, 91, 96, 101
  and adjustment, 95–96
  and well-being, 221
  attorneys, 92–96
  defenses, 96
  dissatisfaction, 91–96
  divorce law reform, 90
  effects on reconciliation, 91–92, 94, 96, 97, 101
  grounds, 94
  lack of support, 92
  legal fees, 94, 95
  no-fault divorce, 91, 97

satisfaction, 93–95, 101
Lerner, R. M., 140
Levinger, G., 27, 45, 53, 73, 81, 115, 116, 126
Lewis, R. A. 96, 115
Margolis, R. L., 61
Marriage
  and access to sex, 12
  and education, 13
  and family, 12
  and happiness, 14, 15
  and mobility, 13
  and the economy, 12
  and working women, 13
  age at first marriage, 12, 13
  cohabitation, 13
  group marriage, 60
  history, 18
  length, 13, 23–24
  norm, 11–12
  outside influences, 59–101
  quality, 14–15, 60, 62, 83–84
  rate, 11–12
  stability, 14–15, 30, 60
  teenage marriage, 12
  trends, 12
Miller, A. A., 167
Minnis, M., 91
Mobility
  and marriage, 13
  of separated and divorced, 22
Mowrer, E. R., 91
Mutual conclusion, 53–54
  and blame, 55–56
  and deliberation, 54
Nager, L., 45, 106
No-fault divorce, 15, 24
Nord, C. W., 76
Nye, F. I., 126, 224
Parenthood
  and separation, 51
  expectations, 30
  single, 16–17
Peterson, J. L., 76
Postseparation
  and children, 134, 145–147, 158, 159
  and extramarital relationships, 151–153, 157, 160
  attachment, 140–143

changes over time, 144–145
contact, 131–137, 139, 141–142, 143, 144, 157, 158
conversation, 134–136, 139
feelings, 137–144
gender differences, 134, 136, 137, 139-140, 141, 142, 144, 147, 148–149, 150–151, 152–153, 159–160
loneliness, 141, 155
new relationships, 153–156, 159, 160
recollections of marriage, 148-151, 159
services, 133
sex, 132, 155
tables, 132, 134–135, 138, 146
tension, 136
Pregnancy
and contraception, 12–13
premarital, 36
Premarital
history, 18
pregnancy, 36
sex, 35–37
Race
and divorce, 13
Rahe, R. H., 111
Rands, M. G., 41
Raschke, H. J., 184, 209
Raush, H. L., 43
*Recycling the Family,* 7, 10, 198
Reeder, L. G., 214
Religion
and divorce, 15, 23
extramarital sex and religiosity, 61
Remarriage
and well being, 232
data, 14
rates, 12
timing, 14
Renne, K., 209
Responsibility
commitment, 54
companionship, 54
for breakup, 53–56
gender differences, 53–56
harmony, 54
role expectations, 54
source, 55–56
table, 55

Rheinstein, M., 90
Robinson, J. P., 214, 215
Role expectations, 30
Rosenberg, N., 214
Ryff, C. D., 140
Separation
and certainty, 49
and dating, 187–208
and divorce, 10
and extramarital sex, 66, 68
and sex, 35–40, 187–208
and the legal system, 90–97
and well-being, 209–234
aspects, 10
associated emotions, 9
determinants, 18
help for marital problems, 97–99
no-fault divorce, 24
relationships after separation, 131–161
Sex
and marriage, 12
and separation, 35–40, 52–53, 58, 187–208, 231–232
after marriage, 37–40, 132
extramarital involvements, 19–20, 59–72, 99–100, 125, 127–128, 151–153, 157, 160, 219–220
frequency of intercourse, 38–39
gender differences, 39, 59
group marriage, 60
premarital, 35–37
satisfaction with intercourse, 39–40, 58, 194–195
sexual freedom, 12
sleeping arrangements, 39–40
table, 39
Shaver, P. R., 214, 215
Significant others, 163–185
and children, 175, 176, 177, 180–181
attentiveness, 169, 181
changes after separation, 163, 167–185
empathy, 166
family, 173–176
friends, 178–179
gender differences, 163, 164, 174, 175–176, 177, 178–180, 181–182, 184

in-laws, 164, 176-177, 182, 184
new friends, 170, 179, 184
support, 171, 173, 174–185
tables, 169, 172, 183
Singh, B. K., 59
Single parenthood, 16
and race, 16
single fathers, 16-17
Spanier, G. B., 7, 10, 18, 40, 61, 73, 77, 95, 96, 97, 103, 112, 115, 129, 197, 198, 202, 209, 221
Spicer, J. W., 164, 165
Stetson, D. M., 91
Straus, M. A., 43
Support, financial, 20, 21, 24
child support, 75, 146
Sussman, M. B., 24, 27, 29, 111, 115, 118
Tender years doctrine, 17
Therapy, marital, 97–99, 101
Thompson, L., 104, 112, 129, 209
Thurnher, M., 30, 115, 118
United States
and death of spouse, 7
divorce rates, 7
Visitation, 75, 76–77
Wallerstein, J. S., 75
Walster, E., 61
Weaver, C. N., 45, 59
Weingarten, H., 209
Weiss, R. S., 27, 39, 43, 45, 53, 81, 82, 84, 103, 106, 108, 115, 118, 121, 122, 126, 136, 137, 140, 142, 144, 148, 151, 154, 155, 164, 167, 169, 191, 192, 193, 195, 209, 231
Weitzman, L., 24
Well-being, 209–234

and acceptance, 226–228
and children, 221–223
and dating, 231–232
and economics, 223–225
and extramarital sex, 219–220, 231–232
and legal barriers, 221
and outsiders, 218–225
and remarriage, 232
and separation, 216–218
and support from others, 230
disapproval by others, 220
gender differences, 211–212, 215, 222–223, 224, 226–227, 230–232
physical health, 210–212
psychological, 212–216
psychosomatic symptoms, 210–212
tables, 215, 216, 225, 232
Whitehurst, R. M., 61
Wilson, W., 215
Witney, S. B., 216
Women
adjustments to divorce, 106, 107
and abuse, 15
and divorce, 13, 15
and economics, 86, 126, 129
and education, 224
extramarital sex, 59
negative feelings, 44–45
work and marriage, 13
Working women
and children, 86
and economics, 86
and marriage, 13
and well-being, 224
Wright, G. C., 91
Zill, N., 76

## About the Authors

GRAHAM B. SPANIER is Vice President for Academic Affairs and Provost at Oregon State University. He has authored, edited, or coauthored eight books among his over 100 scholarly publications. Spanier is currently President-elect of the National Council on Family Relations and has served as Chair of the Family Section of the American Sociological Association. He was the Founding Editor of the *Journal of Family Issues*. Spanier's research interests focus on the quality and stability of marital relations across the life course, divorce and remarriage, family demography, and family policy. He received his Ph.D in sociology from Northwestern University.

LINDA THOMPSON is Associate Professor of Family Development at Virginia Polytechnic Institute and State University. Many of her articles have appeared in the *Journal of Marriage and the Family*, for which she now serves on the editorial board. She is also Series Editor of the New Perspectives on Family book series sponsored by the National Council on Family Relations and is an Associate Editor of *Journal of Family Issues*. Her research interests include feminist approaches to the family, couple decision making and negotiation, and intergenerational relationships in adulthood. She is currently working on a biography of Jesse Bernard. Thompson received her Ph.D. in human development and family studies from Pennsylvania State University.